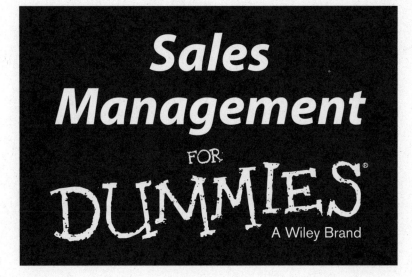

Sales Management For Dummies

A Wiley Brand

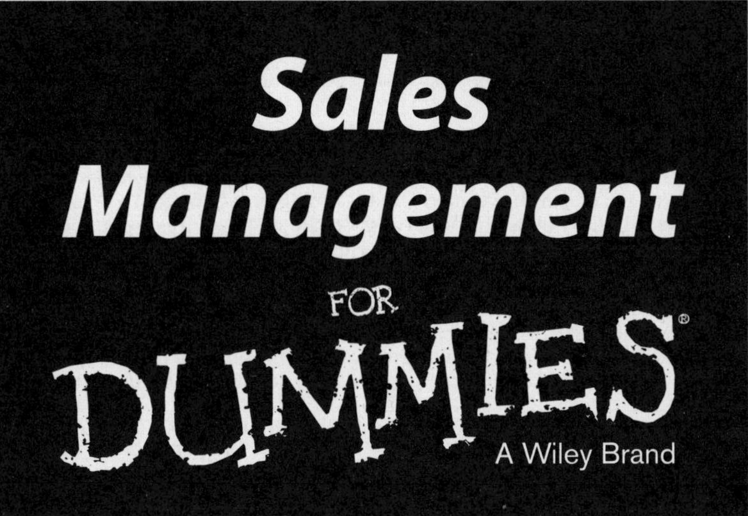

by Butch Bellah

Sales Management For Dummies®

Published by: **John Wiley & Sons, Inc.,** 111 River Street, Hoboken, NJ 07030-5774, www.wiley.com

Published simultaneously in Canada

For general information on our other products and services, please contact our Customer Care Department within the U.S. at 877-762-2974, outside the U.S. at 317-572-3993, or fax 317-572-4002. For technical support, please visit www.wiley.com/techsupport.

Wiley publishes in a variety of print and electronic formats and by print-on-demand. Some material included with standard print versions of this book may not be included in e-books or in print-on-demand. If this book refers to media such as a CD or DVD that is not included in the version you purchased, you may download this material at http://booksupport.wiley.com. For more information about Wiley products, visit www.wiley.com.

Library of Congress Control Number: 2015948998

ISBN 978-1-119-09422-7 (pbk); ISBN 978-1-119-09420-3 (epdf); ISBN 978-1-119-09405-0 (epub)

Manufactured in the United States of America

10 9 8 7 6 5 4 3 2 1

Contents at a Glance

Table of Contents

Introduction

"I'd like you to consider taking over as Vice President of Sales." I can still hear those words ringing in my ears more than 20 years after they were uttered by the man who is my mentor to this day.

At the time, he was president of the company and had called me into his office one afternoon in early 1995. Was I in trouble? Had I done something wrong? He and I had a great relationship, but a closed-door, spur-of-the moment meeting was a bit strange.

"Uh, I'm not sure . . . are you . . ." I stuttered and stammered for a few moments trying to let what I had just heard sink in. "I'm not bucking for a promotion right now," I can remember managing to get out through the hemming and hawing.

"I realize that. But, I want you to take over the entire sales department."

I'd be lying if I said this wasn't my goal, but now? I hadn't even been with the company for a decade yet and had entered below the lowest rung on the ladder. In fact, I couldn't even see the ladder. I got promoted twice before I found the ladder. I'd only been a division sales manager for a few years at the time.

Being a vice president was part of my goal, but not necessarily this fast.

The tone of his voice let me know this was a bit more than a request — it was a challenge. It was time to get in the game or shrink back to the bench. "I'm really not trying to take anyone else's job, I'm just trying to do the best I can as a division sales manager."

His next words let me know it was now or never: "If you don't do this, I'm going to have to hire someone else who will." And so began my career in sales management.

I inherited an entire sales department of more than 25 people, most of whom had been with the company or in the industry a lot longer than I had. I took over with no direction, no roadmap, no instruction book, and really no past experience to draw from. To say I was flying blind is an understatement.

If I was going to learn to be a leader, I was going to have to go with gut instinct and make it up as I went. I didn't have a fall-back plan and failure wasn't an option. I'd been hired at 21, been made division sales manager at

25, and now, at not even 30, I was being handed the job of managing a sales department generating about $75 million a year in sales.

"Do you think I'm ready?" I asked.

"If I didn't, we wouldn't be having this conversation."

I took the job. And through a lot of missteps, mistakes, and complete melt-downs, grew that company to more than a quarter-of-a-billion dollars a year in sales before acquiring controlling interest in the company with a business partner just five short years later.

I always wished I had a book in which to look things up. Now, I give you what I never had.

About This Book

You're holding the book I always wished I had. In it you'll find real-world experience drawn from many years (more than I care to remember) and even more mistakes while I was suffering through a lot of OJT. (For those of you new to the world of management, OJT stands for On the Job Training.)

This book truly is my gift to you: my experiences, lessons learned, and all the broken bones and skinned knees of learning to manage a sales team laid bare. I won't tell you this book will keep you from making any mistakes — we both know it won't. But, it can help you learn from the ones I made and minimize the ones you have to experience firsthand.

Throughout the book I use real-world stories and situations I believe you can relate to. I use a lot of sports analogies because I think a sports coach is as close to a sales manager as you can get. The two share similar philosophies, goals, and ideals.

Some of the examples I use may describe the exact situation you face, and you can see how I handled it — and whether that was the right call. Spoiler alert: it wasn't close!

If you're like most managers, you've said to yourself more than once, "I'll bet this never happened to anybody else." Well, yeah, it did. It happens to everyone. All that stuff you think is exclusive to you isn't.

All sales managers go through similar if not identical situations. And all sales managers tend to think they're the only one who has to deal with their particular issues. Just wait until you go to a trade show or industry function and talk to other managers — you'll come home thinking, "Wow, I'm glad I'm not that guy!"

I attempt to paint you a picture of the world of sales management, and that picture isn't always pretty. There are ups and downs, highs and lows — but I can say without hesitation I have never wanted to do anything else. You represent the greatest profession on earth. Unfortunately, there is a low barrier of entry into sales and it seems as if anyone thinks he can just "go be a salesman."

As you probably know, it takes a strong, disciplined, creative sales manager to make things work. Anyone can call himself a salesperson, but that doesn't make him a professional salesperson. That's where you come in. You're the reason I wrote this book — so you can help me create more professional salespeople in this world. That's what I ask of you in exchange for all these years of knowledge and experience: Help me produce more *professional* salespeople in this world.

I use the term salesperson throughout the book. Let me say upfront that I've found that great salespeople and duds come in both genders. I alternate pronouns with each chapter: even-numbered chapters use female pronouns and males get the odd-numbered chapters.

Although my experience was primarily in business-to-business sales, I worked hard to include those of you in retail sales and other business-to-consumer organizations. From automobiles to . . . to . . . well, something that starts with a *z,* I try to include everyone.

Also, this book isn't written just for those who are managing world-wide teams doing hundreds of millions of dollars in sales. You can certainly benefit, if that describes you, but my advice is also applicable to managers whose sales team consists of herself and a part-timer. Hey, you have to start somewhere.

Within this book, you may note that some web addresses break across two lines of text. If you're reading this book in print and want to visit one of these web pages, simply key in the web address exactly as it's noted in the text, pretending as though the line break doesn't exist. If you're reading this as an e-book, you've got it easy — just click the web address to be taken directly to the web page.

Foolish Assumptions

Any time an author writes a book, they have to make certain assumptions about the reader — and I did. My first assumption is you're a sales manager (or you're about to become one) who wants to improve your performance and the performance of your sales team. I assume you understand the sales process and the role you — the sales manager play in it. But, perhaps my biggest assumption is that you know there are things you don't know. You understand there are things you still have to learn, questions you need answered and a guiding light through some tough situations.

If that sounds like you — I'm glad we met.

Icons Used in This Book

Throughout this book, I use certain icons to call your attention to specific text. These are the places where your highlighter generally comes into use. Here's what they each mean:

This is a tip from me to you. This entire book is filled with useful information, but there are times I want you to be aware of a certain passage. These little tips are your chance to learn from my experience.

Again, I hope you find the entire book memorable. Heck, I want you to highlight the whole thing. But, when you see this icon, pay close attention. Whether you need it now or not, this denotes something I believe is worth filing in your mental bank.

Pay special attention when you see this one; it's called "Warning" for a reason. These will save you time, money, embarrassment, and heartache. I know from experience.

I use this icon for situations and passages of text where you may think you know the answer, but I want to make sure. These are things my late mother would have prefaced with, "I've got news for you, young man." Well, you get the picture.

Beyond the Book

In addition to all the information regarding becoming a great sales manager included within these pages (or in the e-book) I put together a few little bonuses that you can access any time, anywhere on the web. I include some questions to ask when hiring a new salesperson, offer advice on how to handle conflict between two salespeople, and give you several more goodies at `www.dummies.com`. Just click over to `www.dummies.com/cheatsheet/salesmanagement` and see what all I have for you there.

You can also access some bonus material at my website, including a *free* digital copy of my previous book, *The 10 Essential Habits of Sales Superstars: Plugging into the Power of Ten,* by going to `www.butchbellah.com/free10habits`.

On top of several hundred blog posts on sales, sales management, and more at my website at `butchbellah.com`, you can also find out information and sample videos on my speaking at `butchbellah.com/speaking` and information and ways to contact me regarding sales training at `butchbellah.com/coaching-and-training`.

Finally, I'd love to hear from you, the sales managers making a difference in this world. Share your stories of triumph and tragedy (hopefully more of the former) by emailing me at butch@butchbellah.com.

Where to Go from Here

This book wasn't written with the idea that you'd sit down with it and read it cover-to-cover in one sitting — unable to put it down. It doesn't have any wizards, vampires, or zombies, and I didn't have the opportunity to kill off a main character during the slow parts to keep you interested. (I am the main character so that was definitely out of the question.)

Here's the good part: You don't even have to like to read to get something out of it. It's not really designed to be used as a textbook or something you sit beside your bed like the latest novel of romance story. In fact, you're probably not going to read it cover-to-cover and that's okay. You can start anywhere — just pick a spot and jump in.

This book is assembled so you can easily find the chapter or heading on what issue you're facing right now. Read it, absorb it, highlight it, and then keep it nearby to be referred to the next time a fire is ablaze and you're searching for an extinguisher.

However, if you want a suggested place to start (especially if you ever want a suggestion), check out Chapter 4, where I guide you through assessing what you have to work with in your organization right now, or Chapter 7, where I dive into the fun of training your team.

Part I

Welcome to the World of Sales Management

getting started with

sales management

Find additional content at www.dummies.com/extras/salesmanagement.

In this part . . .

- Understand the role of a sales manager. Find out what you are and what you are not.
- Define your expectations and establish your own management style. The old manager isn't there any longer; now it's your turn.
- See the importance of establishing good working relationships across departments. You're now in a position where every other department in the company is affected by you and can affect you. It's important to have good rapport.
- Find ways to communicate clearly and consistently. Your ability to communicate is one of the most important parts of your job.

Chapter 1

You're a Sales Manager — Now What?

In This Chapter

- Getting to know your new role
- Making the leap from salesperson to sales manager
- Inspiring, coaching, and guiding your team
- Getting to know your inherited team
- Establishing your own management style

You've probably worked for years to get to be a sales manager ; you've put in the time on the sales floor or in the field and now it's your turn to take the next step. You've been offered and accepted the job. And now, you're chewing antacids like gum, sweating bullets, and feeling nauseous. Hey! Welcome to management!

Seriously, it's perfectly normal to be nervous and question whether you can do the job. Anyone who ever gets promoted goes through similar feelings, and if they tell you they don't they're probably not being totally truthful.

Now calm yourself; you can do this. In this first chapter I explore the traits and functions of a sales manager and briefly touch on a few topics I cover in more depth later. By the time I'm done, you'll be a confident, successful, efficient manager leading a team of great salespeople.

And, if it doesn't work, just take two aspirin and call me in the morning.

Understanding Your Role as a Sales Manager

It's important to know how great sales managers operate; how they manage their team and how they remain productive themselves. The role is ever-changing but has several core duties and responsibilities which cross almost all industry lines:

- Managing the sales team
- Establishing goals and quotas
- Training and developing sales skills
- Assigning and defining geographical territories
- Counseling and leading individual salespeople
- Reporting data to upper management
- Creating incentive programs
- Establishing budgets
- Hiring and firing salespeople

Are there other tasks you do as a sales manager? Sure. You'll always add new responsibilities to your plate, but you can pretty much expect to handle the jobs on this list when you get the job. In fact, many of them may have been in your job description.

Acknowledging what you are and what you're not

As a professional sales manager you assume many roles: motivator, cheerleader, sounding board, ear to vent to, teacher, judge, shoulder to cry on, and everything in between.

As the leader of your department, the buck really does stop with you. The responsibility that comes with the job is enormous and can be a bit overwhelming.

You can only do one thing at a time, and you can only do your best. When in doubt remember these words, "Do the best you can with what you have to work with."

At some point you will wonder whether you're in the sales department or management. The truth is you're in both, and you have to be able to mold and shape yourself to fit the situation you're in.

There will be times when you must make very hard management decisions and times where you have to defend your sales department against the decisions of others. Sometimes you won't know which role you're playing. There's no cut-and-dried way to tell when to be more sales or more management. There's no right or wrong answer; there's a lot of gray area. You have to go with your gut.

As long as you're consistent, you'll be fine. Don't try to please everyone. Be consistent in your actions, decisions, and how you run your department, and you'll be ahead of the game.

You're the conduit between management and sales. You're the person other department heads are going to look to for information regarding what's happening to the company's sales. The next minute you're answering to salespeople and explaining something the company decided to do.

It's a juggling act, but a manageable one if you just "do the best you can with what you have to work with."

As important as it is to know what you are, it's just as important to know what you are not. You're not a psychic who can read minds and predict the future of the company's sales down to the penny. Everyone is going to ask you to, but you can't. You have to use past history and your instincts to set budgets, goals, and sales forecasts — all of which now come from your desk.

You're also not the secretary for the sales department. Don't get me wrong, I'll be the first to say you work for your sales team instead of them working for you. But, don't let yourself get caught up in doing their tasks. That's not what you're there for. I point out ways to help you avoid this huge bear trap in Chapter 2.

If you set the tone early of doing things for people, they will continue to expect that behavior. Your job is to make your people better, not dependent.

It's now about how your team performs, not how you perform — a feeling that can be both invigorating and scary.

Inspiring, coaching, and leading

When it really comes down to it, your purpose is to inspire, coach, and lead your department. Sales is the only department in the company that contributes to profits — everything else is an expense. If your company is going to not just survive but thrive, it will be in large part due to how your department performs.

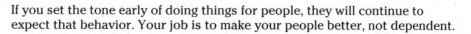

Inspire your sales team to want to achieve more and to believe they can and will. Note I didn't say motivate them. I believe motivation has to come from within — you can't motivate your people; they have to motivate themselves. However, you can and must inspire them.

Coach them to improve their skills. Your job is to observe, provide feedback, take corrective action, and go again. Then observe, provide feedback, take corrective action, and do it all over — over and over and over. You're in a constant state of coaching and training as new techniques, new systems, and new ways to communicate with your prospects and buyers are created.

Lead your team in a manner they want to follow. A leader doesn't say, "Go do this!" a leader says, "Let's go do this!" How you conduct yourself has as big an impact on your sales department as any words coming from your mouth.

Poet and philosopher Ralph Waldo Emerson said, "What you do speaks so loudly I cannot hear what you say." Leadership is taking action, not only speaking.

As a sales manager, you have a lot to digest, but understand you take this journey one step at a time. You're not the manager today you'll be a year from now or five years from now. If you had all these answers and knew how to do all these things already, you would've been a sales manager years ago. Be patient and learn.

Transitioning from Salesperson to Sales Manager

It may be only one step on the ladder of your career, but it's a big one when you move from being a salesperson to becoming a sales manager. Gone are the days of having to concern yourself only with your own sales and keeping up with what's happening only with your customers in your own territory. Now you're responsible for the whole ball of wax.

The nice thing is, although the skill sets of a great salesperson and a great sales manager are drastically different, the same drive, attitude, and burning desire that put you in this position is what will help you excel at this position.

Just because you have a new nameplate on the door or a new title on the business card doesn't mean you forget everything you've learned up to this point. In fact, you'll find yourself relying a lot on your past experience especially as you coach and train other salespeople to grow their business.

The transition from salesperson to sales manager can be especially tough on salespeople who are replacing a previous manager who was either ineffective or fell short in some way. You may face a situation where your immediate predecessor didn't set the best example. That's okay. You want to make the team your team and if you're stepping into a situation like this, it won't take much to look like the knight in shining armor.

Same barn, different stall

Many a new sales manager's biggest obstacle is going from sitting in the sales meeting and listening to sales training to now being the sales trainer. You need to take this role with a certain amount of humbleness because nobody wants to follow a leader who is constantly regurgitating, "Let me tell you how I used to do it."

Your first order of business is to earn your team's respect through your actions — not your words. When you approach the job focusing on how you can help them, not how they can help you, your entire mindset shifts. You use different words, and you have a sincere desire to serve.

Your job is to make your salespeople successful. As you take on the role of the leader, manager, and trainer, step back and let them know that you're viewing their process and practices from a slightly different angle. You get to see what they're doing through a new lens.

I can promise you I managed salespeople who were much smarter, more talented, and better salespeople than I was. Nobody ever said the best salesperson is the next sales manager. It doesn't work like that. There's no correlation between being a great salesperson and being a great sales manager. The skills that make a great salesperson have nothing to do with being a great manager. Some of the biggest mistakes I've ever seen have been when the best salesperson was put in charge of a sales team. Great salespeople can be great at sales, but terrible at managing. To be a great sales manager, you need to be a strong manager first. That's the skill you use more than any other.

Think of your new job this way: You have a racehorse capable of winning the Kentucky Derby but the current trainer just isn't able to get the best out of that horse. So, the owner turns the training over to you. Same horse. Different trainer.

If you know anything about sports or horse racing, you know a small change can have a big impact on a horse just the same as a team responds differently to a new coach or manager.

As sales manager, you're not there to upset the apple cart and start over completely; you're simply there to take what you have and make it the best it can be while adding new talent to the roster.

Your best strategy is to simply find out how you can help each person.

Past experience can lead to future success

The "this is how I did it" style of management gets old very quickly with a seasoned sales team. They aren't interested in what you did; they want to know what you can do for them.

I'm going to hazard a guess that when you first became a salesperson you devoured training materials, read a lot of books, and really studied your craft. You put in the time to be good at what you did and the results were there.

The same holds true for sales management. You're not expected to be a superstar from day one. Everyone in the organization understands (or should understand) that you have a nice little learning curve ahead of you as you navigate not only your own department but how it interacts with other departments.

The experience you gained as a salesperson dealing with different personalities, being committed to learning and growing, and having a burning desire deep within you to be the best you can be are the exact same traits that can make you a great sales manager.

You've displayed the characteristics of a sales manager already or you wouldn't have the job. The single biggest thing you can do is to give yourself time to learn — you're starting over again, and Rome wasn't built in a day.

Assessing Your Current Team

One of the first orders of business after a new sales manager gets settled in is to take an accurate, honest look at the current sales team to see who you're working with.

I refer to the salespeople like a professor would a classroom full of college students. You want to know who are your A students. You need to figure out how to continue to keep their fires lit and challenge them to grow and progress from where they are now. Nobody on your team is as good as they can be, trust me.

You need to identify your B students and find out how you can move them into the group with the A's. You need to identify your C students because you'll spend some time with them to determine if they have a future with you or not.

Most importantly, you need to get to know the D and F students. They're the ones who run you ragged. These are the people who constantly complain and fret over every little thing and blame their lack of sales on the government, global warming, and anything else they can come up with. These are the ones who can drag you down and take your focus away from the salespeople who really need your attention. Don't let them.

Grading on a curve

One of the interesting parts of your first few months as a new sales manager is assessing your team. Although looking at their sales numbers is good, as the sales manager you now have access to data you never had before — namely, the gross profit each salesperson generates and their accounts receivable.

So that explains it

Not long after I started my first position as Vice President of Sales, I had a division sales manager who had let a customer build up tens of thousands of dollars in accounts receivable. This was a customer I was a bit leery of in the first place, so I didn't have a real warm fuzzy feeling when he got behind on his payments.

I called the salesperson one day and read him the riot act, "You've got to get out there and get the money. No excuses. I don't care what you have to do, GET THE MONEY!"

I was steaming hot because this was about to blow up in his face and mine, too. I was not only trying to protect the two of us but keep the company from losing a ton of money in the process.

He said, "Butch, calm down. This is why I'm selling them so cheap. That way when they beat us out of the money we aren't losing as much!"

Yes, he was kidding, it broke the tension, and we both laughed. And, yes we eventually got the money — but it just goes to show how some salespeople rationalize away anything.

A great salesperson doesn't just do a lot of volume, he generates profit and collects his receivables.

Now that you have the ability to see all the numbers, you can determine who is actually producing for your company. Just because someone is on the top of the board every week with the most sales dollars doesn't make him your top salesperson. If his gross profit is low and receivables are high, he could very likely be costing you money.

Those are things you don't see as just another salesperson. But, in your new position you need to take in all the facts and make your own judgment about how your team is assembled and who your top producers really are.

Finding out where you need help

In analyzing and grading your current team, you will be called upon to make some decisions about individual salespeople and where their strengths and weaknesses lie.

Even though you've probably worked with these people before, I doubt you've really stood back to see what part of the sales process they excel at and where they struggle. But, now, it's time you do.

The only way to discover your sales team's strengths and weaknesses is to watch them in action. Salespeople are seldom accurate judges of their own talent levels in any area of the process. Even though everyone wants to be a great closer or be able to answer every objection, if they aren't spending an appropriate amount of time prospecting, they're going to be staring at their desk all day. No prospecting equals no prospects and no prospects equals no sales.

Two things you can do immediately to give you better insight into individual team members are

- **Work with them:** Jump in right alongside as they wait on customers, make their calls, or run their sales route. Note this is called working *with* them and not *for* them. You won't learn anything about them or how they operate if you take over and do everything yourself. That's not what this is for. Just be an observer at this point. There's plenty of time to cover your findings later.
- **Role play:** Whether it's one-on-one, just you and the salesperson or in a group setting during a sales meeting, you can learn a lot about how your people respond to certain situations by role playing. Don't go easy on them and throw them softballs. Making it easy for them is not a learning experience. Treat them like they're out in the field and bring up as many real-world objections as you can.

As you go through these exercises, take good notes. I mean really good notes so that you can go back over what happened when you and the salesperson are back within the safety of your own office.

By identifying strengths and weaknesses in each and every salesperson you get a much better idea where to spend your time when you work with them.

If someone is the best prospecting salesperson you've ever seen but doesn't have any new customers, the breakdown for them is obviously somewhere between that initial contact and the close. On the other hand, if you have a master closer who's not afraid to ask for the sale who's struggling, it's likely he isn't making enough new calls.

Don't assume you know how your salespeople work just by past experience and what you've heard from the previous manager or the salespeople. See it and hear it for yourself.

I can't stress enough how much of your job is simply to make each member of your sales team better, and until you know where each person needs to improve, you really can't do that, can you?

Establishing Your Management Style

As crass as this may sound, your job isn't to have your people like you. Being the sales manager is not a popularity contest. Now, don't get me wrong — given the choice of being liked or not, you always want the former. But, it's not about making your sales team like you.

People will respect you when you earn it, and they will like you when they find out your motives are in line with theirs. Respect is earned every day and it can be lost in a millisecond.

If you go into each day asking yourself how you can help your sales team improve, be more profitable, and more professional, you'll be ahead of 90 percen of the sales managers in the world today.

My management style was somewhat laid back. It's just who I am. It's what came naturally to me. Could I throw a fit and scream and chew someone out? Sure, if I had to, but I didn't manage that way. I didn't like to be managed like that and never liked to be perceived as that type manager.

Running your department by fear isn't managing. It's a very short-sighted view of how to handle your people. I always said I would treat people as adults until they proved to me they shouldn't be. And sadly, you'll have some of those.

Deciding what legacy you want to leave

The bottom line in sales and in life is how do you want to be remembered? What legacy do you want to leave? What is it you'd like your salespeople, other department heads, and senior management to say about you and how you do your job. "He sure screams a lot" isn't a compliment to your management style.

As you wind your way through your management career, your management style will come to you. Your personality will show through and your own moral compass will take over.

If you're wired one way, you're not going to be able to fake that and manage another way. It's why I couldn't be the drill sergeant screaming in people's faces. It's just not who I am. There's nothing wrong with any one style (well, I'm not real fond of the screamers), but the issue is to be authentic — to be yourself. If you try to come off as something or someone you're not, your salespeople and customers are going to smell it a mile away. And nothing looks worse than being phony.

Your first priority is to be true to yourself. Be who you are. Secondly, you must represent your company with the utmost respect, dignity, and honor. Finally, you have to continue to professionalize your sales team and the profession of sales.

You have a responsibility to all those who have gone before you and those who will come after you to conduct yourself in the most professional manner possible.

If you do those things, your style and legacy will be fine.

Valuing the story of the three envelopes

As I close this first chapter, and you get ready to take on what is going to be the most enjoyable ride of your career — the job of sales manager — I want to leave you with a story. A story told to me many years ago and one you can share with the person who replaces you (check out Chapter 16).

The story is about three envelopes.

A new sales manager had just been hired by large multi-national company. The previous sales manager, who was retiring, asked to meet with him privately at an off-site location.

When they met, the retiring manager handed the new manager a large manila folder containing three sealed envelopes numbered one through three.

"What's this?" the new guy asked.

"Any time you have a problem you can't seem to solve, open one of these in order starting with number one. It'll get you out of some tight situations," the experienced manager stated.

Things went great for the new sales manager for the first six or eight months, then all of a sudden the company lost a contract from its largest customer. Sales were about to be hit and hit hard. The new manager remembered the envelopes, went to his desk, and opened number one. Inside was an index card and printed on it was, "Blame everything on me."

So, the sales manager went before the board and blamed the loss of the client on the old sales manager. It was his fault for not securing a longer term deal and the new manager was doing all he could to bring on a new customer to replace the former client.

The board was satisfied with that and seemed a bit perturbed at the old manager. Crisis averted.

Close to a year went by before sales hit another snag and went into a slight decline. Wanting to head off any issue, the manager went to his desk and opened up envelope number two. The message inside read, "Reorganize."

So, that's what he did. He shuffled people around and told the board he was making the needed moves. Once again they seemed satisfied and even a bit impressed with his being proactive. With his reorganization, sales began to inch back up.

Then almost three years later, problems befell the company again. The top salesman left, taking three of the top four accounts. At his wit's end, the manager went to his office, opened the drawer, and slowly opened the final envelope.

The message read, "Make out three envelopes."

Chapter 2

So You Got the Job, Now What Do You Do?

In This Chapter

- Defining the position of a sales manager
- Establishing your management style
- Presenting yourself effectively as a manager

Congratulations! You got the job. Now the work begins. And, more than likely, you're experiencing equal parts pride and terror. You've worked many years to get this opportunity and now you feel a bit unsure where to begin.

Or maybe you've been a sales manager for a while, but you're finding yourself running into the same issues and aren't sure what to do. Well, lucky for you, there's an instruction manual: this book.

Relax and take a breath. You've been given the opportunity of a career that will reward you financially, emotionally, personally, and professionally. You're about to enter the world of sales management — where the lines can sometimes blur between what is sales and what is management — and you're expected to respond in the correct manner every time. Note: You won't.

Let me get this out of the way before I go any further: You're going to experience days and perhaps weeks when you sit in your chair and quietly say to yourself, "I know I'm supposed to be doing something, but I have no idea what it is!" Guess what? That's normal. If you knew all the answers, you would've had the job years ago. You're going to go through a learning curve, and although I do my best to make it as short as possible, there's no way to eliminate it.

This chapter will define what your job is and what it is not, show you how to balance work and home, and give you the foundation to be a successful sales manager. I give you advice on setting expectations for your team and maintaining standards for those working for you. Finally, I look at ways to earn your team's respect.

Understanding Your Role as Sales Manager

As the sales manager for your organization, it's your responsibility to lead and manage the sales team. If you're like many first time sales managers, that one statement leaves you glassy-eyed with a bead of sweat forming on your forehead.

Again, relax (I say that a lot, but it's usually the first thing you need to remember to do). That broad definition can be overwhelming and being overwhelmed kills the very traits you've exemplified in your career: creativity, a positive attitude, a desire for growth and leadership.

More than likely, your roles as sales manager includes:

- **Managing the sales team:** This simply means that you're responsible for your people. You are now the manager and anything (positive or negative) affecting the sales of the company begins and ends with you. You're the face of the only department in the company contributing to revenue.
- **Establishing goals and quotas:** In a perfect world, each salesperson sets goals and quotas that allow her to stretch and reach new heights every year. Unfortunately, that doesn't always happen. It's up to you to set the goals, objectives, and quotas for individual salespeople and for the team as a whole.
- **Training and developing sales skills:** This is where your past success as a salesperson comes into play. You must help each member of the sales department improve her skills. Everyone can get better at some part of the sales process — your job is to identify weaknesses and help convert them to strengths. And contrary to what they tell you in the initial interview, they all have weaknesses.
- **Assigning and defining geographical territories:** After you're in management and can see more of the big picture, some things jump out at you as obvious. Why are two people spending time in the same market on different days? One of the greatest wastes of time for salespeople is *windshield time:* those countless wasted hours between appointments where instead of seeing a prospect, you're staring at the road. At some point in your job, you'll need (and want) to address this and make things more efficient.
- **Counseling and leading individual salespeople:** In order to get the entire team pulling in the same direction, you must work on the individuals first. Because you're their sales manager, your team needs you to take the lead and create an environment where they can succeed. Don't

wait for people to ask for help (some never will). Understand that you most likely manage each person differently, so in order to find out what makes each person tick you must get to know each and every member of your team.

- **Reporting data to upper management:** Good news, bad news, any news — it all comes from you. This is one particular area you should never accept the answer, "That's the way we've always done it!" I hate that answer. That has killed more organizations than anything. It's up to you to find ways to use data to drive sales and provide yourself and others in management with good, actionable information. The things you wished you'd known as a salesperson are now the things you must know as a sales manager.
- **Creating incentive programs:** Whether you're using in-house programs or working with manufacturers and vendors, it's important to keep your salespeople engaged; keep them interested and striving to grow. Build and maintain a special incentive calendar and make the job fun! Additionally, a good sales manager will create team or departmental based incentives to reward the achievement of overall goals. This is just another way to create an atmosphere of working together and not against each other.
- **Establishing budgets:** Working out the budget is the second worst part of the job. The skills you used to become successful probably aren't related to sitting and going over spreadsheet after spreadsheet of numbers and projections. However, you now have the responsibility to create the budget for the sales department. It's not necessarily fun, but it has to be done. I will go into detail on the difference between budgets, goals, and forecasting in Chapter 12.
- **Hiring and firing salespeople:** If budgets are the second worst part of the job, this is the worst (especially the firing part). But the buck stops with you. It's your responsibility to continually upgrade the team in the field. To do so, sometimes you have to fire the bad ones and hire some more good ones.

If you ever get to a point where firing someone doesn't affect you take some time off. No matter how long you hold this position, it never gets easier. I talk about this more in Chapter 15.

Obviously this list is not all-inclusive and can change daily. The best managers are the ones who can handle the day-to-day issues, which inevitably come up without losing focus on long-term goals and objectives.

There will be situations every day which make you take your eye off your goals — just don't let them take your mind off them!

Remembering you work for the sales team, not vice versa

If there's one thing first-time or young managers need to know it's that you work for the rest of the salespeople, they don't work for you. They can function without you — you can't function without them.

There is absolutely nothing wrong with telling your salespeople as a group or individually, "My job is to work for you, not have you work for me." Not only will they respect you for your candor, but you set the stage for how you want to run your department.

This statement and mindset is crucial to your success, so you must understand exactly what it means: You come to work each day asking how you can help your sales force, not how they can help you. It's as simple as that. You run a bottom-up organization, not a top-down one.

Does Addie need you to help close a deal? Does Beatrice need you to place a phone call from a higher authority? Find out what each of your team needs from you. You're there to make them successful and many times that means simply helping them overcome some obstacle in the sales process.

Each day, ask yourself what you can do to make each member of your sales team stronger and better.

The easiest way to grow your sales

Without oversimplifying this, the easiest way to grow the sales of your company is to help each individual salesperson increase her sales. It's almost impossible for one person alone to move the needle very much on an organization's sales. However, if you can get each member on the entire team to grow her own business by just 10 percent, you can have a great impact on your company's sales and bottom line.

By attacking your job with a "how can I help my sales force?" attitude, you will find yourself with the opportunities to make a difference for each person whether she's a million-dollar producer or someone barely making her quota. Each person needs and deserves your leadership and management.

Begin your day, your week, and your month by asking yourself what you can do to help each of your people grow her sales. When you begin to lead in this manner, manage in this manner, and perform in this manner, you'll be amazed at the results.

You cannot demand people follow you as their leader. However, you can create an atmosphere and environment where others want to follow you because of how you lead.

Finally, you're the head of your department, and you must make decisions as such. The mindset of working for the sales team doesn't mean you let them run the show. You're in control, you're in charge — you just accomplish that by pulling rather than pushing.

Ultimately, you are the person who will answer for the performance, or lack thereof, of the sales team. You have to set and enforce the goals, critique and improve performance and develop your salespeople.

Understanding the line between sales and management

Are you in sales or are you in management? Well, the short answer is both. And it's not always easy to separate the two. You should never be anything less than authentic and genuine, but there are times where you must wear one of the two hats and do so diplomatically.

For example, the powers that be will make decisions that adversely affect your department. As a member of management, you must fully support what's best for the company first and foremost. Although you may not agree with all the decisions, you must keep those opinions behind closed doors and never share them with your salespeople. Their attitudes and their opinions are shaped in large part by yours. How you respond and react is how they will respond and react.

While there are things you cannot share with the sale department, understand there will be things senior management doesn't share with you. It's not because they don't trust you, it's simply not something you need to be involved in. Don't get upset because you don't know every single thing going on just because you're a manager now. One of these days you'll be glad to be left out of a few.

If you have to come down on one side or another in a certain situation, your first responsibility is to management. Even if you completely disagree with decisions made, when you stand in front of your sales team, you need to toe the company line. Is that easy? Absolutely not. It's even painful at times. Internally you'll be conflicted, but you are a member of management for a reason.

The value of going to bat for your team

Although agreement with management is a good call, there are also times when you must support your sales team or an individual sales person and go to bat for her. As a young salesperson, the company I worked for was acquiring another. As the lead salesperson on a project, I had made a commitment to a new customer that some members of management disagreed with, and at one point, overrode. My sales manager at the time backed me up and stood his ground basically saying, "If Butch told them we'd do it, we need to do it." He knew my personal credibility was on the line and knew I felt betrayed by those who sought to overturn the decision. I could not have been more indebted to him for sticking up for me and having my back. I felt a great need to show him that his confidence in me was not misplaced and though that happened more than 20 years ago, I still remember it to this day.

I always looked for and sought out opportunities to show my salespeople I had their back. I didn't create situations or orchestrate drama, but if the situation presented itself, I remembered how I felt and wanted them to feel the same.

When conflict occurs and the line between holding the company line and supporting your salesperson becomes blurred, you have a choice: you can fan the flames or put out the fire. I've known and seen people do both and I can assure you you'll be far more successful if you find ways to put out the fire.

There are no hard and fast rules as to how to pick your battles — it's just something you need to get a feel for. You'll know it when you see it and if you put the customer first, the employee second, you'll make the right decision the majority of the time.

But, never be afraid to change course. If you make a mistake, admit it and move on. You're human.

Empowering your sales team to make decisions (Don't do it for them)

It's clear that you work for the sales team instead of the team working for you. However, one of the biggest traps to avoid is to not let yourself be drawn into being nothing but a secretary for the sales team. And trust me, it's easy to get drawn in.

As far as you can according to industry and company policies, provide your salespeople with not only the responsibility but also the ability to make decisions for themselves up to a certain point. Whether it's pricing, terms, or other considerations, there is no way you can make every decision needed to operate a successful sales team. If you could, you wouldn't really need all those salespeople.

One of your first orders of business is to provide your sales team with the tools, resources, and other data needed to make decisions. Otherwise you'll spend your day on phone call after phone call discussing minute pricing details and so forth.

After you give your team members the resources to make their own decisions, you must establish parameters where they have the capacity to make good decisions — decisions that produce profitable results. With that you have two kinds of salespeople:

- **The doer:** This person makes every possible decision. She makes commitments not only on areas you've given her authority to, but may well step over that in an effort to not let anyone stand between her and her customer. Your biggest challenge with this salesperson is to keep them reigned in; keep them from becoming a Maverick who is off doing their own thing regardless of company policy.
- **The thinker:** No matter what you do, this person won't make a decision. She wants your input, feedback, and endorsement on everything she does — before she does it. The thinker overthinks and develops the old paralysis by analysis on even the smallest decisions. Your biggest challenge with this type of salesperson is to have her understand something I heard a long time ago: "Done is better than perfect."

Here's where being a manager comes in. You must successfully handle both types – the doer and the thinker. Let the doer have enough room to maneuver but keep her from breaking ranks and encourage or prod the thinker to make a decision.

Let all team members know that if you have an issue with a decision they make you'll sit down and discuss it in private.

Never call a salesperson out in public. Praise in public and critique in private.

The only way your team learns to make better decisions is by making mistakes and having you tell them and show them how to better handle that situation in the future.

It pays to solve problems sensibly

A few years ago, I had an issue with my satellite television provider — a provider I'd been with for almost 20 years. For whatever reason, the box atop my television went out and required a service technician to come out and replace it. I got in touch with the company, and the company set the appointment for 11 days later. Eleven days! Needless to say, I wasn't happy. You can bet if I were ordering its service I would've seen someone the next day, and I felt I was being pushed down the priority list.

So, I requested the entire month free (roughly $130) or I would call the competition, who I was sure would gladly accept my business. Believe it or not, I was told my provider could not give me a free month, but it could offer me a one-time $50 retention credit to stay with it and it'd discount my bill $50 a month for a year.

Do the math: I offered a $130 solution and the company countered with a $650 answer. How crazy is that? After literally laughing at the absurdity, I accepted the offer. Whatever you do, don't let yourself be in this position! Give your sales team and customer service the ability to make sensible decision to solve problems.

You have to do the same thing with the person making all the decisions. The doer will overstep her bounds at times, and you'll have to let her know you appreciate her desire to satisfy the customer, but that she must follow proper protocol.

The bottom line is to empower your people to grow their sales and solve customers' problems. Avoid creating a hierarchy where the simplest solution to a customer problem requires moving heaven and earth.

Managing, not babysitting (but sometimes both)

Your job consists of a certain amount of sales and a certain amount of management. Unfortunately, what you're usually not told prior to accepting the job is how much of your time is going to be spent as a babysitter. Obviously, I say that tongue-in-cheek. But, you are going to have to be the mother hen to a certain extent.

Make it clear early on that you expect your team to conduct themselves professionally at all times — on and off the job. Any time they're representing the company they're under your direction. Too many times at particular functions where alcohol is involved, someone ends up making poor decisions and you have to treat her like a child and punish her. (Hopefully, it's not severe enough to warrant dismissing her). Let your sales team know what kind of behavior you expect and that you won't tolerate petty infighting, rumors, and the like.

You're managing professional salespeople, not children. But, like in a group of children, some of your team will test you. Someone is always going to want to talk about someone else.

One of the greatest ways to stop team members complaining about each other is to interrupt the speaker when she starts to talk about another person on the team, go get the other person, and involve her in the conversation. This immediately brings that sort of thing to a halt.

The following is a creed I developed many years ago. I recommend copying it and having each of your people sign it:

- I will conduct myself each day as a professional and will represent my company and my product in the highest possible manner.
- I will be part of the solution and not part of the problem.
- I will readily help others and not hesitate to ask for help if I need it.
- I will talk to others and not about them.
- I will work to foster an environment where everyone can be successful.
- I will come to work each day ready to enjoy my job and display an attitude of gratitude.
- I will work with other departments to understand their needs.
- I will set a positive example for others in my actions, attitude, and communication.

Having everyone sign a document like this lets them know you're not there to be a babysitter; you're a manager, a mentor, and a confidant. They will appreciate your honesty and your dedication to the things that truly matter: helping them grow their sales.

Now, there will be times when someone needs to vent. It's inevitable. One day soon (if it hasn't happened already), someone will walk into your office shut the door, and you'll see the steam rising off her head. This is not the time to have her recite the creed. (Not if you want to see your family again).

It may be a disagreement with another department or any number of issues, but this one is serious and it's time for you to listen. However, ask one question before the rant begins: "Do you want me to do something about this or just let you vent?"

I mean this sincerely, find out what the venter expects of you because it changes how you listen and respond. More times than not, the person simply wants to vent and get whatever is bugging her off her chest. Your job is to sit and listen. On the other hand, if the person wants you to help solve a problem, you need to be prepared to ask a lot of questions and get to the root of the issue before flying off the handle. But, if she just wants to vent, let her. Everyone needs to at one time or another.

Keeping your relationships professional

In many cases, being a new sales manager means you were recently a member of the sales team — your friends, your buddies, your girlfriends. Well, not anymore. One of the changes you must make as you accept your new position is that you can no longer have the same type of relationship with your salespeople as you did before.

Let me guess: Of the people on your sales team, there are some you really like and some, eh, maybe not so much. That's all in the past. As a leader and a manager you can't play favorites — positively or negatively.

It's difficult, uncomfortable, and awkward at times, but it's imperative that you keep all your relationships as professional as possible. In some cases the people you're now managing have more experience and are older than you — and you have to earn their respect by how you conduct yourself.

My own personal career path led me to be a division sales manager at 25 and vice president of sales at age 30. The problem was I was supervising, managing, and leading the exact group of people I'd just been laughing with, hanging out with, and talking about management with. Well, those things had to stop immediately. It's the only way the job can be done professionally.

If you find yourself in the awkward position of becoming the boss to your former teammates, immediately schedule one-on-one meetings with every member of your sales team. Have the following discussion with those who may feel like they are in trouble because they weren't your best friend or you'd had some disagreements:

> "Mary, I know we've had an issue or issues in the past when we didn't see eye to eye, but I want you to know that's all in the past. My main goal in this position is to make you as successful as possible. Anything that's happened before is in the past, and I want you to know I'm professional enough to make sure that I don't let it influence how I make decisions or lead the department. I'd like to ask you to give me the opportunity to prove this, and I am going to ask you put our differences in the past as well and let's move forward today, together, focused on growing your sales and satisfying your customers. Fair enough?"

Guess what? Nobody has ever said, "No that's not fair enough." This speech accomplishes several things:

- You acknowledge the past issue. Don't try to ignore it and hope it goes away.
- You express your own professionalism. You put past difficulties behind you and pledge to make Mary successful.
- You ask someone you had disagreements with to work *with* you to make her successful.

That's a pretty strong statement and one you should seriously consider.

You also need to deal with the person or persons who were your good buddies when you were a member of the sales team. As important as the conversation you have with people you had issues with, the conversation you have with your friends is even more important. You need to let friends know from the beginning that you're going to keep the relationship professional.

Now, there are different schools of thought as to whether you can socialize with these people. Personally, I believe it's a bad idea and creates situations you're better off without. That's not to say you can't ever go out to dinner or over to a friend's house, but the relationship has to change — it has to be one of manager and salesperson, not two friends.

Just like you sat down with the people you'd had negative issues with, you must also sit down with your friends:

> "Hey, Marisol, I know we go way back and I hope you appreciate the position I'm in. Everyone is expecting me to treat you differently because we're friends — and, I am going to treat you differently. I'm probably going to be harder on you than the others for two reasons: I don't want there to be any perception of playing favorites, and I expect more out of you. I'm not going to let you get by with average work. Please understand this is extremely hard for me and I'm going to have to make decisions that you and I may not agree on, but I've got to do what I feel is best. Fair enough?"

Again, what can Marisol say? "No, I want you to treat me like the teacher's pet!"

What you accomplish with this conversation includes:

- Your friend knows you're still friends, but the relationship must change.
- Your friend also knows she's going to be treated differently — but because you expect more from her than the others.

Wow, how powerful is that? Do you think your friend will come out singing your praises? If she's a true friend, she's happy for your promotion, and if she's a professional, she understands the predicament you're in.

The main thing is to not ignore the situation with former peers — face it head on and keep all your relationships professional. Setting those ground rules in the beginning will serve you well in the weeks, months, and years to come.

Establishing Your Own Management Style

Early in your tenure as a new sales manager, it's important to establish and communicate your expectations to each member of your sales organization. Some have their own ideas of where the lines are drawn, a few may be living in the past with your predecessor, and still others may have no preconceived notions and need the direction immediately.

Whatever the case, you are now the responsible party and it's up to you to set the ground rules of what is and is not acceptable and not just from a performance standpoint.

Sadly, some will test you and see what they're able to get away with. Get ready — it's probably going to happen. You're going to have to flex your manager muscle for some who just want to see if you will. Although I've never liked to lead or manage in that manner, it's unfortunately all some people respond to.

Write your expectations for your team members so each person has a copy and understands what's expected of her. Although this document may not be drastically different from the one in operation with their prior manager, you must put your stamp on it.

You can use the Three P Method:

- **What are your Performance requirements?** Put in writing the required number of calls, new accounts, or any other metric you use to measure performance. Your people must know what criteria you will use to judge them. Don't keep this a secret — they always need to know if they're doing a good job or not.
- **What are your Participation requirements?** Do you require attendance at sales meetings, group meetings, department meetings, or other functions? Will you send team members to trade shows, continuing education, or other opportunities? Make clear what you expect and/or require them to participate in. Don't wait until the last minute to notify them.
- **What are your Professionalism requirements?** Whether or not your company has an official conduct policy, have one for your department. Be specific on how they are to conduct themselves with customers, other associates, and the general public. If you have a dress code or other codes of conduct, get it out in the open now. Professionalism includes integrity, honesty, and attempting each day to satisfy customers. Being professional isn't difficult. Set the guidelines and most of your people will meet and exceed them immediately. Those who don't probably don't need to be part of your team in the first place.

How to handle what others think of you in your new role

Even if you've been with the company for years and just got promoted, you're the topic of conversation throughout the sales department and the company, "What do you think about the new sales manager?" People form opinions — some good and some not so good. Some will be happy for you and some not so much. But, how you establish and communicate your expectations will go a long way in either strengthening the good opinions or dispelling the myths.

Here's a tip: Even though salespeople generally have extremely positive attitudes, they're some of the most self-conscious people on earth. A salesperson can add two and two and get seven and convince themselves they're correct — it's just part of their nature.

Instead of letting the grapevine establish the ground rules for how you manage and what you expect, do it yourself. Get out in front of it and control it. This will save you tons of time and save them a few ulcers.

Being a great sales manager is ultimately about being a great person. If you treat others with respect, lead your team with honesty and integrity, and conduct yourself professionally you'll be miles ahead of the game.

Listening more than you talk

As a salesperson you're successful in large part because of your ability to listen and honestly hear what your prospects and customers were telling you. As a manager you must put those same skills to use in dealing with your sales team. Early on you're going to want to solve all the world's problems overnight. While that's a worthy goal, it will sometimes cause you to make knee-jerk reactions and poor decisions.

Be quick to listen, slow to speak, and ensure you understand the entire situation before making a decision. You've heard your entire life that there are two sides to every story, and in some cases there are three and four sides. You just have to make sure you have all the information available at your disposal.

This is especially true when dealing with interdepartmental conflict. Listen to everyone — you have to put on the judge's robe here. Don't assume anything. Ask questions and listen before ruling.

Sometimes you must make a quick decision. Someone has to make a call and you're the manager so it falls to you to decide how to proceed. In those cases, consider the following questions:

- **What's best for the customer?** If every decision you make is customer-centered, you'll win far more than you'll lose. Are there times you have to go against this? Sure, there are no hard-and-fast rules, but keeping the customer first makes you a better manager and your company a better provider.
- **What's best for the employee?** A close second to your customers are your employees or associates. Be very conscious of decisions and how they impact them and their lives. And, I'm not just talking about safety or other obvious issues. Most salespeople I've met would much rather you mess with their safety than their commission check, so be very aware of how decisions affect their income or potential for income.
- **The company's need to make a profit.** Is there a reason this point is last in the list? In my opinion, yes. If you keep the first two questions in the proper order this question takes care of itself.

But, when all else fails, and you must make a decision simply do the best you can with what you have to work with.

Being consistent

Nothing costs you credibility with your sales team more than inconsistency — inconsistency in your decision making, communication, or administration. If you want to drive your salespeople crazy, have an "idea of the week" mentality where you get all fired up and change everything only to lose interest in it, stop measuring it, and change the focus the next week. I've seen this happen hundreds of times.

Good salespeople want consistency. After you establish your ground rules and operating procedures, don't deviate from them. And, before you go trotting out a new program, check it, double-check it, and triple-check it. You never lose credibility for yourself or the company faster than rolling out a program that hasn't been well thought out.

Setting the bar high, but not too high

Your first instinct when you take over the department is to raise everyone's quota 50 percent (okay, so that may be a slight exaggeration). Again, take your time. Be careful not to set the bar too high in the beginning. As you establish yourself, you want to be seen as someone who asks and helps your team stretch, but is also in tune with the market enough to be realistic.

Taking the time to get it right

I had a superior entrust me with creating a commission program — one that was much needed. In this case the sales team was getting paid on sales dollars instead of gross profit (a huge no-no in my book). As you may know, paying someone strictly on sales dollars doesn't necessarily benefit the company. For instance, they could be making hundreds of thousands of dollars in sales with little or no gross profit and getting paid like they were the greatest thing since sliced bread.

However, by paying on gross profit — you are truly being rewarded for what you bring to the company. Being the new guy, the rest of the team was already a bit leery of me and now I start talking about messing with their paycheck. Needless to say, the mood was tense.

As I dug in, I kept running into areas where I wasn't confident that the gross profit numbers were accurate.

Don't be shocked to know that some companies struggle to determine exactly how much they're making. And, as you well know, everyone thinks the company is making far more than it actually does — there is a general sense that revenue is being hidden from the salespeople.

The deeper I got into this program the more obvious it became that the data I needed wasn't easily accessible. So what should've been a relatively easy project took almost a year. But, we tested it, re-tested it, and then tested it again.

When I met with the sales team I told them I would never do something that I wasn't completely confident in the results and I kept my word. I was consistent in my communication and my style.

I kept them informed at every turn — even though it created even more distrust and uncertainty in their mind that it was taking so long. But, in the end it proved to be a very positive move.

I lost three salespeople during that time, but if they had that much distrust for me or the company, I didn't really want them on my team anyway. And, if they couldn't see the need to be paid on gross profit dollars rather than sales dollars, I certainly wasn't going to miss them.

Throughout the entire process I was consistent in my communication and the way I handled myself. I never shied away from questions or failed to keep them informed. The news won't always be good, but consistency is critical. And, as any manager will tell you, bad news never gets better with age.

You can always increase your goals and quotas, but the last thing you want to do is to decrease them because you were a bit overzealous.

Far too many decisions are sent to the field from the Ivory Tower of Sales Management. I want you to set big, bold goals but once again listen — get input from your salespeople and let them be a part of the process. This will greatly enhance their interest in and achievement of their goals and quotas.

Just as you can set the bar too high on quotas, you can do the same with your time. Understand going into the job that everything is going to take twice as long as you think it is — that's just how it works. It's extremely easy to overcommit and get yourself into sticky situations you could have avoided if you had just slowed down a bit.

If you finish something prior to deadline, nobody is going to complain, but if you miss a few deadlines early in the job or end up burning yourself out because you overcommitted, you'll know it and feel it.

Learning the magic words: No and delegate

There are two words you must use in order to become a successful sales manager. They're both small words, but they have to be a part of your vocabulary on a daily basis. If you have a highlighter or a way to mark this section of the book, do so — underline this, it's that important.

The words are no and delegate. Nowhere in sales training do you learn to use these words, but as a sales manager they can save you time, frustration, and heartache.

As a new manager you will have not only salespeople try to dump their problems and issues on you but other departments trying to do the same. It's almost as if they smell fresh blood. Everyone knows you're eager to please and be a part of the management team. But, never let someone else hand you their problem — and trust me, many people are just waiting for you to get your desk unpacked so they can.

Some people trying to foist their problems on you act as if it's natural and insist that the previous sales manager did the same thing. Before you accept their burdens, ask yourself these two questions:

- **Am I the best person to handle this?** Just as you aren't a secretary for the salespeople, you're also not a data entry clerk for another department. Don't accept handoffs without asking yourself, "Am I the best person to handle this?" If you aren't, don't be afraid to tell that person no. Don't agonize over letting others down — you haven't. Instead of letting them down, you've let them know your time is valuable.

  One of the biggest problems I see in young sales managers (and I was as guilty as anyone) is that they take on tasks and projects in order to keep from putting others out and end up put themselves out. I used to bring on so much unnecessary stress and worry over things I had nothing to do with because I let others hand me their problem. Don't be like me.

- **Does this task directly lead to sales growth?** Every project, task, and program you take on should be with the express intention of moving sales forward and growing your team. Now, there will be projects you work on as part of a team that don't fit these criteria, but that's not what I'm talking about. You can certainly sit on a company committee working on the annual employee appreciation day, but be sure to spend your sales hours on projects or tasks related to sales.

No is a perfectly acceptable answer. You don't have to qualify it or explain yourself, but if you'd like a great way to answer when someone tries to drag you down one of these rabbit holes, try this: "I'd like to help, but I'm really not the best person to do that. I need to focus on the sales department right now. Thanks for asking, though." That's the best way in the world to not accept that handoff.

Very close behind no is delegate. Think about this: You didn't get your position so you could do everything yourself. You're the sales manager — notice the word *manager.* Your job is to lead and manage — not do everything by yourself. As you develop your task list, ask yourself the two questions in the preceding list. But, this time, ask whether someone in your department should be doing the task.

If you have an assistant, you may experience a bit of uneasiness in asking her to do things for you. But that's her job. I had a manager one time who said success came down to three little words: del e gate.

There will be times where upper management may hand you tasks that take away from your job of managing the sales department. Once again, clarify what is most important. Simply ask, "Just so I'm understanding and prioritizing correctly, I am going to put aside working on the new account development program (or whatever you were working on) and get this done for you."

Sometimes that's all it takes for them to suddenly think of someone else who would be better suited for the job. I'm not in any way suggesting you don't let your superiors hand you projects — that means they have confidence in you — but it can be a juggling act. Just make sure your time is being used properly and they are aware of what you are not doing while you're handling their new project.

Industry associations have some sort of sixth sense when it comes to new managers. You will be invited to be a part of every board, committee, meeting and association possible. Choose wisely. Some of these can turn into full time jobs will little or no direct benefit other than being seen as a mover and a shaker in your industry.

Don't bog yourself down with menial tasks — spend your time on the big picture and pass off the rest.

Finding your balance between work and home

One common issue facing all professionals is the battle to keep your personal and business life in balance. I've had people tell me, "When I'm at work I feel guilty that I'm not spending time with my family, and when I'm at home I feel guilty that I'm not working." That is one of the great paradoxes of successful people. Get used to it. It's going to happen — especially in the early part of your career.

People tend to focus on what they think they should be doing instead of what they are doing. Instead of enjoying where they are, they long for where they aren't.

I know it sounds like a cliché, but keep your focus on the here and now. That's all you can control. Live in the moment and block out everything else. Develop your plan, work it, and don't let outside influences pull you away from what you determined was important. Easier said than done? Absolutely.

Worry and stress come from thinking about, focusing on, and placing yourself in positions where you have little or no control. Today. Now. This moment. That's what you can control. Make the best of it and the rest tends to take care of itself.

It takes not only practice but a commitment to saying, "no": "No, I'm not taking that on right now" or "No, I'm going to delegate that to someone else." Or "No, I'm going to focus on what I can control at this time."

As a young sales manager, I had a job that covered everything west of the Mississippi River. It seemed as if I would fly in on Friday, dump a suitcase, and fly out on Sunday to another rental car and hotel room. With three young children at home, that got old quickly. I had to force myself to take more time off than normal because of the travel schedule. On weeks I wasn't traveling, I was home right on time. Nothing can replace lost time with children as they grow.

I had a friend tell me recently of his father's funeral, and how for over five hours he and his siblings greeted mourners, all of whom wanted to stop and share a story about his dad. Not a single one talked about his work or how nice his truck was. They all talked about what kind of person he was.

As a new manager, you'll feel like you're on a treadmill at times. That treadmill led me to open-heart surgery at 43 years of age.

Keep your balance. Enjoy your family time and your work time.

Displaying the Characteristics of a Successful Leader

You're the sales manager. You got the job for a reason — you're good at what you do. You've not only exhibited the skills to be a great salesperson, but you've got what it takes to be a manager, as well. If you've been promoted into this position, you'll find yourself now supervising people you recently were working beside.

Although you should be proud of your accomplishment, this isn't the time to flex your muscles. I actually knew a gentleman who took over a sales department and opened his first meeting with the words, "There's a new sheriff in town." Um. Really? Needless to say, he didn't win over many people. You can catch more flies with honey than with vinegar.

Stay humble

The most successful sales managers (or managers in general) are those who don't even have to introduce themselves as the boss. Everyone knows who they are by the way they carry themselves, the way the act, and the way they treat others.

It's much easier to pull your team along with you than to push them. And, it's even easier still if they trust your leadership enough to follow you without having to be pulled along.

Make it your mantra to accept less credit and take more blame than you deserve. If you do that, you'll have the respect of your sales team, your clients, and your coworkers. If there are wins to be celebrated, make sure your team gets credit for the win — this is not the time or place to feed your ego.

Being humble is one of the greatest qualities a true leader can demonstrate. And we've all known (and probably worked with or for) someone who was just the opposite — it was all about them. They were the smartest, they were the best, they were the reason anything good ever happened. Is that the legacy you want to leave? Humble yourself and your sales team will want to run through a wall for you.

Be firm but fair

Establish a reputation of being firm but fair early on. If and when you must counsel, critique, or otherwise discipline one of your salespeople, do so in a manner that doesn't undermine your position and doesn't damage her confidence. Have all the facts in front of you and take personalities and your likes and/or dislikes out of the equation. The salesperson you're talking to should know exactly what happened, what you found to be the problem, and how you feel it should've been handled. There's no place for veiled, vague criticism.

Your position should be firm — no wavering. Don't show one ounce of uncertainty when it comes to handling difficult personnel situations. Understand the employee will have excuses, an opinion, and other ideas about what happened or should have. Listen to the employee, but ultimately, you must hold your ground.

Just as much as you should be firm, you should also be fair. Never, ever, ever play favorites. Always document any disciplinary action in writing. Remember that nobody is immune — even your superstar who exceeds quota every month. When you display fairness, it's noticed by everyone. Trust me. The only thing noticed quicker is if you make a decision that shows or even hints at favoritism.

As you grow into your position, many of these things will become second nature, but there's only one way to learn these skills and attitudes and that's by doing.

One of the easiest ways to establish yourself as a fair manager is to never ask your salespeople to do anything you wouldn't or haven't done. Don't put them in a position where they resent you for simply asking them to do their job. You've most likely done everything they're asked to do, but if you enact a new policy or put in new requirements, humble yourself to do the same.

The greatest manager I ever knew was a gentleman I worked with for almost 15 years and is my mentor to this day. He displayed humility day in and day out and made it a point to let everyone know we worked together — nobody worked for him, even though he owned the company.

He never flaunted his position or pulled rank on anyone; he just had the persona of being a natural leader. I've talked to several people whom I worked with and who worked with him who felt the same. He's the type person you not only wanted to follow, but someone you wanted to be proud of you. It was almost a strange feeling. He just had that aura of a great leader.

He always made the right decisions, which weren't made because he was motivated by money but because they were the right thing to do; money just seemed to follow that.

One of the simplest things he ever did had a profound impact on me (I'm talking about it almost 30 years later) was where he parked when he came to work. I asked him one day why he didn't have a reserved parking spot next to the front door instead of having to park well away from the building at the back of the lot.

I'll never forget his response: "I was going into a business one time as a customer and parked close to the building. The receptionist told me I'd have to move because I was in the owner's parking spot. Now, I'm a customer and was told I'd have to park somewhere else? So, I got in my car and left and never went back. I don't want to create that environment at our company. Our customer is most important, then our associates. A little parking space isn't going to help me, but it could certainly hurt me."

Did he have a right to park where he wanted? Absolutely, but he saw the bigger picture and humbled himself. It made him a leader others wanted to follow.

Be flexible and open to input

I spent a lot of time telling you to be firm. Now, I'm telling you to be flexible. Wait, Butch, I'm confused? Let me clarify: When you're meting out discipline, you have to be firm but fair. However, as you set the tone for how you're going to run your department, the best thing you can do is get input from other departments and your sales team themselves.

If you're tasked with creating a policy manual or something similar don't feel like you have to be the sole person working on the project. Recruit some assistance and not just from your top salespeople. Sometimes getting your weaker salespeople involved in side projects does them more good than it does your top-tier folks.

As you enact policies and programs, there's no shame in changing direction if you feel the need to do so. The only exception to that rule is if you're working on a commission program. Make sure you have that figured out from every angle before you ever trot it out in front of everyone.

Part of being a leader and a manager is to help others grow, and by soliciting their opinion you show them respect and that you value their input. While you can limit this to just the sales department, asking for input from other departments strengthens your position as a manager and a leader within the company. I'm not talking about pawning your work off on them, but about sincerely soliciting their input. The more opinions you get involved in a project the better.

I don't mean to infer you should involve everyone in the your project, but simply you should get their input, ideas and suggestions. If it's part of your job, you have to do it but that doesn't mean you can't benefit from others' experience and knowledge.

Chapter 3

Establishing Good Working Relationships across Departments

In This Chapter

- Understanding the importance of communication
- Remembering to listen as well as talk
- Getting along with various personalities
- Getting your point across well in writing
- Using other forms of communication well

As a sales manager you're a member of management, and as such you'll be called upon to work with and through other departments within your organization. One of the most useful non-selling skills you can develop is the art of communicating and working with the other people in your company.

Communication used to predominately mean talking face to face, but today that's no longer the case. You leave voicemails and send text messages, type emails and communicate via social media. Each form of communication has certain pitfalls, which I discuss in this chapter. Much communication takes place via email these days, and I outline some do's and don'ts with email communication and discuss the tightrope walk needed to deal with the many different personalities within your company.

Communicating effectively and having good, professional relationships across departments makes your job much easier; you need each and every one of these departments in order to succeed.

In this chapter I talk about how your actions affect others, the overall value of good communication skills, and the need to know what others do every day.

The more you know about how your entire company operates, the better you can manage your department — and share this information with your own department.

If you've been promoted from within the company, you may already have a working knowledge of how things flow through your organization. However, if you're new to the company and/or industry, it's critical to understand the role each department plays in satisfying your customer.

Communicating Effectively as a Sales Manager

As a salesperson, you know the value of effective communication. If your prospect doesn't understand your product, what it does, and the need it fills or the problem it solves, you're not going to make the sale.

By the same token, it's vitally important to communicate effectively within the walls of your own building. Being able to share your point of view and understand that of others is only part of the job. There are going to be times when you must sell other employees, managers, or departments on your ideas, projects, or programs.

The best managers are extremely good communicators. They not only make it easy for others to understand them, but they easily understand others, as well.

I believe effective communication can solve 99.9 percent of problems faced in business today. If each of us would go into every interaction with the goal of understanding the other party, listening intently, and asking questions when needed instead of just trying to get our point across, we'd have far fewer problems.

Understanding how your actions affect others

Every time you add a new customer, make a sale, or even handle a credit or other customer-related issue, a waterfall of actions takes place throughout your entire company. In order to be the most successful manager you can be, you need to know exactly what happens throughout the entire chain from start to finish.

For example, when you have a new customer application in hand, think to yourself, "Where is this going from here, and then from there to where, and from there . . ." and so on.

Now, if you aren't aware of what has to occur just to set up an account, you may not understand why it takes a few business days. It isn't as simple as just checking someone's credit before setting up the account.

Figure 3-1 is a pretty realistic example. In fact, your company may have even more steps. To see how the process works for yourself, take some time and walk an application from department to department. That way you not only know what happens, but you get to see what each person does in order to accommodate a new account.

I am in no way trying to talk you out of generating new accounts. However, it's important that you see the big picture and what happens every step along the way.

Salesperson
forwards credit application to
Sales Manager
ensures proper information available and forwards to
Credit Manager
places calls, checks references, and runs appropriate reports and forwards to
CFO
declines or approves and establishes credit limit and forwards to
Data Entry/IT
sets up account in computer with pertinent information and forwards to
Purchasing
builds necessary inventory or adds required items and forwards to
Production
makes any needed changes and forwards to
Transportation
routes account for proper delivery and sends back to
Sales Manager
logs new account and notifies
Salesperson

Figure 3-1: Mapping the sales process.

The next thing you need to be mindful of is what happens when something gets fouled up — for whatever reason — and the customer has to be taken care of. If your salesperson forgets to turn in an order on time and puts the purchasing, production, and transportation departments to the test, do you know what happens in those departments? Does your sales team understand the lengths these other departments go through? They should.

You, as the sales manager, must understand the process well enough to teach it. You also need to be sensitive to what other departments spend on human capital and other resources when they have to fix a mistake or correct a problem. There's a cost associated with everything, and you should at least have a sense of what it is.

Every department in your company has to support the efforts of your sales team. The more in tune with their world you are, the more likely your colleagues in other departments are to want to help you because they know you spent the effort to get to know them, their jobs, and their challenges.

Sales may be the only department in the company that contributes directly to revenue — all others are an expense — but the people in other departments don't want to hear you tell them that. You need them to help satisfy your customers. In fact, you're nowhere without them. So it only makes sense to treat them professionally and understand their world a bit and what they go through to fill, deliver, and bill the orders you and your salespeople sell.

Take the time to learn the entire process. If you must ask your boss to allow you to spend a day with each department, do so. It will be one of the best investments of your time all year and an investment that will pay dividends for a long, long time.

Communicating without over-communicating

There's a fine line between communicating enough and over-communicating. Some people say you can't over-communicate, but you can. If the accounting department tells you they're working on processing an application, there's no need to check with them hourly. In fact, if the person you call every hour is the vindictive type, he'll move your application to the bottom of the stack for that sort of thing. (I know, I've been on the bottom of the stack.)

The best way to discover how to communicate with other departments is to observe what other managers do. Find someone you feel is a good communicator and watch and listen to what he does. See how he really expresses himself. Pay attention to how he asks questions. Observe that he seems genuinely interested in others and always seems to know what to say and when to say it.

Developing a professional vocabulary

The more time you spend with other managers, the more you communicate verbally. Your vocabulary is crucial. Many people judge you (fairly or unfairly) by your command of your language and how well you can express yourself. A strong vocabulary will serve you well your entire career and is an investment in your future.

Don't be one of those people who does nothing but throw around big words just to try to impress someone. If you want to really improve yourself, improve your vocabulary. Take an online course, or read, or otherwise learn to make yourself sound professional.

Understand the proper use of technical terms within your industry. Nothing makes you look worse than trying to sound like you know what you're talking about only to be so far off base it's embarrassing. Sadly, those sort of things stay with you for a long time.

A professional should always avoid any jokes, comments or words which could in any way be taken in an offensive manner. When in doubt, don't. A quick laugh from the guys isn't worth it.

There are also numerous books in various formats available on the subject of communication, including *Communication Skills For Dummies* by Elizabeth Kuhnke (Wiley), to guide you to being a better communicator.

Proper, professional communication is essential in being able to work with other departments. The world of technology has opened up so many forms of communication. Past generations would simply get up and go to someone else's office or perhaps page them on the telephone. Today you have email, voice mail, texting, and more. It can be tempting to employ all of these at once, but that can come across as impatient and definitely over-communicating.

Again, communications is the key, but over-communication is a nuisance to others. After you ask someone to do something, give him time to do it. Over-communicating sends the message that you don't have confidence in him to do the job or don't think he will do the job. Until someone proves you wrong, assume he'll get the job done.

Listening Carefully and Asking Questions

One of the greatest examples you can set for your salespeople is showing a burning desire to learn; to be curious; to ask questions, and to know as much about your business as possible.

The best way to create meaningful dialogue and communicate effectively with other departments is to truly understand the role they play in your organization.

When you have knowledge of how other departments operate, you not only become a much greater communicator, but you have a really good idea of the big picture and where you and your department fit into it.

Spend time with each department — preferably a day — so that you can see how and what they do. Don't waste that time! Soak up knowledge like a sponge.

Create a notebook for each department and write down everything you can during your time there.

I'm not suggesting you must be able to step in and run the IT Department if someone calls in sick, but you have to understand what the IT world is like. What upsets the routine? What battles does it face on a daily basis?

One of the side benefits of these sit-in days is that you earn a lot of respect from your fellow managers if — and this is a big *if* — you go into it with the right frame of mind. If you go into it really wanting to learn, being curious, and digging in deep, they'll notice. At the same time, if you just show up, watch the clock, play on your phone, or otherwise waste their time, they'll know that, too.

As you visit with other departments, offer them the opportunity to have one or more people ride with your sales team. After you set the tone with your day in their department, most will take you up on the offer.

Almost without fail, other departments think the salespeople don't do anything but play golf, entertain customers, and take off early. They really have no idea what your people do. Let them come experience it first hand, but welcome them as a guest and treat them with respect.

Think about this: your salesperson calls on a customer and has someone from production, or purchasing, or whatever department with him. The introduction should go something like this, "Mary, I want to introduce you to Mike from our production department. We're always looking for ways to better serve our customers, and we think it's important that every department in the company get to know our customer's business as well as possible. When Mike goes back to his job, he'll be able to share with the rest of his team how what they do impacts your business and get them started thinking of ways to innovate and grow." That, my friends is powerful.

Make sure the people riding along understand that they're guests and their role is to observe. Suggest they hold their questions until they're back in the car or at the office. And by all means, hold them to the same dress code you do your salespeople.

Navigating Personalities at Work

Most successful businesses and organizations are made up of many different personality types. In fact, that's what makes them successful — if everyone thought the same, responded the same, and performed the same, any business would fail pretty quickly. It would be a pretty peaceful place to work, though . . . while the business lasted.

The strengths and weaknesses of each member of the team are needed in order to provide a balance allowing the company or organization to progress, innovate, and succeed. But, along with that comes the inevitable minefield of different personalities.

If you're new to management, understand that not everyone was promoted to his position because he has the same skill set you possess. The truth is that other managers probably have skills you don't have or are strong where you're weak — that's what makes the entire management team strong and diverse.

Although it's important to have a varied set of personalities running an organization, remember that the rest of the team processes information or makes decisions based on a totally different set of criteria than you do. What's important to you isn't necessarily important to them and vice versa.

Remembering why you aren't in accounting

The skills that make a great salesperson probably make a horrible accountant. And what makes a great accountant more than likely makes a poor salesperson. Each department within the company is made up of different personalities, but perhaps the two most diametrically opposite are accounting and sales.

You need the folks in accounting and they need you, but there are going to be times when you cannot figure out how they think like they do. They think the same thing about you!

A salesman and an accountant are crossing the street . . .

For a true picture of how differently the sales and accounting departments operate, let me tell you about the salesman and accountant crossing the street.

The accountant looks to his left and sees that it's clear. He then turns to look to his right and again, there's nothing coming. To be sure he turns back to look to his left, just in case something happened over there while he was looking to his right. Once again, the coast is clear. With that in mind, he thinks, "*Well, I better check that right side again*" so he waits to cross before he looks right yet again.

Just as before there's nothing coming from the right. But, before he crosses he wants to check one last time to be double sure, so he looks back to his left only to be distracted by screeching tires, honking horns, and people shouting obscenities. He looks up to see the salesman who took off across the street, having not looked either direction and ignoring oncoming traffic because he thought he could make it.

You will have a much longer, happier, more productive, and ulcer-free career if you realize early on that other departments don't operate with the same value system you do. That's not to say either one of you is right and the other is wrong; you're just different. You're concerned with sales and gross profit, and although those drivers ultimately determine the overall success or failure of a company, you have to grasp the fact that accounting, purchasing, production, transportation, and other departments don't wake up every morning with those being their sole focus.

The more you can understand and accept how the people in other departments operate and what makes them good at what they do, the better manager you'll be, and the easier it will be to pass that information down to your sales team.

Just as with learning to communicate with other departments, discovering how those departments operate, what's important to them, and how they're graded gives you a much greater understanding of the big picture of how your company operates on a day-to-day basis.

For example, assume you have a customer who has a last-minute request you have to fulfill. Your thoughts are on satisfying that customer, but you need to be aware of the fact that the production and transportation departments are also dealing with overtime, production numbers, and efficiency criteria. Your little favor on a Friday afternoon could affect their entire month.

Again, that's not to say everyone in the company doesn't want to satisfy the customer, but when you see the challenge through others' eyes, you're much more sensitive to what they deal with.

When you truly understand and appreciate what other departments do in order to solve a problem, satisfy a customer, or otherwise pull a rabbit out of a hat, the people in those departments are much more likely to work with you.

There's a big difference between calling the transportation manager and telling him you need a special delivery for a customer and calling and saying, "I know you're always working to make our deliveries more efficient and to save time, fuel, and other resources, but I need to help a customer, and it's probably going to hurt your numbers for the week. How can we make this work?"

Has the problem changed? Has what the transportation department got to do changed? No. But, your attitude and how you approach the issue makes all the difference in the world!

If you have a purchasing department in your company, be aware that they're not judged on sales like you are. On the contrary, they're judged on turning inventory and maximizing the company's capital. Although you may like them to keep a year's supply of every single item on hand, that's not going to happen. There will be times where you're out of stock on something you need — in fact, if you're not, your company is carrying too much inventory (but that's another book).

The more you can understand and appreciate how each member of management is judged on their job and how that figures into their daily decision making, the better you can be at navigating through that minefield. You'll also be seen as a leading member of the management team because few of your peers have the same grasp of how the entire company operates and works in harmony.

Picking your battles

You're well versed in communicating with other departments and have a good handle of how they work, process information, make decisions, and judge their work. Yet, you still have a disagreement. Oops!

Disagreements happen. They're a part of business. If everyone got along, you'd have that defunct company where everyone thought alike, acted alike, talked alike, and so on. And you'd probably be out of business before you finish this chapter.

It's important to understand you aren't going to win every dispute. Nobody does. And, if you did, you'd be the most disliked member of management. You'd be resented by everyone else, have your birthday ignored, and otherwise be ostracized.

Therefore, you have to pick your battles. You're only going to get so many wins every year, so you have to ask yourself if what you disagree about is really worth giving up one of your few victories. Is this one worth it or should you save the digging your heels in and holding your ground for another issue?

A manager who can disagree without being disagreeable is more respected than one who throws a fit every time something doesn't go right. Also, it's a sign of strength, not weakness, when you hear everyone out and decide to do it how the other person wants it done instead of how you think it should be done.

Every time you have an issue with another manager or another department, you represent your entire sales team whether you realize it or not. Keep your disagreements professional and never let them get personal.

For the most part, your team members won't understand that you can't win them all. That's why you're the manager and they aren't. Your salespeople are going to want you to fight till your last breath for every issue that arises. Part of being a good manager is balancing the two — keeping your team satisfied while not inciting every other department in the company to let the air out of your tires.

Trust your instincts. You'll know when the times comes for you to really put up a fight. But even when you do keep it professional and focus on the solution, not the problem.

If you're solving a problem created by a mistake in another department, there is no value in pointing out who made the mistake. Solve the problem, take care of your customer or whoever was inconvenienced first, then work with the manager of that department to prevent future problems. It doesn't matter how it happened, what matters is how you solve it.

The more you approach problems, disagreements and disputes in this manner, the more wins you'll have in your bank because other managers will respect your management style.

Just as you do with customers, when dealing with other departments understand that just because there is a winner doesn't mean there has to be a loser. The more you can find, create, and produce win-win situations, the more success you'll have at dealing with other departments and other managers.

Getting along with everybody

Getting along with everyone sounds crazy, doesn't it? Oh, that only happens in the movies!

I'm here to tell you that it can be done, and that you can do it. It only takes a commitment on your part to not forget the things you know about communication and what other departments go through.

When you approach your fellow members of management with knowledge of what they value, how they think, and how they're judged you'll be amazed at how they respond to you.

Sometimes I'm amazed at how some people get through life with their negative attitudes. You've seen them: mad at the world, grumpy, the people nobody likes to be around. Don't be that person.

You can get along with everyone if you simply become a person everyone wants to get along with. Use these tips:

- Be a problem solver, not a problem finder.
- Be a fountain, not a drain.
- Attract people, don't repel them.
- Find the good in others instead of focusing on the bad.
- Be positive instead negative.
- Recognize other people's strengths; don't point out their weaknesses.
- Be a leader, not a follower.

As you work your way through the ups and downs of day-to-day business, understand that you're dealing with other people. The departments I talk about are made up of people. Being a professional sales manager means you treat people as you want to be treated — with dignity and respect. If you do that, you'll not only get along with everyone, you'll have everyone looking for ways to help you, and you'll ultimately score a lot more wins.

Writing like a Manager

Aside from verbal communication, your ability to communicate in writing says a lot about you as a person, a professional, and a manager. Whether you're constructing a sales letter, a memo, or writing an article for the company newsletter, nothing looks worse than misusing *you're* and *your* or *there, their,* and *they're.*

Like it or not, people judge you on your ability to write properly. You don't have to be William Shakespeare or Stephen King (and yes, I made sure it isn't Steven), but you should be able to put together a few paragraphs without looking like a high school dropout.

I am continually surprised at the number of seemingly professional people who misspell words or simply cannot construct a logical sentence. I see it a lot. Note: There is no such word as *alot*. Stop using it. Now.

Again, if business writing is an area you feel uncomfortable with, then by all means seek help. There are far too many avenues to get better to sit there and wallow in your lack of skills. Do something about it.

You're a manager now, you need to not only act and sound like one, you need to write like one. If you're several years removed from an English course and aren't sure how to properly format a good business letter, look it up. Although many of the rules I learned in typing class many (many) years ago are no longer accepted as proper, I try to keep up with current styles and acceptable forms.

One of the main things to focus on when writing is to ask yourself, "Who is my reader?" Then simply write to that person. Don't try to write below his level or above it — just write to him.

Finally, it's great to use spell-check and all the handy, dandy little tools built into your word processor, but nothing — and I mean nothing — beats reading what you've written aloud. When writing a letter, print it out and read it out loud. Slowly. Read it slow enough that you read what the letter says, not what you intended to write — sometimes those two are entirely different things.

Seriously, proofread

Many years ago, I was vice president of sales for a large wholesale food distributor. The company was sending out letters to our top customers. I don't remember the subject, I just remember I wrote the letter and forwarded it to my assistant to add the addresses and salutations.

Well, we had one customer whose first name was Butch and his last name started with a *C* and ended with *son*. The letters were given back to me to sign after being personalized, and I was busy just scribbling my John Hancock across the bottom when for some reason my eyes were drawn to the top of the page.

I have no idea why because I hadn't really been looking at to whom each of them was addressed. But, in this instance I did. And, thank goodness I did!

Thanks to spell-check, I had just signed and was about to send a letter to one of our largest, most valuable customers — Butt Collision.

Proofread everything . . . slowly.

Avoiding the Pitfalls of Email

Email has made communication more convenient, efficient, and timely, but I wonder whether we've sacrificed clarity for that convenience. Email makes up the majority of written communication in any business and is something you need to be well versed in.

Although it's easy to dash off a response from your smartphone or laptop, if that communication is poorly written, it delivers the wrong message and you've wasted your time and that of the reader. And that doesn't even take into account the time it takes for the recipient to ask what you actually meant and for you to respond yet again.

Email communication should be taken as seriously as any other form. Perhaps more seriously than verbal discussions because there is a record of written communication.

Unfortunately, the ease with which you can send email leads some people to think quicker is better. It's not.

Remembering emailing is not like talking

Email creates several potential communication issues. You don't want to write a book, but you don't want to be too terse. You don't want to be unfriendly, but you don't want to play email ping-pong, either. Here are some ways emailing can be tricky:

- **Lack of communication:** Most people tend to shorten emails to make them informal. Don't lose the meaning of your message in the process. When writing, it's true that less is more, but don't sacrifice clarity for brevity.
- **Miscommunication:** Ignore the Internet jargon and texting abbreviations. If you have time to send an email, write it as you would a letter. Be brief but to the point and read it back to make sure you're not miscommunicating.
- **Over-communication:** Have you ever had this type of email exchange:

  You: The information you need was left on your desk yesterday.

  The other person: Where on the desk?

  You: On the right corner, I think.

  The other person: I can't find it.

You: I left it there.

The other person: Never mind, I found it.

You: Okay.

The other person: Thanks.

You: You're welcome.

The other person: Have a good day.

You: You, too.

Stop, please! This is absurd! It just took more than ten emails to do what one could've done! And this nonsense and time-wasting happens every single day.

The first email should have said, "The information you need was left on the right corner of your desk yesterday under the Thompson folder." That is all that's needed. Period. End of story. End of the vicious cycle. By the time this conversation is over, the two of you sound like Chip and Dale, the overly polite cartoon chipmunks.

Email communication does not require an affirmative response like verbal communication does. There's no need for "you're welcome" and other nonessential responses.

Just because someone doesn't say thank you in a separate email, don't take it personally. It's unnecessary. It starts a cycle of compliments and acknowledgements that is a tremendous waste of time. Take the initiative to be the person to stop the conversation. It's enough already.

It's never a good idea to send a mass email out and expose recipients' email addresses to each other. If you must send out a mass email, address it to yourself and then blind copy everyone else — that's what BCC is for. It protects the recipients' privacy and displays a level of professionalism, too.

There's no crying (or laughing or joking or winking) in email

The Internet is known as the information superhighway. I believe there's an exit on that highway where all the sarcasm, jokes, and tongue-in-cheek remarks get off before arriving at their intended recipient.

The biggest problem with email (or any written communication) is that there's no way in it to express the emotion you feel when you write your message. There's no sarcasm font on your computer. What may seem like a joke or wisecrack to you may be taken totally different by the person reading your message. An innocent, off-the-cuff comment can cause a lot of problems.

The one thing people know about email etiquette is that when you type in all caps, YOU ARE SCREAMING AT THEM!

Err on the side of caution. Keep your email communication professional and don't try to get cute with it. The recipient can't see the look on your face or hear the tone of your voice. Just because you read something one way doesn't mean your recipient will follow suit.

Don't write emails like you talk. Eliminate all the slang terms and casual tone. Write like you're writing a formal business letter. Just because it's email doesn't mean it carries less weight. Start with your email message being very formal; you can always soften it a bit as you read through before you hit Send.

If you receive an email and think the writer is being less than professional or says something that makes you angry, stop, take a deep breath, and read it again. See if there's a chance the sender was trying to be funny or cute.

Not everyone is going to be as professional as you in their email communication. Before you blow your top, give the sender the benefit of the doubt and don't read things into a note that aren't really there.

Adopt this professional email policy with everyone you communicate with including your salespeople, vendors, peers, and especially customers. Don't ruin a relationship because of a misunderstanding that could have (and should have) been avoided.

Reading twice, sending once

If you've been using email for more than a month chances are you've had one of those panic-stricken moments when you scream at the computer when you realize you've sent something you shouldn't have or you notice an error after it's gone. Unfortunately, email doesn't come back.

You may have heard the old saying, "Measure twice, cut once" about being very sure of yourself before taking action. Email is the exact same way except it's "Read twice, send once."

These few tips, if followed, can save you some heartache, time, and potential embarrassment:

- **Don't put the recipient's address in until last:** I love this little trick and have been using it for years. This prevents those "Oh no!" moments when you accidentally hit Send before you're ready. It's a great habit to develop and will save you aggravation often.

- **Read it aloud:** Slow down and read it out loud. Don't rush through because you know what you wrote. Well, you know what you *meant* to write, but that may not be what's in the body of the email.
- **Check for spelling and grammar:** Don't get so dependent on spell-check that you assume everything's okay if there are no red, squiggly lines under anything. If you have a word not recognized in your software's dictionary, make sure it's spelled correctly and then add it to the dictionary for future reference. Grammar is also important. Don't send an email telling the customer, "Your going to love our product." Neither spell-check nor grammar check catches *your* instead of *you're,* but your customer will — and if he's like most people, it will drive him nuts.
- **Use cut and paste sparingly:** Yes, it's easy to just cut and paste from one document to another, but be very careful. I've had emails sent to me I knew were cut and pasted because they had someone else's name in the body of the email. This looks very amateurish.
- **Double, triple, and quadruple check for attachments:** If I had a nickel for every time I've had to send another email with "Okay, here's the attachment I forgot to include," I'd be retired living on my own island somewhere. Certain email programs recognize the word *attachment* in the subject line and notify you before sending if nothing is attached.

  If you can get in the habit of adding the attachment and then the recipient's address as the final two things before you send, you'll be miles ahead in your email communication.

Sharing email tips is a great topic for a sales meeting. Make your people better communicators and it makes your entire organization look more professional.

Replying to all: Probably a bad idea

It amazes me that my laptop or computer asks me to confirm every single task I start to perform with the old, "Are you sure you want to close this document? Really sure? Do you pinky swear?" GEEZ!

But, when it comes to Reply All, I'm thoroughly convinced there's a maniacal little voice in there just laughing and laughing every time I hit that by mistake. Couldn't the machine ask me at least once if I'm sure I want to Reply All? Until the email hosts wise up, it's up to you to police yourself.

Seldom is it a good idea to hit Reply All without giving it some thought. Unless you're several emails into a lengthy discussion with several parties, I don't recommend it at all.

If the sender initiates the conversation and includes several people — especially some you don't know, my preference is to respond only to the sender with a note in bold or otherwise highlighted, "I replied only to you, feel free to forward to the other recipients as you feel necessary."

If everyone would get in this habit, I'd have far less email in my inbox. It's especially aggravating when my phone pings, or my email alert sounds for conversations between two or more people that have absolutely nothing to do with me.

Try to be the person in your company who starts not hitting Reply All and suggest others follow suit. You'll be amazed at how much useless email you don't receive anymore.

After all, if you reply only to the sender, you can always go back to your Sent folder and forward that email to everyone else. But, after you hit Reply All, you can't reach through the screen and pull it back. Trust me, I've tried!

Communicating via text or Intranet or chat program

Just as email has taken the place of the handwritten letter, text messaging and various chat programs have replaced phone calls and face-to-face communication. While some studies show people would rather receive a text than a phone call, be mindful of spelling, grammar, and the other issues as with email. Once a text is sent, it can't be pulled back and though you're limited in the number of characters you can use, there's still enough there to get you in trouble if used improperly.

If someone is in a meeting or otherwise unable to take a phone call, don't assume he can answer a text. You're distracting him from what he's doing (especially if he's driving).

Be respectful with a short text of, "Call me when you have a moment" or something to that nature. Don't feel the need to write a soliloquy, and by all means use group text only as a last resort. Scientists have proven that next to fingernails on a chalkboard, group text notifications are the most annoying sound to human ears.

Okay, I made that part up, but you get the idea. Simply allow technology like this to make you better, not make others bitter.

Part II

Building the Team

Top Five Places to Recruit Sales Talent

- Shop your competitors and see how their salespeople handle prospects and customers. Find out who's the top salesperson for your competition, and if you can't beat 'em, hire 'em!
- Industry conventions and meetings are a great place to network and meet other salespeople. Who stands out? Who impresses you? Seeing people outside their normal selling environment where they're working or have to be on can tell you a lot about them.
- Check within your own company. Many people have tremendous sales talent within their own organizations but don't realize it because those people aren't in the sales department. Don't overlook in-house talent — people who know your product and your company already.
- If you have to place an advertisement for a salesperson, radio advertising can be some of the best available to you. Generally people reading newspapers are already unemployed and that's not good for a salesperson. On the other hand, someone listening in his car or who has the radio on in his office is a working salesperson. That's generally a much better choice.
- Perhaps the greatest place to find sales talent is by asking your customers. Rarely are your customers only doing business with or buying from one person. Ask them who else they do business with that they think would be a fit for your company!

For more about building your team and being a team player, go to `www.dummies.com/extras/salesmanagement`.

In this part . . .

- Discover how to grade your current sales team. Find ways to help your best get better, your middling people raise their games, and get your unproductive people to move up or move out.
- Find out how to conduct a professional interview and how to spot those people who interview great but are horrible salespeople.
- Realize the importance of proper onboarding for new salespeople and provide them with the best chance for success.
- Understand how to clearly define a salesperson's job description and your initial expectations for performance.

Chapter 4

Who's On First: Building Your Best Team

In This Chapter

- Assessing your current sales representatives
- Understanding what makes a successful salesperson
- Hiring new sales representatives to your team
- Conducing a professional interview
- Defining what you're looking for in a new salesperson
- Avoiding the professional interviewees

Working in sales management you'll likely find that your job, at times, resembles that of a coach, and your sales team is much like a roster of players. (Hopefully without the spitballs.)

You hope to have some salespeople who are A-level players, but the great majority of your team is likely to be made up of B and C players and, undoubtedly you have your share of D and F players. Now, this is not to say these players are bad, but sales works on a scale: If someone is the best, then, unfortunately, someone else has to be the worst.

Your job is determine who falls into what category and how best to manage each of them to reach their full potential, which is the subject of this chapter. Although everyone would love to have a team of nothing but superstars, that's rarely the case — being a B or C player may be the best someone can do. And, it's up to you to get that maximum performance out of her by training and coaching her along the way. Not everyone can hit home runs; some players are solid singles and doubles hitters.

Of course, there are the D- and F-level players. They're the ones who constantly cause problems, have issues, and cost you and your company time and money. Not to mention the effect they have on customer service and other departments.

Although you work to help your B and C players improve and meet their objectives, the strategy for handling the D and F players is a bit different — and I explain both methods in this chapter.

By properly assessing each person's potential and setting goals accordingly you can get everyone to perform at her best and beyond. Don't get caught up in trying to make all your players superstars; just get them to be the best they can be.

Whether you're assessing your current team, weeding out the weaker links, or looking to add talent to your staff, this chapter covers how to recognize successful salespeople and how to identify those you are better off without.

Let me end this introduction with something I had a manager tell me years and years ago that I've never forgotten: "Hire hard, manage easy. Hire easy, manage hard."

Evaluating Your Current Sales Team

Depending on how much past information is available, you should be able to tell a lot about your current sales team. What are their individual sales for the past year? Are they increasing their business? Are they selling new products, developing new business, and growing your clientele?

A professional salesperson is seldom static — meaning, she's either growing upward or downward. She's moving forward or falling behind. Oh, you'll have those who tell you they're just in a rut, but as I once heard, a rut for a salesperson is simply a grave that's open on both ends. You get out of that rut by continuing to move forward. Don't linger.

Is a salesperson part of the solution or part of the problem? That's the real question you have to ask yourself — and be prepared for the answer. As the sales manager you need to know:

- **Where to focus your time and energy:** The D and F players all have one thing in common: They're a giant energy drain. And, not just for you, but for every department in the company. They prevent everyone from moving forward. If you allow them to, these team members will take an inordinate amount of your time and energy away from the thing you should be focused on: growing your sales. Should you solve their problems? Absolutely, but they are the Chicken Littles of the sales world and you'll soon find the sky is not always falling.

- **How to establish realistic individual goals:** Individual goals allow each person to stretch herself. Sales is like a muscle — you don't get stronger by lifting less weight. It's important to know not only what each person is doing, but what she's capable of doing and many times you have to show her and get her to believe in her abilities.
- **How to separate the excuses from the real issues:** Is it a complaint or an excuse? Who knows, right? Sadly, the D and F players are full of excuses for why they can't sell: It's too hot, it's too cold, it's too wet, it's too dry — I've heard them all. And the one thing they have in common? You never hear them from your A players who go on selling anyway. Real issues need to be addressed and excuses need to be squashed! As a new sales manager, you may find yourself wanting to solve everyone's problems. While that's a worthy goal, don't get pulled into people's personal issues. Valid business issues should be resolved, but they are to be expected to find solutions to problems outside of work.
- **Find players who can be part of the future of the company:** Any company or organization should always be looking for the leaders of tomorrow. Establishing early those who need and deserve your time will ultimately be the seed for your future growth.

So, get started and find out what kind of talent you have to work with.

Identifying the A players

Identifying the A players isn't as hard as you might think. Have you ever heard the expression, "the cream rises to the top"? Well, it's true in salespeople, too. As you make your way through your entire sales roster, identifying the A-level players is perhaps the easiest evaluation to make.

A-level players tend to hold themselves accountable — they don't wait for you do it for them. They are the superstars and separate themselves from the rest of the group very early on. These are your leaders, and they aren't hard to spot.

Generally, A-level people make up about between 10 and 15 percent of your sales team. They're the high performers — the first in and the last to leave. They work Monday through Friday (what a novel idea, huh?). They have the knowledge and ability to handle customer issues without bringing the entire company to a screeching halt and can make a decision without consulting you, the company president, their senator, or member of Congress.

A-level players are hard to keep in captivity — they love to be out and about in the field working with their customers and growing their business. They are fueled by competition and absolutely hate to lose. A players tend to be the early adopters of technology — finding ways to work smarter, not harder.

They have it down to a science and are very self-reliant. They also understand the difference between sales and gross profit and understand not all sales are good sales. They aren't afraid to walk away from an unprofitable account, and they know the value of their own time.

However, their self-reliance can lead to problems. It can cause you to ignore them, thinking they have it all under control. Therein lies the great A-Level Paradox! (I just made that up). Yes, they can handle 99.9 percent of the issues that come up in the day-to-day world of selling, but never, ever let that cause you to take them for granted.

A-level players have certain needs you must feed:

- **The need for recognition:** Recognition can take many forms — believe it or not, it's not always money. Your A-level people need to be recognized for their achievements. That's what drives them to be at the top.
- **The need for materials:** If your salespeople ask you for something, it's because they need it. Whether it's help with a proposal, new marketing materials, or whatever, know that your best people aren't going to bother you with unimportant details. They're out in front of your team and know what the market calls for long before you do. Listen to them.
- **The need to keep score:** This one is critical. The A-level personality is driven to compete and will get bored and fall into the B and C category if she cannot see how well she's doing. You should have scoring metrics in place, but if not, let your sales team keep score — in whatever manner possible.

Your top performers are what make your business work. And, even though they seem self sufficient and easily managed, you need to give them as much or more of your time than anyone else.

The last manager's evaluations

If you're taking over for another manager (for whatever reason), use her evaluations with caution. I've seen many cases where the previous sales manager's A players were nothing more than her buddies that she could count on to go to lunch with and be her yes men and women. Make your own judgments based on your own data.

Never assume that D and F players are there by choice. Sometimes they simply need a leader — and that may be the reason you got the job in the first place. Don't throw the baby out with the bathwater. Take the time to make your own judgments based on facts, not assumptions.

It's easy to spend all your time doing drills with your D- and F-level players, and take your eye off your superstars. It's easy to get dragged to the back of the classroom with the rowdy D and F players, but remember why you're there: You're there to make your superstars the best they can be. Don't ignore that fact, or them.

When you know who fits into the A category, immediately let them know you see them as the leaders. (That's part of the recognition they need). Make sure they know you value their opinions and that you're there to work for them! It's your job to make them better.

This isn't Little League where everyone gets to play and gets a participation ribbon. A good sales manager understands she must manage and treat each person differently because what drives and motivates one person isn't what another needs. At the same time, if you correctly assess your team, you soon have others wanting to have what this group has.

Letting your top performers know who they are

So how do you let your top players know that you recognize them? In the sections that follow, I give a few tips for how to let your top performers feel acknowledged, and how to give them what they need to ensure they want to stay and stay motivated.

These are your superstars, the cream of the crop, and while some may know it, it never hurts to hear it. I can assure you no employee ever got upset because someone bragged on her or gave her a pat on the back.

Too many times we only recognize poor behavior; here are some ways to recognize superior performance, as well.

Share your assessment

Your top performers or A players need to know that they're your A players. Don't hide that from them. Let them know you consider them your leaders and that you expect more of them than the others (don't worry, they love the responsibility). Let them know you respect their drive and determination.

Let your top people know that you're there for them. They most likely have never had a sales manager tell them that — most have felt they were there for the manager but not vice versa.

Solicit input

Want to get the most out of your A players? Get their input on how to grow the business. Guess what? They know! But, again they've probably never been asked what they would do or what changes they would make in your product or service.

Here's the irony about getting good ideas from your sales team: The ones who have good tips may not feel they have the relationship to share them because the previous manager spent all her time cleaning up after the D and F players, and the teams members who have no clue about how to improve the business are more than willing to tell you exactly what needs to change around here.

Create an open door policy

This should go for all your salespeople, but especially the crème de la crème: Let everyone know without hesitation that you are always available for her no matter what.

More than likely, the top 10 to 15 percent of your team is responsible for 75 percent of your sales or more, and perhaps an even greater percentage of your gross profit. Nothing is more important than what they need — even if it's someone to talk to or to vent to. (Helpful hint: Let them vent occasionally; it's good for everyone.)

If you feel it appropriate, create a President's Roundtable or some other exclusive group tasked with meeting on a regular basis to mastermind and brainstorm ideas, solutions, and plans for the future. Create a program like this where opinions matter and people get to be a part of short-term and long-term solutions. Your A-level players will gravitate toward it. Let them be a part of the process. Remember, they're out in the field every day so they know the customers' needs and wants better than anyone. Listen to them, and they'll make your company better and you a better manager. Meet with them regularly — just them — and get their input and opinion on what needs to be done.

Ask how can you help them

Finally, make it crystal clear you want to help your best salespeople continue to grow. I can't stress enough that the job of a sales manager is to work for the salespeople and not have them work for you. Ask regularly, "How can I help?" or "What can I do for you?" — and don't make it just lip service. Listen, respond, and keep these eagles flying high!

A word of caution: These are professionals, but some will try to take advantage when you solicit their suggestions. You need to keep in mind that you're in management, not sales. Ultimately, you have to do what you believe is best for the company and the department. If you solicited their opinion or input and decide to go in a different direction, be upfront with them and let them know you felt the need to do what you did. This doesn't mean you don't want their ideas, but you have to be responsible for the team's performance.

Identifying the B and C players and assessing their potential to improve

The B and C players aren't your superstars, but they're still important to your team's success. And they're likely the majority of your team, making up 70 to 75 percent of your sales team.

You cannot ignore your top talent, but the fact is that most of your time will be spent on this group — the B and C players. Your job is to determine what's keeping this group from reaching the top tier and what you can do to help them maximize their potential.

Determining which players have the most potential

To determine which of your B- and C-level performers can rise, you must first figure out why they're in this group to begin with and what's holding them back. You have to ask yourself:

- Are they here because of talent level — is this the best they can do?
- Are they here because of poor practices?
- Are they here because of a lack of training?
- Are they here because they're satisfied with this level?
- Are they moving up or down? Are they A players regressing or D and F players improving?

Let's tackle talent level first because it's probably the easiest to identify. If these members of your sales force are truly trying and simply performing at this level, that's completely acceptable. One of the quotes I've built my training on is this one, by yours truly: "It's okay to settle for less than the best, but not less than *your* best!"

If your mid-level players are making the required number of calls, asking the right questions, qualifying the prospects, asking for the sale, and doing all the things a salesperson must do in order to be successful and their results are just not at superstar level, that's okay. There's no crime in that. It's something you can work with. Their talent level may define where they are today, but it doesn't have to be the key to their destination.

Your job as a sales manager is to take the natural talent of your team and help them get the most out of it. You have to assess the reason they're underperforming: Is it lack of ability or lack of desire? The former is solvable, the latter not so much.

Your B- and C-level players are the ones you work with to improve every aspect of the sales process. They can potentially land in the A group with the right challenge, support, and continued training.

It may take a bit of research and time spent with the individual to determine whether some team members aren't using the best practices. Perhaps they've fallen into some bad habits — they're not making the calls, they're not giving it their all. If this is the case, you owe it to them, their family, and the company to raise the bar immediately.

If some of your salespeople have accepted mediocrity when they shouldn't, you have to take that crutch away. This involves training them, coaching them, and helping them grow. Will they ever make the top group? Maybe not, but you can get them to be better than they think they can be, and that's the most you can ask for.

If members of your team are underperforming due to a lack of training, it's not their fault and it can be corrected.

Salespeople hate to ask questions because in the back of their mind they're thinking, "I'm supposed to know the answer to that, and I'll look stupid if I ask." It's happening right in under your nose. I promise. (For more on training and professional development, see Chapter 9.)

Give your salespeople the opportunity to ask questions — almost like an amnesty period when they can ask anything. You'll be surprised at the questions uncovered. And you get a great idea of what areas your team needs to be trained in. Is it prospecting? Asking for the sale? Qualifying? Who knows until you get them to tell you where they feel the most uncomfortable.

But, please let them know one thing: You don't care if they don't know everything . . . today. Now, if they still don't know a month or six weeks from now, it's their own fault.

Although everyone needs your attention on your team, the B and C players are the ones you're paid to really help. This is why you have a job. If everyone were in the Top Performers group, the company probably wouldn't need you. And, if everyone were in the D and F group, you wouldn't need the company!

Be prepared to spend the majority of your time with this group of individuals: finding each of their weaknesses and helping them grow.

Recognizing that some are content not to excel

Sadly, a certain number of people fall into the B- and C-level group because they want to be there. They may not admit it, but for whatever reason, they're comfortable where they are. They aren't the best, but they're not the worst either. They don't stand out in a crowd, and they like it that way. They aren't prepared to put in the extra effort to improve and aren't driven by a desire to drastically improve their performance.

Accept it. It's part of the gig. These people will frustrate you to no end if you let them. It's hard to look at so much wasted potential. But, you cannot help someone who doesn't want to help herself — it just doesn't work. Keep your content-to-be-B-levels comfortable and let them be a part of the team. Just watch and make sure they're influenced more by the positive forces than the negative ones.

Helping those who most want help

Now how can you help those who want to — and can — improve? Some of the salespeople in this group are here not of their own choosing — they're superstars in waiting. These are the people you gear your training toward; don't dumb it down for the ones who are just too lazy to work the program and have no desire to improve.

Let the people you determine can improve know that you want them to improve. Make sure you tell them that no matter what the situation was before you, you're here to help them reach new heights and fulfill their potential. Last month or last year's performance isn't good enough — you expect more.

Even though they are advanced in some ways, you must start with the basics of the sales process. Even if you gave them an amnesty opportunity to ask questions without judgment, not all your team take such opportunities.

Focus your training program on what your B- and C-level people need and what you want them to know for a few reasons:

- **They're the majority of your sales team.** These players make up as much as three-quarters of your team so the skills they need to improve and the knowledge they need impact most of your team. You get a lot more bang for your buck focusing your training and coaching on making these people better than you do from any other place you spend your time as a manager.
- **Your top performers benefit.** The A-level players are at the top of their profession and the top of your sales board for a reason: They love to learn. And, it never hurts to have a refresher course. One of the greatest benefits of sales management is having one of your people come up to you after a meeting or session and tell you, "I really needed that!" And the best feeling is that many times, the speaker isn't the one you expected.

- **The D- and F-level players don't care.** Okay, I'm not going to sugarcoat it: your low-level players are at the bottom of the roster for a reason. You can't set your training program around them or you risk dragging everyone else down. Don't get caught in the trap of trying to save the weakest of the bunch — you'll lose your strongest players in the process.

Focus on improving every single person in your B- and C-level group. Some will advance to the top performers group because of the extra training and attention while others will simply improve from a C to a B. But, hey, that's a step in the right direction, and it just may be the spark they need to light a little fire under them.

Dealing with the D- and F-level players

At almost every bar at closing time, the bartender uses the old line, "You don't have to go home, but you can't stay here." Think of your weakest performers in the same way: You don't have to fire them, but they can't stay here.

A true tale of guiding a team member to success

I once had a young man who started in the mailroom of the company but wanted to get into sales. When I took over the department, I probably would've classified him as barely a C. But, it became apparent early on he wanted to learn and was hungry for someone to teach him. Up to that point his training had consisted of what far too many are made up of: "See payroll, see human resources, see ya later!"

I'll call this young man Tony (because that's his name). Tony couldn't get enough guidance. He was constantly pushing himself — reading, learning, and asking questions. By just paying him some attention and focusing the training on his needs, the fuse was lit. Tony soon became a division sales manager (DSM) for me, then he quickly became the top DSM. I can happily say that today, some 20 years later, Tony is an amazingly successful businessman. All it took was someone to show him the how and he found the why!

Now, had I focused the training on the A players, Tony would've felt left out. If I'd focused it on the D and F players, he would've gotten bored. I can't stress enough how important the B- and C- level salespeople are to your success. They're your bread and butter. Help them improve and you're in for a long and successful career in Sales Management.

I bet you have a few Tonys on your team. One of the most satisfying feelings in the world is to help Tonys achieve what others thought was impossible.

Your lowest performers have to either get up or get out. They have to work their way into being at least a C, or you need to let them go to work for your competition and perform as a D and F player for them. You don't have the resources to devote to someone who isn't going to provide you with the proper return on investment. It's just that simple.

There's a fine line in dealing with this group of salespeople: You must identify them quickly, but take a bit of time to act on your judgment. Don't shoot first and ask questions later. However, when someone proves she belongs in this group (and it doesn't usually take long), you must take action.

So how do you know who these weakest links are? These salespeople are the first to complain, they probably have collection (accounts receivable) problems, and any number of other issues that are a giant drain on the company. They're definitely not the future of the organization. In fact, they're the bottom ten percent former General Electric chairman Jack Welch suggested firing each year. Hey after all, if you replace them with even a C-level player, you've upgraded the team, right?

After you identify the people in this group, you have to decide whether they're salvageable or not.

Don't put a lot of effort into making an F performer a D. You can use that same time taking a B player to the A level and provide much more benefit for the employee, the company, and your sanity.

Firing someone is never fun, but you must remember:

- **These are not your top performers.** Don't get caught up in estimating sales you might lose if your underperforming players leave the team. They're not your top performers and therefore aren't going to take much, if any, business with them when they leave. In fact, assigning their account lists to someone else could prove to be a huge win for everyone — including the customers.
- **They're costing you money.** Plain and simple, these salespeople aren't paying for themselves. Your budget and your psyche are better off without them dragging you down. They're literally costing you money.
- **They're not a threat if they go elsewhere.** Many times managers are scared the representative will go to work for the competition. Well, if she's a D- or F-level player, you hope so! Let her drag that sales manager and sales team down. Let her cost that company money. Let her put all the departments at your competitor in flux. If the competition hires your headaches, you can only benefit!

- **Your team is ultimately stronger without them.** The rest of your sales team sees what the underperformers are doing. And trust me, they don't appreciate poor performers being able to skate by while the rest of the team works. Taking a stand of not tolerating poor performance or lack of performance only strengthens your team. The rest of the group not only will appreciate the gesture but also will respect you for it.

Once you make the decision to fire a player, don't wait. Do it sooner rather than later. The reasons in the preceding list are all you need to see the benefit of pruning the dead branches.

Key Elements of a Successful Salesperson

Successful salespeople all have certain traits in common. I don't subscribe to the theory of anyone being a born salesperson, but I do believe each successful, professional salesperson must possess certain qualities.

Anyone can be taught to sell, but they must have the desire to learn. Just like anyone who really wants to can become a doctor or a dentist, those who have a desire to learn what it takes to be a top salesperson can be taught. There's nothing magical about sales — no secret handshakes, special recipes, or ancient scrolls handed down from past generations. If you want to learn it the craft, you can.

As a sales manager, part of your job is to determine whether someone really wants to be a professional salesperson. Unfortunately sales is treated as almost the last resort for many people, "Well, I can't get any other job so I guess I'll go into sales." Really?

I can't just show up at the courthouse Monday morning and call myself an attorney! What makes people think they can just grab a box of business cards and be a salesperson? It's that mentality and lack of training of the "sales as a last resort" people that has given the profession the stigma professionals are still trying to shake. You have to take the lead in changing that one person at a time. And the best way to do so is know what a successful salesperson looks like and what skills and traits they need.

Product knowledge

If you sell cars, you train your people to know everything in the world there is to know about the vehicles you sell. If you're selling advertising, you make everyone on your team an expert in marketing. You have no excuse for not being at the top of your game when it comes to product knowledge. All you and your sales team need is the desire for the knowledge and access to the information.

In today's world, there's no excuse for not knowing all about something you really want to learn about. If you, as a manager, need assistance, you have access to untold outlets for data on the Internet, through your company's resources, or your industry's resources. Lack of product knowledge is completely unacceptable.

Successful salespeople:

- Know the product inside and out
- Can explain the benefits to a 5-year-old
- Constantly learn and grow

Although product knowledge is only a third of what makes up a successful salesperson, you can't get very far without it. You can't fake it.

As a manager, test your people regularly — perhaps every sales meeting — on one aspect or another of your product. Let them role-play going through the features and benefits just as they would do with a prospect. This is critical because if they can't perform in front of their peers, they certainly can't do it in front of a prospect. Not to mention that the last place you want them practicing is on potential customers! The great thing about role-playing is that it benefits everyone — the two people involved in the role play, and those who watch and take notes.

The best way to make role-playing effective is to let everyone participate and talk about what she saw, heard, and learned. Did someone say something wrong? Could she have asked better questions? Did she properly explain everything? Understand that your sales team is going to learn a lot from their peers and product knowledge is the best place for that to happen.

Any time a new product is introduced or a new model is updated start over. Never assume your sales team automatically knows about new products or features. This is most important with new salespeople entering your organization. In addition to company orientation, company history, the mission statement, and other relevant information, they need to see how the product works for the customer and how their sales fit into the grand scheme of things.

Sales skills

The second component of a successful salesperson is basic *sales skills* — the knowledge and ability to perform the tasks involved in the sales process. Just like product knowledge, sales skills can be learned. The desire for the education must be there, but the process can be taught.

As sales manager, you must constantly work with your team to improve their sales skills. Today's buyers are sophisticated and knowledgeable, and your competition is investing in training and development, so you must always be improving just to stay even. The days of just winging it are long gone.

As a manager, you not only set the tone for professionalism of the sales process, but continue to upgrade your team's performance. Each prospect is an opportunity and wasted opportunities can never be regained.

One of the first orders of business is to ensure your sales force understands your sales process, whatever that process may be. Whether it contains 7 steps or 27 steps doesn't matter. What matters is that your sales team knows the process and the steps and can properly perform the required functions.

The only way to determine this is to see them in action. Again, role-playing can be extremely beneficial, but it has a tendency to be fake or unrealistic no matter how hard the participants try. It's just not easy to replicate the process of calling on a real, live prospect. The next best thing is to ride with your salespeople and observe each one in action.

Note the word *observe.* Any time you, as a manager, ride with a salesperson, you're there to see her work, not to show off how well you can perform. You have plenty of time for that.

During your ride along, let the prospect know that you're the manager and you're just observing. Resist the temptation to get involved if at all possible and try not to rescue your salesperson unless she's at death's door. Simply sit quietly and take notes; notes you use to help this salesperson improve.

Back in your car or office immediately go over the notes while the meeting is fresh in both your minds. Find at least one positive to start with before working to where the representative can improve. Don't crush her confidence or self-esteem. You're there to build her up and make her better.

One final note on sales skills: They're like a muscle. If they go unused, they can atrophy and die. Don't get so involved in the management side you lose sight of the sales side of your job. There's nothing wrong (and a lot right) with going out and making your own sales calls periodically. It keeps you in practice, helps you understand the reality of what your people are hearing in the market, and earns you a lot of respect from your team. If you're going to have your team run a mile, strap on your shoes and run alongside them. That's when you're a real leader and not just a boss.

Natural ability: What you can't train or teach

Product knowledge and sales skills are only two-thirds of what it takes to be successful in sales. Together they make for a strong salesperson, but one who will fail if she doesn't possess certain intangibles:

- **Attitude:** I don't care how much a person knows about the product and how skilled she is at the sales process, if she has a negative attitude, she's done . . . finished . . . kaput. You can't train or teach a good attitude. A salesperson has to bring the proper attitude to the table herself, and it's something a person either has or doesn't. It's not something you can grow into or develop. No, you need to have the proper attitude or everything else is worthless. A good, positive attitude sees the rainbow, not the rain, a salesperson with a good attitude sees the good, not the bad, and finds solutions, not problems. Good salespeople understand issues are going to come up daily, but they never let problems bring them down.
- **Goals:** Show me a salesperson who has become a top performer and I'll show you one who is goal oriented. The elite sellers love to set big, bold goals. They stretch themselves and aren't satisfied with anything but the best. You know these people by the fact that you don't have to set their sales quotas because they've already done so. And in most cases, their goals are written down where they can see them daily. But, if you do have to help them set them — set them high!
- **Motivation:** There's no denying sales is a tough job. The best of the best hear far more no's than yes's and they have to be able to pick themselves up, dust themselves off, and keep coming back for more. Is it easy? Absolutely not. As salesman extraordinaire Zig Ziglar once said, "People often say that motivation doesn't last. Well, neither does bathing, that's why we recommend it daily." Your top salespeople understand this and are constantly finding ways to motivate themselves.
- **Honesty:** Another quality that a person either has or doesn't is honesty. You can't teach someone to be honest. And, it's not a sometime thing either. Honesty is not negotiable and there's no gray area. I've always heard honesty is doing the right thing even when nobody is watching.

- **Character:** The best description I ever heard about character was almost 35 years ago when a former sales manager of mine described it as, "The ability to follow through with a commitment long after the mood in which the decision was made has left you." Once again, this isn't teachable or learnable — it's bred in.
- **Desire:** Every successful salesperson has this thing deep down inside they can neither describe or turn loose of: It's a burning desire to be the best, to win, to succeed, and to achieve. Perhaps the most elusive of all the intangibles, a salesperson will never achieve superstardom without it.

The truth about motivation

Many of your salespeople may expect you to motivate them. But, that's not going to happen. You can't do it. Nobody can motivate another person. Now, you can inspire them to want to be motivated, but they must motivate themselves.

Don't feel the need to keep your team motivated. Instead keep them inspired with positive, uplifting words and actions. Unfortunately many are more motivated by the fear of loss rather than the desire of gain and you can't spend all your time threatening for them to lose their job or take away some perk. Motivation has to come from within. Inspiration is up to you.

Chapter 5

Adding New Players to the Team

In This Chapter

- Recruiting new sales talent
- Interviewing candidates
- Sidestepping professional interviewees
- Knowing when to make the offer

Recruiting and hiring new salespeople is a key part of a successful team. If your company is growing you need salespeople. If you're managing the sales department, you may be in an upgrade mode frequently. Whatever the reason, you want to find the best possible person available. If you're going to build a team, build it right! That's what I cover in this chapter.

Recruiting New Sales Talent

Inevitably you need to add new team members. Whether you're growing or replacing an existing representative, successfully bringing a new person into the fold starts long before the interview.

Answering basic questions

You must answer several questions before you ever think about moving forward to hire a new salesperson:

- Are you required to post the job in-house first?
- How will you promote the job opening?
- Do you require an experienced salesperson?
- What qualities does the ideal candidate have?

If you don't know whether you're required by your company to post this job in-house before you advertise for outside applicants, contact your human resources department to find out. Many companies today require jobs to be posted for current employees either prior to or at the time you solicit outside the organization.

To be honest, there's little chance your next superstar is walking the halls working in another department, but play by the rules as necessary.

That's not to say you'll never find the perfect candidate right under your nose, so don't dismiss someone based on the fact he works for the company in another department.

What's your plan for promoting the job? Newspaper (please don't — see the upcoming list), online, industry trades, or other means? Where are you most likely to find your next great candidate?

Many people lose sight of what they're ultimately after when they're in the hiring mode. Some want to see 500 resumes and applications come through. Really? Why? In all honesty, you just need to see one for your ideal candidate. Be careful not to substitute quantity for quality here. It can be a tremendous waste of time and cause you to settle for less than your desired results.

My personal preferences (depending on how high-end the sales position is) are the high-end job boards and LinkedIn, for several reasons:

- **Newspapers are dead:** Every year newspaper readership falls, newspapers lay off more of their staff and raise their advertising rates. It's a dying medium and hasn't performed well for anything more than minimum-wage positions in a while.
- **Quality of candidates:** If people are searching the so-called "Help Wanted" ads, they're probably out of work. My best recruits were already employed when I recruited them. That's not to say someone who's out of work is an automatic no-go, but a good salesperson seldom finds himself out of a job.
- **Choice of candidate:** Through sites like LinkedIn and other online job boards, as the employer you can solicit the potential employee. This gives you much greater control over whom you talk to, what resumes you look at, and the quality of applicant. At the same time, you will get inquiries from candidates via professional boards like LinkedIn, and these tend to be extremely high quality candidates. Professional salespeople generally do everything professionally — even look for a job.

Believe it or not, you can state in the ad that you require a four-year degree with a masters of business administration (MBA) and 47 references, and you still get a stack of applications and resumes from people with just a high school diploma who have never worked in sales. Try to save yourself the time of weeding through all that mess.

You can find a lot of information on how candidates are using the Internet and social media in *Job Searching with Social Media For Dummies* by Joshua Waldman (Wiley).

Do you want someone with experience either in sales or in your particular industry? Think about that, because some people won't talk to someone without experience while others don't want their new hire to have a lot of baggage and bad habits from years of doing it according to someone else's system. Whatever the case, decide now — it obviously affects how you structure your job description. Narrow down whom you want to talk to as you start the hiring process.

Finally, think about what your ideal candidate looks like. I'm not talking about how tall or short they are or what they weigh, but who are they as a person. Before you ever construct your ad or job description create an avatar — a best-case scenario of your dream candidate based on psychological make-up and psychographic characteristics such as attitude, personality, lifestyle, and values. Don't shortcut this step. It's vitally important to the process.

You can get a very definite picture of what and who you're looking for — so much so that, in many cases, you know them when you see them.

Get a sense of where your ideal candidate spends time then go where that person is most likely to be. Don't necessarily wait for him to come to you.

Placing ads

I'm not a fan of ads, but if you must place them, I strongly suggest you work backward. By that I mean create your ideal salesperson profile, and build the ad around that. Don't make it a wish list; make it a must list.

Write the ad in a way that properly describes the job (and be realistic). One of the best ways to do this is to refer to the job description for that particular position. If there's not one, take the time to write one.

What do you want this person to do? How are they going to be evaluated? Who will they be reporting to? These are all things to include in your ad.

Choose your ad locations carefully, and if at all possible run split tests — run two ads at once and see which one provides the better candidate. For example, if you run an ad at `www.careerbuilder.com`, have the person email their resume to `jobs@yourcompany.com` attention Mrs. Castle (C for careerbuilder). Now, chances are you don't have a Mrs. Castle, but because it comes addressed to her, you know that person came through that ad. At the same time you run a slightly different ad at `www.monster.com` and have resumes sent to the attention of Mr. Mason (M for monster.com). This makes it remarkably easy to know at a glance which job site generates your best candidates.

After you determine that one of the ads or locales outperforms the other, double down and increase your ad placement there. After all, that's where you're getting your best candidates. It's not unlike fishing — after you find the bait that works, you put as many lines in the water as possible.

Soliciting people you want

When a sports team look to bring in a new short stop or a quarterback, they don't put an ad in the newspaper, do they? No, they scout out players they want. So, why can't you find the person you want instead of letting the person find you?

You can. You must make soliciting candidates part of your hiring process. Don't just place ads and wait for people to come to you, spend a certain amount of your resources recruiting and soliciting candidates you identify as ones you'd like to talk to.

Although it's easy to go out and poach someone from a competitor, that's not always the best idea. If your competitor is willing to let someone go, he may not be worth having. Don't think just because a salesperson comes from the competition he's going to be an asset that adds lots of new business. In fact, I've found the opposite to be true. Many times these job-hoppers are just looking for a place to cash their next paycheck.

If you place ads either in newspapers or online, I strongly suggest creating a company profile on LinkedIn and searching for applicants there. Look through the professional groups that align with the type of person you're looking for; see who's engaged in good conversation on there. You don't have to pounce on day one, just lurk a bit and see who draws your attention.

LinkedIn (and other online forums) have groups and subgroups where professional people gravitate to discuss business and some of the challenges they face. Now, I don't know about you, but I want a salesperson who's interested enough in his job to make it a point to seek out answers. There's no shame in that — I love it!

At the same time, visit some business mixers or organizations you targeted as a guest — look around and ask yourself, "Who in this room would I like to have representing my company?" Is that pretty simple? Uh, yeah! But, too many times hiring managers or HR directors want to make finding talent harder than it has to be.

Here's the key to finding good employees: Approach and look for people who are working. Introduce yourself (or have your HR department get in touch with them) to see whether the people you're interested in are interested in talking to you about your opportunity.

This is all designed to eliminate the people who have no business applying for the job in the first place as soon as possible.

Never, never, never give your phone number to jobseekers. They will drive you nuts — trust me.

One more approach is to ask your top performers who they know outside of work. Do they know someone they think would make a productive member of your organization? Birds of a feather flock together, and if you have a superstar salesperson, I can assure you he doesn't spend his free time with non-superstars.

Depending on your industry you may have luck with headhunters or employment agencies. Talk to others within your organization or perhaps industry peers and find out who specializes in your field.

Finally, don't settle. Don't let yourself get into a situation where you settle for less than your ideal candidate. Good people are out there; you just have to find them. You're going to get frustrated, you're going to get tired, you'll read so many applications you'll see them in your sleep, but hold your ground. Your next superstar is out there, and the reason he's hard to find is the same reason you want him!

Remember, you have to move a lot of dirt to find a diamond, but you don't go looking for the dirt!

Interviewing Candidates

You've narrowed your search to a handful of lucky candidates you'd like to interview. But, where to start? What to say? Prepare yourself for the interview and know what you want to say about your industry, your company, and the specific job available. At the same time you're interviewing them, they're interviewing you, and you certainly want to be able to highlight the benefits of your company if you find your next superstar. Although there are no hard-and-fast rules, keep a few things in mind as you conduct interviews with candidates:

- **Don't be too easy on them.** Ask hard questions and don't let them off the hook. If someone is truly going to be one of your top performers, this is the time to find out how he handles pressure. Resist the temptation to be likable and make friends. That's not what you're there for.
- **Listen more than you talk.** From easy questions like, "Tell me about yourself," to tougher ones like "Who was the hardest manager you ever worked for and why?" let the candidate do the talking. You're there to interview him, not vice versa.

- **Remember these are salespeople.** Even in an interview a good salesperson asks questions, and it's a great sign that a candidate asks questions. Gently lead him back through the interview process, but note this is as very positive reaction.
- **Don't oversell the job.** More than once I've seen managers or human resources directors feel the need to sell the person on the job. That's not the purpose of this interview. This interview is for the candidate to sell himself to you. If he gets to a second interview that's when it's more appropriate for you to do a bit more selling, but never oversell the job.
- **Discover why they're looking to change jobs.** If a candidate is currently employed, you *must* ask this question, "Why are you wanting to leave ABC Company?" The reason may be something as simple as the company has been acquired (which is happening a lot these days) and the candidate doesn't feel comfortable with the direction of the future. Or, it could be he's padding his resume and is one step ahead of his manager at his current job. Ask the hard questions and get the answer you want before moving forward.
- **Look for gaps in work history.** Years ago if someone had more than two jobs in a five-year period, it was a sign of a job-hopper. That's not the case any longer. More and more today you find people who have moved around more than they used to — partly due to the economy and consolidation in commerce and partly because of the changing landscape of the job. If an applicant has any gaps of more than a month, ask about the gap and don't stop until you're satisfied with the answer. Many times an applicant leaves out a job he doesn't want you to know about and creates an unexplained gap. Get a satisfactory explanation of all gaps.
- **Have some standard questions of every candidate.** Have some go-to questions you ask in almost every interview. Ask these no matter how the conversation is flowing. It's okay to write these down. Feel free to use the following questions, which are some of my favorites, but come up with some of your own as well:
  - Tell me about yourself.
  - Who's the best manager you ever had and why?
  - Who's the worst manager you ever had and why?
  - What criteria do you use to judge your performance as a salesperson?
  - What is the last good book you read and what did you like about it?
  - Tell me about a time when you had to satisfy an upset customer by going the extra mile.

The bottom line to the entire process is this: Would you buy from this person? After all, you're hiring a salesperson. Ultimately what you really want to know is that if he were selling your product or service would you buy it from him? Remember, the person you're interviewing wants the job and is likely to do and/or say almost anything to get it — especially if he's currently unemployed.

Verbal skills, body language, and eye contact are my three main areas to note other the actual answers to the questions ask. It comes down to a candidate's ability to communicate, which is exactly what you're going to ask him to do as a sales professional. If he can't do it here, he can't do it there. The following sections outline some important flags to watch for in an interview.

Watching body language

The single biggest nonverbal communication tool humans have is body language. While you're asking questions and writing down answers, note the candidate's body language. Is he leaning back? Are his arms crossed? Both of these indicate a person wants to be distant from the situation. Is he leaning forward, interested in what you have to say and listening intently? That's a good sign that he's engaged with you and what you're saying.

Think of the interview as a sales call. How would you rate candidates if they were selling your product (instead of themselves) to a prospect (instead of to you)? Are they open and inviting and friendly or cold and closed and standoffish?

Don't just listen to a person's words; listen to what he's telling you, not just to what he's saying.

Body language is much harder to control than words. A candidate can come up with a great story and try to buffalo his way through an interview, but it's very difficult to fake positive body language. In fact, if someone is trying to pull one over on you, he'll be so worried about what he's saying, he won't even notice his own body language.

Look to see whether your candidate shifts uncomfortably when asked a hard question. This is a sign he doesn't really want to open up with the answer.

Keep your eyes — as well as your ears — open.

Listening for buzzwords

At one point, if I'd heard the phrase "think outside the box" one more time, I would've screamed. Be very mindful of someone littering his answers with jargon and buzzwords. Many times this is done to cover up a lack of knowledge about the subject matter you're asking about or avoid addressing an experience he's had.

Is a candidate talking because he has to say something or because he has something to say? There's a huge difference. If he's going to drone on and on and on with you, rest assured he'll do the same with a prospect.

A salesperson should be able to talk knowledgeably about any subject matter of interest to you in an interview. That's not to say he needs to be able to discuss world politics or brain surgery. Keep your questions on point and judge candidates based on job criteria.

Part of being a master salesperson is having a very good command of language and how to communicate. This is a very important part of the interview process. How are the answers to your questions structured? Does the candidate speak intelligently? Does he sound like a robot? Does he talk like a teenager and use "like" every other word?

"I left my last job because, like the manager and I, like just couldn't get along. And I was like, 'Hey I don't have to take this, you know?" And he was like, okay then . . . ." Just shoot me now.

And, let's hope your candidates don't use profanity. (That really ****** me off!)

Very simply, ask yourself if the candidate is a good communicator. Yes or no.

Maintaining eye contact

Another test of a person's sales skills is whether he's able to maintain eye contact with you during the interview. If not, cut this one short and move on!

No eye contact? No chance.

I once had an associate who happened to be interviewing a candidate for a sales position. It soon became obvious this person was not going to make it in the world of sales — or perhaps in the world in general.

He was sitting across the desk from the interviewer in a swivel chair on rollers. As the interview progressed and the questions got tougher, the candidate slowly began to turn his chair and roll ever so slightly backwards away from the desk. The harder the questions, the less eye contact and the further away he got. Pretty soon he had his back to the desk and almost rolled his chair out into the hall.

My friend laughs about it to this day because he could see what was happening and didn't let the poor guy off the hook — he just kept digging in harder and harder. He said he darn near had to chase the guy down the hall to finish the interview!

This may be an extreme example, but eye contact is huge in my book. If someone can't look me in the eye, my distrust radar goes off in a hurry.

Eye movement can also be very telling. When you ask a question, note whether the person's eyes dart back and forth nervously or hold your gaze confidently as he easily answers your question.

Avoiding the So-Called Professional Interviewees

If you stay at it very long, you'll find that there's an entire subculture out there of professional interviewees — people who are phenomenal in an interview but couldn't sell their way out of a paper bag.

They look picture perfect, know all the right answers, and say all the right things. But, they can't seem to keep a job. Now, I understand there is a lot more movement in a person's career today than even just a few short years ago, but there are a few things to watch for when sorting through resumes and applications and when you get to the interview itself.

Many of the warning signs are described in the preceding sections about body language and buzzwords, but the most telling of all is a person's work history. A good salesperson may change jobs but he doesn't often change industries. In fact, really good salespeople are recruited by the competition quite often and sometimes the offer is good enough to make them move. But, rarely is a successful salesperson someone whose resume includes selling insurance, cars, real estate, apparel, printing, and seven other totally different products or services.

If an applicant's resume is filled with completely different industries, it's an immediate red flag. This isn't to paint everyone with the same brush — your candidate may have valid reasons for a varied career. But someone with multiple jobs better be squeaky clean over the rest of your criteria if he's going to make it to a second interview. And, if he does make it to the next interview, be very inquisitive about his past and ask "Why?" — a lot.

It's not out of the question to ask, "Why do you think you haven't found an industry you could stay with?" The next words out of his mouth will tell you a lot about him. If he blames anyone and everyone, move on. You've just met a professional interviewee.

On the other hand, perhaps his spouse was transferred and he couldn't find a job in his chosen field and decided to try his hand at something new. That's a completely different set of circumstances.

I'm not saying you should avoid everyone who has worked in more than a few industries, but I am saying that such people fit the profile of someone who can interview with the best of them and sell with the worst of them. And you don't have time for that.

Knowing When to Make the Offer

Seldom have I extended a job offer at or after a first interview. Although it has happened, it's extremely rare. In fact, in my years of sales management, I can count the times on one hand. It's just not good business. For one thing, a quick job offer doesn't give you a chance to check the person's references. And you should always check references and past work history.

Take some time to let the interview sink in. Lay your notes aside and come back to them later. If you liked the person, do you still feel the same way the next day? After reviewing your notes, do you see conflicting statements you didn't catch at the time?

There are any number of things time helps sort out. If you rush yourself, you usually make a poor call.

If you're in doubt, have someone else in your company interview your favorite candidate(s). Everyone has different styles and asks different questions. Your colleague may get a different answer to the same question, which is a huge red flag. I've interviewed people I just clicked with, and they aced the interview with me. But when I sat in for the person's second interview, I saw him fold up like a cheap tent.

Whenever possible, have your superior interview someone you're thinking of hiring.

Consider the impact of the person you're thinking of adding to your team. Will he fit in with the rest of your team? Will he be an asset and make your team stronger, or does he have the type personality (even though he can sell) that could hurt the dynamic of your current group? You always want to add talent; you always want to get better.

Talking to past employers

As strange as it may seem, I have known people who got burned by simply dialing the number of a former employer provided on the applicant's resume or application. It works like this: the job seeker invents a job to fill a gap and provides you with the phone number of a friend or relative. When you call the friend gives a glowing reference — all completely bogus.

Any time you call a former employer or a reference, look the number up yourself — either online, through the company's website, or through a directory. Never use the number provided by the applicant — never.

Chapter 6

Hiring and Onboarding New Staff

In This Chapter

- Signing up new talent
- Understanding the value of onboarding
- Creating an effective Onboarding Packet

No matter how strong your team may be today, there will be a time when you are tasked with adding new salespeople. Chapter 5 talks about how to get through the recruiting process virtually unscathed.

In this chapter, I look at the steps for actually hiring your latest superstar discovery and getting her up to speed. I talk about the importance of making others in your company aware of your new hire (especially the person responsible for ensuring she gets paid), presenting a professional first impression, and properly onboarding your new hire — making her aware of the knowledge, skills, and behaviors she needs to succeed in her new role.

Hiring Your Next Superstar

You sorted through the stacks and stacks of resumes and applications and read through dozens of LinkedIn profiles. You whittled the number down to the handful of people who stand out and you conducted interviews. You decided on the one person you feel would best be an asset to your team and your company.

It's time to call and make the hire. At this point you believe this person is a superstar or she wouldn't have gotten this far, so treat her that way.

Be nothing but professional from your initial contact offering her the job to scheduling her pre-employment drug screening, physical, and other necessary procedures.

Most of the time, the actual job offer occurs through a phone call. Keep in mind that your candidate has more than likely interviewed with several potential employers so don't assume she knows who you are. Your initial conversation should go something like this: "Hello, Marlene? This is Butch Bellah with ABC Company. We spoke last Thursday about our position of sales account manager in the Taylorville market and I'm calling to see if you're still interested in the position?" If she answers in the affirmative, your follow-up is along the lines of, "Well, after carefully considering many qualified candidates, I'd like to offer you the job. Are you available to meet in person tomorrow?"

Set a face-to-face meeting when you can go through the salary discussion (or negotiation, if applicable) and walk Marlene through the pre-hire steps, including what she can expect as far as training and onboarding.

Just as you have options, a good salesperson does, too. Presenting a professional first impression to her is important for Marlene to be excited about her new career.

Creating a New Hire Packet

If your company doesn't have a New Hire Packet already, create one. A *New Hire Packet* contains every single bit of paperwork you need for a new employee, from the application through all the government tax paperwork.

Human resources (HR) and the payroll people all have paperwork to be properly filled out, and it's up to you to ensure it happens. When creating the New Hire Packet, work with your HR Department and get copies of all paperwork needed for your new employee — everything. I talk about creating that list later in this chapter in the section "Designing a Winning Onboarding Packet."

The first thing in your New Hire Packet should be a checklist of everything else that's in the packet. Because you need to make copies in the future, always keep the originals in a separate file so that you can produce nice-looking packets. Nothing looks worse than having a copy of a copy of a copy of a copy. You know the one I'm talking about — it's not even straight on the page, two copies ago something got wrinkled and it's barely legible. Not exactly the look you want to present to your new sales superstar, is it?

Keep a half-dozen or so New Hire Packets in a file ready to go at a moment's notice. Remember to update the information in them with any changes in policy or new procedures. If a true superstar falls into your lap tomorrow with absolutely no notice, you should be able to reach into a file, get out your packet, and give your new superstar the tools she needs to join your team.

Being prepared saves you an enormous amount of time the day your new salesperson shows up.

You don't have to know the answer to every question about insurance, benefits, and those sort of things. Someone in HR answers those questions every day. In fact, it's best to let HR folks explain retirement plans, insurance waiting periods, and so forth.

However, you must be able to explain the compensation program and how it works to a T. The one thing your new salesperson expects of you is to be able to tell her how she gets paid, how she can increase her income, and what formulas are used to calculate any commissions or bonus programs.

Informing all departments of your hire

It's imperative you notify everyone who needs to know of your new hire as soon as possible. The payroll department is clearly important, but have a checklist of others you want to introduce your new salesperson to immediately. This list includes other department heads, your sales team, and any key customers she will be inheriting.

A new salesperson should never meet anyone on her own. You make the introduction — identifying her and giving her the best chance to succeed.

If your new hire needs to spend time in other departments, let that department know prior to your new superstar's arrival. Not only is this courteous, but these other departments have to do their jobs along with having to meet and greet your new person.

I prefer to make as many introductions as possible in person and have a new hire actually meet the individuals she'll be working with and around. Let new employees put a face with a name and see the people behind the company rather than just the company itself.

The list of departments or people to visit with a new employee should include the following, at a minimum:

- **Human resources:** This is a given — HR needs time with the newbie to go over policies and procedures.
- **Upper management:** Make the salesperson feel special by meeting the key players in the organization. Introduce your new hire to as many of the senior managers as possible.

- **Purchasing:** Let the newbie know who to talk to in the event of product questions. Even though you're the person your salesperson calls first in times of trouble, she needs to know how to respond the quickest to a customer's needs.
- **Production:** These people generally fulfill the promises your new salesperson makes. Make sure they get to know each other well.
- **Transportation:** If your salespeople need to know about delivery or routing schedules let them know who the go-to person in transportation is.
- **Information technology (IT):** Your new hire needs lots of hardware and software set up — phone, email, laptop, voicemail, and so on. Make sure to carve out plenty of time for IT. This is one of the departments to notify as early as possible in case they have to order equipment for your new person.
- **Accounts receivable:** Your new hire has to know who's going to be asking for the money!
- **Credit department:** This is another obvious department that needs to be on the list.
- **Security:** If your company requires gate codes, identification badges, or other access tools, it's a good idea for your new person to be able to access the property and get where she needs to be.

There's more to making the rounds with a new hire than just walking her through the halls and introducing her. Make sure you take time with each department to give your newbie time to ask a few questions and feel at home. Starting a new job is a stressful time; make it as comfortable as possible.

Your New Hire Packet should contain a list of all the people you take your new salesperson to meet along with an overall company organizational chart. Let her know not to worry about remembering everyone's name because you'll give her a list with email addresses, titles, and phone extensions. An overall company organization chart also helps.

Human resources, IT, and even Security need to be notified of your new hires before they ever set foot on the property. Your job is to make the first day at a new job as natural and stress free as possible for the employee and your associates. Don't put other departments in the position of having to scramble to set up passwords, gather equipment, or otherwise prepare for your new person.

Don't forget your own department. Do you have a sales assistant or others who needs to know your new person? Make sure you don't leave these people out.

Finally, notify the rest of your sales team. Aside from sending out an email to the department welcoming the new person onboard, gather as many members of your team as possible for a quick meet-and-greet. Although it's doubtful that the whole team can be physically in the building for every new salesperson hired, I always like to have at least one senior representative there to share stories of her first day, first week, and first month.

Having the new salesperson hear about an experienced employee's first few days will make her much more comfortable and let her know she isn't the only one who ever had those feelings, insecurities, anxieties, and questions. It's natural — it happens to everyone.

Having a senior rep participate on that first day also gives the new person someone to address sales specific questions to — someone who has gone through what she's going through. It makes the transition process a lot smoother. You enjoy a little side benefit, as well — your senior rep will take a bit of pride in sharing her experiences and may take the new person under her wing. Now, you're building a team!

Completing the company paperwork

You've probably heard the old line, "The job's not finished until the paperwork's done!" Well, when you're hiring, that line would say, "No one's starting the job until the paperwork's done."

In many cases, HR has a paperwork packet or file already assembled for new employees. You need to go through it and make it sales specific. Add things such as company vehicle policies and procedures or take things out like uniform contracts and warehousing procedures. Whatever the case, have all your ducks in a row the moment your next superstar walks through the front door.

Familiarize yourself with all the documentation a new hire is required to sign. And, be ready to help fill out federal and state employee forms.

You don't have to be an expert in the company insurance policy and retirement plan, but you should know enough to discuss an overview of it, leaving the details to an expert. I always left any discussion of benefits to Human Resources simply because I didn't want to get anything wrong. If there's a 90-day waiting period, I don't want to inadvertently tell my new hire that it's 60 days. Let the people who specialize in your benefits packages do their jobs and explain eligibility requirements, enrollment dates, and options.

As you start your part of the paperwork, let HR know you'll be bringing your new employee there next. Keep the sitting around time to a minimum. Look professional and don't make your new salesperson feel as if she's being an imposition.

When all the paperwork is finished, assemble a nice packet of the copies for your new person to take home. Don't bog her down with a mish-mash stack of papers. Professionalism starts today.

If your company uses a formal offer letter, this should be the very first thing you go over. Make sure everyone is in complete agreement on the terms, compensation, commission structure, and any other benefits offered. The last thing you want to do is have a conversation six months from now about what someone thinks she remembers from the interview or get into a compensation dispute. You can mess with a lot of things, but don't mess with the money!

Onboarding: An Annoying Word But an Important Process

I'm not particularly fond of the term *onboarding* — it makes me think of waterboarding — but the process is important, and a lot more enjoyable than I imagine waterboarding to be. Another term for onboarding is organizational socialization, which is a mouthful.

Why is onboarding so important? Every new salesperson goes go through a period at the beginning of her employment when she's uncomfortable and feels a little bit lost. It takes a bit of time for everything to click. The best way to shorten this learning curve is to have a well-designed, set process you use every time for every new employee. That's really what onboarding is; easing new hires into the company, the sales team, and their new environment.

If you've been in business very long you've probably seen people hired and then thrown to the wolves. First off, it's completely unfair to the employee, and secondly, it almost insures failure — most people simply quit on you if you fail to provide them with proper training and a smooth onboarding process.

Now matter how much experience your new salesperson has, take every new hire through the same process every time. It's better to spend time on knowledge and information a new person already has than to assume she knows something she doesn't. Plus, after you get the process down and know it works, it becomes just like your sales process — no room for shortcuts.

Making a good first impression

Onboarding by definition is the act of acclimating or inducting a new person into an organization. It's derived from "bringing someone on board." Studies consistently show that employees who go through an onboarding process have a much higher job satisfaction rating and success rate, achieve greater success, and become strong assets for the organization.

Have I mentioned being professional with your new person? The reason I stress professionalism in the new-hire and onboarding process is because this is really the first look this person has of your company and how it operates on a day-to-day basis.

The process of onboarding involves more than just you, the sales manager. Make sure all other department heads are on the same page and aware of what information you want them to share with your new salesperson.

You are literally welcoming this person into you company. And, as you know, you never get a second chance at a first impression.

Figure 6-1 shows a sample welcome letter.

If you're at a position to hire more than one salesperson, take each through the onboarding process separately, if at all possible. I realize this may not be possible if you're opening a new division or region and hiring 30 people, but if it's only 2 or 3, handle the onboarding process individually. Give each person the time and attention she deserves.

Being (and looking) prepared

During the interview process, everyone does her best to impress you. Now, it's your turn to impress. Prepare for a salesperson's first day just as you would if you had one of your larger customers visiting your office. If that were the case, you'd notify everyone in the company, wouldn't you? Maybe straighten up the office a bit? That's the mindset you need to have as your next superstar walks through the front door — or even before.

If your new employee shows up to her first day and nobody knows she was coming, and it's a madhouse trying to get the paperwork filled out, do you think your new hire will be inspired to do her best for you? I doubt it.

You can arrange a much better experience if the guard at the gate has her on his schedule, she's greeted by name by the receptionist, and everyone is genuinely helpful and glad to meet her. Now you're looking like a well-run company. Have her work area clean, set up, and ready for her. Perhaps even involve another salesperson to help gather supplies and so forth so your new hire walks into the best possible scenario to succeed.

Dear [NEW EMPLOYEE NAME],

It is with great pleasure that I welcome you to [COMPANY]. I am very pleased that you have chosen and been chosen to represent our organization and know that this is the beginning of a mutually beneficial relationship.

We encourage all our Account Executives to take advantage of the continuing training available in order to improve their product knowledge and sales skills. As we continue to add new and exciting products to our offerings, it is increasingly important for you to be well versed in all of them. This will make you more valuable to your customers and ultimately make you and our company successful.

I have you scheduled for onboarding and to complete all your paperwork next Monday-Thursday. Remember, I'm here to help you succeed. If you have questions, please make a note so we can cover them during that first day.

You're joining an amazing group of people who are all committed to helping our customers grow their business. This is a very exciting time for all of us. Again, welcome to [COMPANY]!

Sincerely,

Butch Bellah
Sales Manager

Figure 6-1: Example of a professional welcome letter.

That's the way to make an impression that will last and inspire your new employees to want to really be a part of your team and perform for your company.

I'm not talking about rolling out red carpet and treating new salespeople like visiting foreign dignitaries, but a little advance planning and communication (there's that word again) with other departments goes a long way to creating a very positive first impression of the company.

Your new hire is the person you selected out of all those stacks and stacks of resumes; the one who came through maybe two or more rounds of interviews; the person you believe is your next superstar. Treat her that way.

Finally, because this is her first day, be aware of the example you set. Don't start the day at 10:00 a.m. and finish at 2:00 p.m. Establish early with your new hire that you start early and aren't afraid to work late. Your employees notice this. Trust me.

Acting like you've been here before

One of the most impressive things you can do for your new salesperson is to make the hiring and onboarding process seem as if it's a natural part of what your company does. Not that you want to seem like you churn-and-burn salespeople day-in and day-out, but you want it to seem as if you've been here before.

A new hire suffers some anxiety and nervousness on her first day, and a complicated process where the right hand doesn't know what the left hand is doing only makes that worse.

Plan the onboarding process carefully and eliminate any downtime when your new employee has nothing to do or when she has to wait for another departments to be ready for her. All these things contribute to the stress she's already feeling.

Focus your energy on introducing your new salesperson to the company and the company to her. Get the paperwork and all the necessary evils of HR procedures out of the way first. This allows you to spend your time on the positive aspects of getting your new hire up to speed.

This is a person you're going to call upon to sell your company's products or services to prospective customers. This is your first chance to sell her on the company. If she feels that you're fumbling around and not really sure of how to do this, it could potentially destroy her confidence and cost you a great salesperson.

Your new hire's spouse or significant other is going to ask her, "So, what did you think?" as soon as she walks in the door at home. What do you want her answer to be? You don't want her to say, "These people have no clue what they're doing!" Make the first-day experience so positive and professional that your new salesperson can't wait to get home share her excitement!

When you get into the specifics of the sales position, have a quiet place for the two of you to sit uninterrupted. Be prepared to provide a pen and notebook and a box, attaché, or binders so that your new salesperson can start assembling all the sales materials she'll leave with that day.

Designing a Winning Onboarding Packet

An Onboarding Packet is designed to act as a roadmap for the onboarding process. Just as the New Hire Packet contains the government forms and company-centered paperwork, your Onboarding Packet is strategically built just for the salesperson.

The New Hire Packet could be used by any department. The Onboarding Packet is for salespeople only.

The Onboarding Packet is designed to

- Reduce the upfront investment for the company and time for the salesperson to see a return
- Increase the account executive's proficiency to produce optimal sales performance
- Reduce turnover
- Provide proper training, assurances, and materials to new salespeople
- Increase the company's ability to properly grow and service their customers

The Onboarding Packet is a fluid document (er, packet) and should always be growing as you and the company grow.

From a written job description to a well-documented explanation of how the compensation plan works, everything needs to be included in your Onboarding Packet to ensure you cover everything with each new representative every time.

It's a good idea to include a company history, industry information and statistics and other relevant data. And, if you work for a publicly-traded company, include a copy of the most recent annual report.

The Onboarding Packet itself acts as sort of a checklist for you, as sales manager, to ensure you go through the same steps every time you hire a new representative.

Keep in mind that this Onboarding Packet starts when you decide to hire your new representative — it's your own personal checklist to keep you on track. Start from the time you select your candidate, and write down everything that has to happen — everything. Each of these items or steps becomes part of your onboarding process and represents an item to be checked off in the onboarding list.

There's no way to include everything — that needs to be customized by your own company — but I provide a sample onboarding guide to get you started in Figure 6-2.

Sales manager onboarding checklist:

New Account Executive: ______________________________

Contact the selected candidate to indicate our desire to move forward with bringing the person onboard. If requested by the candidate, allow time for him/her to give proper notice at his/her current job and/or review the offered position with [COMPANY] and agree upon a date to respond verbally. Put a reminder in Outlook for the agreed-upon response date.

Date Completed: ____________ *Manager Initials:* ____________

Create a personnel file with all required paperwork for the employee to complete prior to and/or on his/her first day. (Use New Hire Packet checklist.)

Date Completed: ____________ *Manager Initials:* ____________

Prepare Training/Orientation schedule for new hire(s). This should begin with a list of people the employee should meet (even virtually) during his/her first day with the company. If possible, the manager should plan to introduce the new account manager via phone (if not in person) to the company president, the vice presidents of sales and marketing, the other people in the sales department, and possibly others within the organization. Confirm with all of these people the time they will be available.

Date Completed: ____________ *Manager Initials:* ____________

Figure 6-2: Sample onboarding packet.

Clearly define job description

Even though you created a job description for your ad or had to describe the job during the recruiting and hiring process, the job description in your Onboarding Packet needs to be a bit more formal, include more specific information, and include some company-specific information.

This particular version of the job description serves to not only outline the functions and duties of new salespeople, but also gets into performance requirements, evaluations, and other areas not covered in the public job listing.

You can use the job description you created for the hiring process as an outline, but you must go much deeper with this official version. When creating this version include the following:

- **Exact job title:** If you call them Account Managers, Account Executives, Business Development Mangers, whatever it is, it should be the exact same thing printed on their business cards.
- **Key duties and overall job purpose:** Be precise but flexible. The job may change with time but construct the description in a way that lists all the duties expected along with the overall purpose (for example, "to maintain and grow business within the assigned territory").
- **Define location:** Be specific about where the new employee will be working.
- **Reports to:** Self explanatory, but needs to be listed.
- **Manages/Oversees:** To be used if anyone reports to this person. Be specific as to the scope of the manager's responsibility for other employees' actions, schedules, performances, and so forth.
- **Compensation:** Give a detailed account of how any commission or bonus program works and if there are any minimums, maximums, or other pertinent information.
- **Performance review information:** Include how often performance and employee assessments will be completed and by whom.

There's really no better way to describe this document than to provide a sample for you to use as a template, so see the sample account manager job description in Figure 6-3. Your description may be longer, shorter, or completely different. That's fine. The key is to get everything in writing you need to have on record.

The job description is not an ad to recruit the greatest salesperson; it's the actual job description by which you will judge your new employee — there's a huge difference. Although it's called a job description, focus your thinking on duties — what do you want your salespeople to do every single day? — as you write it.

Or perhaps the best question is this: "What do you want your new representative thinking about every morning when she wakes up?" That's what needs to be in the job description. That's the best way to ensure you're both on the same page going forward.

Account Executive

Reports to: Sales Manager

Job Description/Duties: The Account Executive (AE) is responsible for the development of new business through identifying qualified sales leads, determining client needs, making proper proposals, presenting programs, and closing the sale. Additionally, the Account Executive will maintain an ongoing relationship with his/her customer base at the decision-maker level and is responsible for overall client satisfaction.

The AE can and should have a goal of ultimately managing approximately $500,000 per week in volume within the geographic territory assigned: Adams County, Baker County, Charleston County, Denton County, and East River County.

Compensation: AE will earn a base salary plus a commission on all sales under his/her control based on the following formulas:

New Business: 5% of Gross Profit

Repeat Business: 10% of Gross Profit

In addition, the AE will receive a company vehicle, fuel card, expenses, and benefits as outlined in the offer letter and New Hire Packet.

Account Executives are expected to conduct themselves in a professional manner at all times when dealing with coworkers, prospects, and customers. Timely communication and response to issues is required.

The Account Executive will have an initial performance review with the sales manager after 90 days of employment and annually after that.

Figure 6-3: Sample job description.

Training schedule

Your Onboarding Packet should contain a detailed training schedule your new representative can plan her first few weeks around. It needs to be a set schedule and the same for everyone who comes through your program.

The key to anyone's success on any job is how well her initial training is conducted. Too many times, salespeople are simply thrown out in a "sink or swim" scenario — expected to learn on the fly and either succeed or fail based on their own desire to pick up training through osmosis. What a shame.

Many great salespeople have quit many jobs because of a lack of training only to go on to wildly successful careers elsewhere. They don't lack talent or ability, but a company's lack of a professional training program can drive away great assets.

When creating and outlining your training schedule for new hires, think back to what you wish you would've been taught — good and bad — about the market, the company, the product, or whatever the case may be.

Not everything is rainbows and unicorns, and if you try to show only the good side of the business, you're sending an ill-prepared person into the field.

The complexity of your product or service determines the length of your training schedule, but if there's one piece of advice I can give you, it's to allow more time than you think you need. If you're going to err, err on the side of over-training instead of under-training.

A typical training schedule looks something like this:

- **Day One:** Complete all paperwork, meet department heads, collect your new sales materials, and begin the introduction to our sales process.
- **Day Two:** Introduction to company policies and procedures with Sales Manager and/or Human Resources. Spend the majority of the day on product knowledge.
- **Day Three:** Ride with or shadow a seasoned salesperson for the entire day, taking notes and asking questions.

  Make sure you send a newbie out with the right person. Your best salesperson is not automatically the person to send her with. Put some thought into which of your current salespeople has the heart of a teacher and can best benefit your new hire.
- **Day Four:** Spend the day in the purchasing, production, and shipping departments to get an idea of how an order is generated, filled, and delivered.

  The more salespeople know about the entire chain of events, the better they're going to be!
- **Day Five:** Testing on product knowledge and sales process.

  Spend a lot of time creating this test. Make it hard. It needs to really dig deep to determine if this person is ready to represent your company in the field or needs more training.

In this scenario, have the new salesperson spend at least the second full week with various salespeople — shadowing and watching (with her mouth closed in front of prospects). This gives her a great deal of real-world experience to draw from. One representative may have an opening and rapport-building tactic that resonates with your new salesperson while another may ask for the sale in a way the new hire can relate to. You want her to take the best of the best from each of your current representatives and put it into her own words and her own style. The best way to do this is to expose her to as many different techniques as possible.

Have a new salesperson keep her ears open and mouth closed in front of clients or prospects. She should be introduced as a new salesperson in training who's there simply to observe.

At the end of the second week, it's question-and-answer time. Let your new salesperson take all the questions she's collected over the previous week and get answers — from you, from product brochures, or whatever source can provide the right answer.

Finally, before sending your new salesperson out into the field (and by this time she's going to be raring to go), she needs to spend a day with you while she makes calls and you observe. Evaluate how she is at building rapport, posing questions, and asking for the sale. See how well she knows the product and whether she can answer a customer's questions with certainty.

Do *not* expect a new salesperson with two weeks on the job to perform as well as a ten-year veteran. However, she should be able to comfortably represent your organization and present your product or service.

It's okay to let new employees know that they never really stop learning. Your job at this point is to simply get them ready to hit the market armed with a good sense of *how* to sell, *what* to sell, and *whom* to sell it to.

If you're not 100 percent comfortable at this stage, there're no reason not to take another few days to make sure your new hire is up to speed on the areas she's a bit deficient in. It's better to take a few more days now than have her sales suffer for months.

Providing a list of key contacts

Another important aspect of your Onboarding Packet is a list of key contacts. This list is one your new representative can take with her, input into her phone (which she should do immediately), and add to her email address book.

The Key Contact list should include all department heads along with their department, phone (extension), and email address. Also include upper management, but you may want to just include email addresses for them, depending on the formality of your organization.

Poll your entire sales force and ask them who they call, what industry websites they use, and which manufacturer or vendor representatives they call or have in their phones. This is a great place to start building your Key Contact list.

Don't forget to include manufacturer or vendor representatives, vendor websites, industry websites, and links and other online sources of information. Again, this is not just a phone list but a Key Contact list.

The Key Contact list is really the who's who of people your new salesperson may need to reach at some point or another — not just the employee telephone list.

You can make the Key Contact list a laminated piece of paper designed to be kept in the salesperson's briefcase, car, or work area. It will be referred to a lot, so make it easy for her.

Outlining your expectations for the first 90 days and beyond

The final piece of the puzzle for your Onboarding Packet is perhaps the most important. You should have, in writing, your expectations for the first 90 days of the new person's employment and your ongoing expectations for her continued growth and success track.

People want to know how to get to the next level. This is where you explain it to them.

A good salesperson wants to know where the next step on the ladder is. A great salesperson wants to know where all the steps on the ladder are. A superstar salesperson wants to know what the record time is for someone to have climbed it . . . so she can break that record.

When outlining your expectations, be specific. Salespeople want to know how they're doing — they have to know — it's built into their DNA. If you're not going to be there to tell them every day, at least give them the targets you expect them to hit so they can see for themselves if they are ahead of schedule or behind.

Be realistic. Don't set targets, goals, and expectations for a new hire at the same place you set them for a 10-year veteran no matter how much experience your new salesperson has. Every new employee goes through a learning curve and the last thing she needs is to feel pressure to live up to some unrealistic expectations.

If your company has a 90-day probationary period, be very specific about the consequences of not meeting those objectives. If they include the old catchall "up to and including termination" language, go over this with your new salesperson and let her know what would trigger the "including termination" part. Is it simply failure to meet goals or is it being less than 50 percent of target? Whatever it is, be specific. It's best for her to know now the standards you expect of her.

The next step is to take her beyond the first 90 days and let her know what you expect from her personally. Let her know you're hiring her for a career, not just a job, and that you want to do everything possible to help her to succeed.

Ask her to consider where she should realistically be a year from now . . . two years . . . five years? Let her know what others have done so she knows what's possible.

Don't embellish expectations or other salespeople's accomplishments and think you're going to trick your new hire into outperforming everyone else. That doesn't work, and it could blow up in your face.

To display your true ability as a leader and a manager, have your new hire fill out the last part of her Onboarding Packet. Have her write down (yes, write down) her goals for the first 90 days. Make a copy for each of you to review at the 90-day mark but also have her look at and read her goals out loud every single day.

Now, take it a step further and have her write down her own goals for the first year, two years, and five years. Let her keep those herself. That's for her to live up to.

If you can get a new salesperson off on the right foot in those first 90 days, keep her on track to hit those first targets, communicate with her, let her know your goal is to make her successful, you're well on your way to building your next superstar salesperson.

Chapter 7

Defining Your Sales Process and Training Your Team

In This Chapter

- Defining your sales process
- Emphasizing planning and prospecting
- Presenting your product
- Understanding how to ask for and finalize the sale
- Training your team to ask for referrals
- Knowing your product
- Making technology work for you

A sales manager wears many hats, but perhaps the most important is that of trainer. It's your job to make sure that not only is your sales team at its best today but that the members of your team are constantly learning and growing.

There's a knack to training someone to sell — and yes, it is an acquired skill. It's not enough to just tell him what you think is obvious. You must set your own ego aside and understand that, as a manager, you're not there to show off but rather to enable your team to improve.

Anyone can stand in front of a group, bark out orders, and regurgitate facts and figures. However, it takes a certain skill to be able to actually teach — to train your salespeople (new and seasoned) in the art of selling.

Once you embrace the fact that it's not about what *you* know, but rather what you can help your team learn, you'll be far ahead of the game and a much, much better trainer.

This chapter focuses on the importance of the sales process — which you must customize to your own product, service, or philosophy — and how to train your team in each step of your specific process.

Although I talk about "steps" in the sales process, train your people to see the process as one smooth movement. Imagine running the bases in baseball after a home run. You don't stop at every base and adjust your pants or tie your shoes, you just keep moving toward your ultimate goal like you were meant to be there.

Understand that training is an action verb. It's a process. You will always be training your team; they will never be trained. There's always something new to learn, a new product to study, and a new way of doing business.

To truly be great at this you must have they heart of a teacher and the mind of a student. Never stop teaching and training your people, and never stop learning yourself.

Mapping the Path from Prospect to Customer: Defining Your Sales Process

The path from prospect to sale is your process. The whole reason behind having a sales process is to simply draw the line your prospect takes in order to become a customer. When you begin to think of it as a process — a series of steps — it becomes much clearer.

Start by asking how you first meet a prospect. What do you want to happen next and so on. Before long, you have your entire sales process mapped.

Although no set process applies to every business, there are some keys each should include. You can use this basic ten-step process as a template and an outline:

1. Prospecting: who is your prospect and how will you meet them?
2. Establishing a relationship
3. Qualifying your prospect
4. Getting an initial verbal agreement
5. Doing a needs analysis

6. Presenting your product or service
7. Reaffirming buyer's needs
8. Converting needs to wants
9. Asking for the sale
10. Overcoming objections

After you complete the basic formula, take some time to review it. Think it through. Is it logical? Is it chronological? Is it realistic?

After you successfully complete this process, you can back up and see your entire sale from start to finish in a timeline. You can anticipate all the roadblocks and training moments you need to prepare yourself for as you begin to assemble your training program.

The key is to start at the beginning and take it literally step-by-step — leave nothing out — in your process.

A great reference for developing your process is *Selling For Dummies*, 4th Edition, by Tom Hopkins (Wiley).

Setting a realistic timeline for your sales cycle

Your *sales process* is the chronological order of creating a customer from a prospect; your *sales cycle* is the time it should take to do it.

For you, as a manager, to be able to establish realistic goals and quotas, you must have a firm grasp on your sales process and the ensuing sales cycle. Create a timeline or an expected amount of time it takes to move a prospect from one step to the next in a perfect world, knowing that the world is never going to be perfect. The idea is to set the bar at a point where if everything goes exactly right at each step along the way, it takes this long to close the sale.

It's far better to err on the side of caution when setting your sales cycle, because at almost every step along the way, you deal with the prospect's timeline, not yours. You cannot force your clients to respond to your needs in a certain amount of time because you're trying to keep your sales cycle on target.

The way to do that is to simply take each step and assign a time period to it. For example, the following scenario sets your ideal sales cycle at five to nine weeks — again, in a perfect world:

Again, if you're in a retail environment this may be five to nine minutes — it all depends on your market and how your prospect makes buying decisions.

- Initially meeting the prospect to building rapport and establishing a relationship to where you both feel comfortable moving forward is two to four weeks.
- Building on the relationship, you begin to qualify your prospect, go over your initial oral agreement, and sit down to do a needs analysis. This takes between two and three weeks.
- It's reasonable to assume you'll invest another one or two weeks before you get the opportunity to present your product or service. During this time, you should be preparing for the presentation, learning as much as you can about your prospect and assembling your sales materials. It's also not realistic to think this is your only prospect. During this time, you'll be working with other prospects and clients at different stages of the same cycle.
- You reaffirm the buyer's needs, convert those needs to wants, ask for the sale, and overcome any objections. Now, if your product or service is usually closed at the time of the presentation, stop here.

If your average buyer usually takes time to make a decision, you can add whatever is standard to this, perhaps another two to three weeks before you have a decision. Now your sales cycle is anywhere from 7 to 12 weeks.

You're looking at spending two to three *months* to bring a new customer from the time you initially meet him. That's too long to spend on a potential sale that could fall through. That's why prospecting is so important.

When you train your team, you need to illustrate the length of the sales cycle because the biggest recipe for failure is to have just one or two prospects working at a time. You must train your team to constantly be adding people to this cycle so they always have forward momentum from some prospect.

Your prospects are in complete control of the timeline at several points throughout the sales cycle. Don't rush them. Be persistent, but professional. This is why the superstar salespeople keep as many prospects "in the hopper" as they can possibly manage.

After you establish your perfect scenario timeline, add about 20 percent to it. In this case, I would estimate the typical sales cycle takes about 120 days from start to finish. Again, this illustrates the critical need to be working multiple prospects at once. Furthermore, it allows you to set realistic targets for your people and to know what to expect as far as "ramp up" time when a new salesperson hits the market with no prospects in hand.

Training Your Team on Planning and Prospecting

You have your sales process and your sales cycle — you know how it should work and how long it should take to complete. The next step is putting together a formal training program for your team, which I discuss in the following sections.

The early part of any sales process is planning ahead and prospecting, so I discuss how to approach training these first.

You train your sales team on *your* sales process. Some members of your team want to tell you how they used to do it elsewhere or to share any number of techniques, and that's fine. But, this is your rodeo and you pick the riders.

No matter what the end result of your own sales process was, planning and prospecting must not only be included, they're the genesis of the entire undertaking. As you train your salespeople, you cannot stress enough the importance of these two tasks or habits. If they make them habits, they will certainly be much farther ahead of the competition. Planning and prospecting are essential to sales success at any level.

Never, ever, ever keep or continue a process "just because that's the way we've always done it." If it doesn't belong, get rid of it.

Emphasize the value of planning

In my own personal sales process, I take planning for granted. Planning is something I actually enjoy doing, and it makes my job so much easier. Ask your salespeople if they would go to the grocery story without a list and just fumble their way down the aisles trying to remember whether they need this or that? That's basically all I'm talking about with planning — make your list of what you need to do, where you need to go and make sure you're doing it in the most effective manner.

Even though it can take on a multitude of definitions, in my world *planning* is simply researching the market. Successful planning involves market research and putting together a list of contacts to call on the next day or within the next week. Planning also involves preparing materials and presentations you need, gathering samples, and mapping out your route, your day, and your week. A few minutes of planning can save a salesperson hours and make him so much more productive.

Before your salespeople can do anything, they need to be in the habit of planning. I highly recommend training your team to spend a few minutes each evening planning for the next day and about a half-hour on Sunday night planning for the coming week. Those few minutes — if well spent — can have a tremendous impact on their success. I don't want to spend half my day driving around looking for someone to call on who could be considered a prospect. I'd rather plan.

The downside of not planning is simply jumping in the car on Monday morning and heading out to make calls. This can create an inordinate amount of windshield time that is totally wasted. If you simply train your team to plan in advance and work in a very structured, efficient manner, you're ahead of three-quarters of your competition from day one.

By the same token, in a retail establishment the lack of planning could leave a salesperson just hoping someone walks through the door rather than having an appointment scheduled to come see the latest fashions or newest arrivals.

Be prepared for some (even seasoned) salespeople to complain about planning time. It may be hard to start, but if they simply make a habit of it, it becomes easier and more natural, and they see the benefits very quickly.

As the old saying goes, "If you don't have time to do it right, you certainly don't have time to do it over."

Always be prospecting

In your role as a trainer, if there is one area to focus on and be your best at, make it in teaching and training your team to prospect, or find potential customers.

If you were to ask them what they all wanted to be better at or improve their skills in, they'd probably answer with "asking for the sale" or "overcoming objections." But if they aren't prospecting, they don't have anyone to ask for the sale and no objections to overcome!

Always be prospecting. That's a good lesson to teach your salespeople and one that will pay far more dividends because no prospects equals no closes. Period.

In my opinion, prospecting is the single most important skill a sales professional can develop. And yes, it is a skill. It takes practice and study.

In almost any sales team the top salesperson isn't the best closer, it's the person who has refined and mastered the art of prospecting. Note I didn't say the person who prospected the most, but the one who prospects the best.

This is where the planning comes in. If you can get your salespeople to develop a plan and stick with it, success will come.

Prospecting should be something each of your salespeople does regularly in order to keep their skills sharp and to have plenty of potential customers to start into the sales process.

If one of your salespeople is having trouble meeting numbers this month, it may be because he wasn't prospecting two or three months ago. Don't overanalyze his presentation or other sales skills until you see how many real prospects he's working.

I've trained salespeople for a long time on four basic principles of prospecting:

- **Have a plan:** I always suggest having a set time each day or each week to do nothing but prospect. Remove anything else that's a distraction and simply find potential new customers whether by phone or in person. Don't try to multi-task — give it your full attention.
- **Be prepared:** When it's time for someone to start prospecting, start prospecting. Don't waste time looking at maps or trying to find out where you're going or who you're going to call. This time is much too valuable to waste. If you're plan to spend an hour every morning prospecting, you're cheating yourself if you only get in 59 minutes.
- **Have a goal:** Know what you want to accomplish before you ever start. Are you looking for appointments? Seeking email addresses to send out information? Whatever it is, have a clearly defined goal before you ever start the process.
- **Enjoy yourself:** Have fun! Smile. Meet and greet people. Introduce yourself and let them know who you are and how they can reach you. Don't get too stressed over whether these are cold calls, warm calls, or whatever — just make the calls.

Train your salespeople to either take good notes or keep a record of what they're doing and how they're progressing. Each and every prospecting session can and should be a learning experience — if they pay attention to it.

Prospecting is an area where your sales manager hat is going to be much needed. Salespeople tend to stop prospecting as soon as they get a few deals working. *Don't* let them.

If your salespeople aren't prospecting today, they'll have nobody to talk to tomorrow. Whether you require some sort of form, report, or just rely on the numbers to tell the story, make sure your team is constantly meeting and talking to potential new customers.

The sales floor is not the place to prospect either. Don't allow your sales team to wait for the company's advertising or marketing plan to bring people to their store or showroom. That's where average salespeople live — and you want superstars.

Today's sales are not a result of today's activities — they're the end result of groundwork laid weeks and sometimes months earlier.

If you aren't planting seeds, don't complain about a barren harvest.

Presentation Is Everything

Your sales process has a multitude of steps between planning and prospecting and presenting, but the one thing you can be sure of is that if your team is going to be successful they must be very good at making a presentation.

Assume your team has completed every step in the process and it's time to make the presentation — it's showtime! It's time to take the stage and present your wares in a way that makes the prospect beg to buy them. (Well, okay — so you know that's not going to happen.)

A well-designed, well-planned presentation is essential to a successful salesperson's career. If you have someone who is great at prospecting but cannot make a presentation to save his life, you might consider putting him in a call center setting appointments or something.

I've found several strategies, tools, and techniques every salesperson should be taught. And, your team is a great place to start:

- **Make the presentation appear customized:** The last thing a professional buyer wants is a cookie-cutter answer for his problems. If the salesperson has done his job and uncovered the need or diagnosed the issues — then shouldn't the prescription be just for that person? Does you doctor give you the same medicine he gives everyone else without asking questions? The patient's name is on the prescription! Include the prospect's logo, use his name in the presentation, do whatever it takes to let him know the presentation is meant for him. If you're showing your client a new suit or an automobile, talk about how they look in it or what it would be like in their driveway. Include them in your story.
- **Ask lots of questions:** I'm amazed at salespeople who do a great job up to a certain point. They're phenomenal at finding prospects, planning their approach, and asking good questions, but when it comes to the presentation, they just show up and throw up.

  The style of communication shouldn't change — this is just another natural step along the way. Train your people to make a natural transition into the presentation — not some glaring, raise the flag, strike up the band type performance.
- **Convert buyers needs to wants:** For years I sang the "needs analysis" tune, and like me, you have probably done hundreds, if not thousands of them. I would find the buyer's need, pain point or other issue and show how my product would solve their problem. But, guess what? People don't buy what they need; they buy what they want! By training your team to effectively present your product and ask good questions, they create the desire — the want.
- **Practice your voice inflection:** If you're talking about a serious issue with a prospective customer, you better sound like it's serious. Words are just words unless they are delivered properly. Teach your people to use passion, conviction, and a true interest in their prospect. Listen to your salespeople; really listen. This is a perfect place to role play with them and test their skills.
- **Use your own name:** If I have a customer who's going to hear several presentations before making a decision, one method I use to stick out in his mind is to use my name or my company's name in the context of the presentation. For example, "I was talking to a customer just the other day who said, 'Butch, the main thing we like about. . .'" or "All my associates back at ABC Materials are committed to making this transition as easy as possible." Teach your sales team to use these small drops that can pay off big time in the end.
- **Make it special:** This is really a combination of the customization and the voice inflection. A salesperson may have given his presentation hundreds of times, but make sure each of your team members keep their presentations fresh and interesting. Remind them constantly: This is the prospect's first time to hear it!

People buy what they want, not what they need

If I would've been asked on May 18, 2009 if I wanted triple-bypass heart surgery at 43 years old my answer would've been, "I don't want it, I don't need it, and I can't afford it."

Those are the same three things your salespeople hear every day! "No want, no need, no money!" But, on May 19, 2009 when my cardiologist showed me I had a 70 percent, two 80 percent and a 90 percent blockage in the pathways around my heart, I changed my tune! I was all in! Sign me up!

Not only did I want it, need it, and find a way to afford it, but I wanted an expert doing it! But, amazingly, the only thing that changed in those 24 hours was the information available to me. My heart didn't just get blocked up all of a sudden. My finances didn't change.

But, after I was shown the blockage, a need became a want.

How can your salespeople show their potential customer's their blockage? How can they diagnose the problems and then be the expert their customer needs?

It's not about needs. It's about wants and desires.

The presentation is show-and-tell time. Your people should be proud of what they're offering and presenting to your prospective customers. Train them, test them, and test them some more.

Role playing is one of the best ways to become a better presenter — not only do your people get to practice, but they also get to observe presenters better than they are and pick up some great habits.

Teaching "Asking for the Sale"

Even though I have gone on record as stating that prospecting is the most important part of the process, I also tell you that I believe you'll spend the majority of your teaching and training time on asking for the sale. It is the most dreaded, least-liked, most feared part of the process. But it doesn't have to be.

When training salespeople to ask for the sale, the first thing you have to do is have them change nothing. Don't shift positions, don't change their body language, voice inflection, or anything else.

This is just a natural next step in the process and the process flows from one step to the next.

Prior to the actual training and teaching of how to ask for the sale, you must build your people's confidence. They have to know what they're doing and expect positive outcomes.

If they're timid or show the least bit of uncertainty, they're done.

Teaching someone to ask for the sale boils down to three parts — three parts you could easily use in any part of your training, but it's most effective at this juncture.

1. **Education:** Educate your team and actually teach them the art of asking for the sale. There are correct and incorrect methods to use — I go through those later in this chapter. But, you must make this part of the educational process.
2. **Demonstration:** Have you ever heard, "Don't tell me, show me"? Demonstrating the correct procedure and technique is very important. This is something you should be very good at — or you probably wouldn't be the sales manager. Now, you have to make yourself equally good at sharing that knowledge with others.
3. **Observation:** This is not something where you can talk about it, show it a couple of times, and say, "Okay, you got it? Good! Now, go get 'em!" That's doesn't work. Period. You need to use your educational time on the techniques, your demonstration time on the art and actions involved, and then observe your salespeople doing it.

But here's the kicker: Until you're comfortable with their ability to do this professionally, why in the world would you put them in front of a live prospect?

Have your salespeople practice asking for the sale until they get it to where it's second nature to them!

Confidence is king. Your people build confidence through repetition, practice, and a general knowledge of what they're going to say. For example, if you have a scripted, well-rehearsed, natural-sounding way of asking for the sale, your confidence is going to be exponentially higher than if you're just flying by the seat of your pants.

I prefer to have a script when it comes to asking for the sale. I want to know exactly what I am going to say, although I want it to sound natural. This is planned, not canned! Have your people write out the script and use their own words. Nothing is worse than talking to a salesperson, and when it comes time to ask for the sale, having him sound like a ventriloquist's dummy — as if someone else is talking and the salesperson is just moving his mouth.

It should be as natural as if someone asked for his phone number — it should just roll right off the tongue.

Here's one technique for asking for the sale that I've used and can personally endorse. It's not a be-all, end-all you can use for every product, scenario, and person. But, you can use this template then fill in your information to make it your own:

> Mr. Prospect, you've stated you like our service and we both agreed together that it would solve your problem in tracking turnaround time. Here's the best part: After working with my team, I put together two options for you.
>
> Option one includes full installation, a 12-month maintenance package, and full technical support for a year for just $12,500 (pronounced *twelve-five*).
>
> Option two also includes installation, but it has a three-year maintenance package along with full technical support for just $15,500 *(fifteen-five)*.
>
> Now, after we've spent time together and I've learned what I have about you and your company, I believe option one is really the best fit (use whichever option is actually best for the customer) because of the strength of your in-house team and their ability to get it set up and take care of you after that first year.
>
> But, we both know it's not my money, it's yours, so which would you choose?

Still another way would be if your salesperson was showing someone two different refrigerators:

> This first model has the built-in ice and water dispenser and has the deluxe stainless-steel finish and has the full warranty for $1,495. The newest member of the line is the built-in ice dispenser without the water. It still has that beautiful finish and the warranty and it's available today for just $1,195, saving you $300.
>
> From what you've told me, I believe it would fit your needs and your budget, but it's not my money — it's yours, so which would you choose?

Again you've given the buyer a choice and suggested the lower of the two.

What do you think the customer expected you to suggest? That's right, the most expensive! You earn a bit of trust by having the offer you suggest in your close be the least expensive of the two!

This entire process only works if you have gained the prospect's trust, truly done your homework, and are sincere and confident in your suggestion.

Train your people to be confident, sincere and prepared. If you train your people to handle every situation like that, when it's time to ask for the sale, their numbers will go through the roof.

Training your team in asking for the sale isn't something you can go over in one sales meeting and then never touch again. This is an area you should be working on constantly — practice, practice, practice!

Training Your Team in Finalizing the Sale

You trained your sales team to take the prospect all the way from the planning stages to becoming a customer. What started out as a cold lead became a hot prospect, but is not yet a happy new client. Now you need to wrap this puppy up and finalize the sale.

> Oh wait, what?
>
> The prospect has an objection? Really?
>
> Well, of course he does. Everyone has an objection.

Buyers think they must always have an objection so they don't look too easy. Sometimes the objections are legitimate, other times they're not. It's up to your salesperson to be professional enough to find out whether the objection is real or imagined — or just an excuse to have an objection.

The job isn't finished and you cannot allow your team to let up here. All the groundwork has been laid, it's time to bring it home, do the paperwork, and welcome this new client into the fold.

Overcoming objections

Allow me to step onto my objection soap box for a moment: If a salesperson has done his job for the entire sales process — asked the right questions to determine where the blockage is, qualified the prospect to make sure he has the ability and responsibility to make a binding decision, presented an adequate, fair solution, there should be no objections. But, before you scream out loud, I realize that is a one-in-a-thousand scenario.

My point is the best way to overcome objections is to keep them from ever arising in the first place. Because there's little chance of that happening, take a look at the best way to overcome them when they happen.

An objection — no matter what it is — is simply the prospect telling you, "I am not sold on your product or service . . . yet." That's it. It's just that simple. From the old "I want to think about it" to "I have to talk to my husband/wife/cousin's sister's brother's uncle," it's all the same. The prospect isn't sold on your product yet.

Please make sure any new salespeople understand this and know objections are going to come, and that an objection doesn't mean the sale is lost. In fact, objections mean just the opposite — the prospect is giving you an opportunity to gain his business.

The best answer a salesperson can get when he asks for the sale is "yes." The second best is "no" because then and only then do you have something to work with.

As a sales manager, the best way to train your sales team to overcome prospects' objections is to first find out what they are. Make a list of the ten most common objections your salespeople hear on a regular basis. If you were to ask each individually, you're going to end up with about the same ten, but ask as a group and have them buy in to the fact those are the most common.

Then simply go through them as a group and determine the best way to overcome each objection with the benefits of your product or service. That's right: Make a list of the ten most common objections and then work with your team to come up with how to overcome them. No salesperson should ever be en route to a sales presentation thinking, "I hope they don't say (fill in the blank)."

If you know a customer is going to have an objection, be ready to overcome it. How to deal with objections should be a training topic exactly as how to ask for the sale is. Your sales team's ability to overcome objections should be natural and conversational. When the prospect says "X," your salespeople should immediately know to reply with "Y." Practice. Practice. Practice.

I personally don't consider "I can't afford it" a valid objection simply because if the prospect is properly qualified, that information would come out. If you have a salesperson who consistently gets the "no money" objection, work with him on his qualifying process. If the salesperson had asked the proper questions and uncovered the prospect's actual budget — which is how you train him to qualify a prospect — "I can't afford it" isn't a real objection; it's a smoke screen, meaning you've got to dig deeper to find out what is holding your prospect back.

Objections are the opportunity for your people to show prospects how your product or service can fill their needs. Throwing out an objection is simply asking for more information.

Training in following up for success

You can break down follow-up opportunities into two segments:

- **Pre-sale:** The pre-sale follow up is important when you have a product or service that tends to have a lag time between the sales presentation and the actually awarding of the sale. If you're answering an RFP (Request For Proposal) and make a presentation, you likely have to follow up with the prospect after that presentation and before the sale is finalized.
- **Post-sale:** The post-sale follow up is the ongoing process of following up after the sale is complete and customers are using your product or service. The last thing you want is to leave prospects and/or customers with the impression that you disappear as soon as the sale is complete.

In both instances, it's important to have a set follow-up plan that you, as the sales manager, can monitor.

Let your prospects know the salesperson's job *starts,* not stops, when they become customers!

As you train your team to be professional and consistent in their follow up, there is one thing you must stress: Never go to a customer to just touch base. This is one of the most amateurish things a salesperson can do.

Always have a reason to get in touch. You can share information or data with your prospect in the pre-sale follow up. Be as much a part of the decision-making process as possible.

As far as the post-sale follow up is concerned, a professional salesperson is always looking for ways to increase his business with a client. In fact, the easiest way to grow your business is to increase the business you do with your current customers who already know you, like you, and trust you. Have a set follow-up program to continually introduce them to either new aspects of your offerings or perhaps add additional products and services to what you already sell them. This is not only the easiest sell you'll ever make, but the most profitable because you have almost no acquisition cost in that customer.

Challenge your sales team to always be increasing the penetration at their current accounts. New business is critical, but don't overlook current clients.

Socks go with shoes; sell them. Ties go with shirts; add that to the sale. If you're selling barbeque grills, you should be adding all the cleaning tools and the big forks and everything. Don't let your customers go home without everything they need to fully enjoy your product.

If you sell a service like insurance, make sure your team is always looking for ways to add more coverage for your clients. My insurance provider started out with just my automobiles and now has my homeowners, some insurance on some rental property and a few other products.

Never stop looking for ways to increase the business you do with a current client.

A good, effective, planned follow up system can do that — and allow you, as the manager, to measure its effectiveness.

Training Your Team to Request Referrals

If the easiest sale you'll ever make is to your current customers, the second easiest is to a referral. The problem with referrals is salespeople don't ask for them! I've known salespeople who had no fear at all when it came to asking for the sale but couldn't bring themselves to ask for a referral.

If you're asking your customer for a referral, you're implying you trust his judgment and appreciate his business. Believe it or not, most of the time your customers want to help you. I have trained salespeople for years to keep the client involved in the process throughout.

I don't recommend asking for referrals on the first post-sale follow up. The current customer comes first — make sure he's well taken care of before you start trying to add more to your plate.

In order to have a consistent supply of referrals, you must have a referral tracking system. I suggest challenging your salespeople to generate a certain number of referrals every month. However, in order to succeed at this, they must track the referrals they get.

Create a referral log spreadsheet so each salesperson can log his referrals for the month. Keep up with not only how many each salesperson received, but note who gave the referral and the results of contacting the referral.

A referral comes from someone who already likes, knows and trusts you, and if you end up securing business from a customer's referral, let him celebrate the win with you! Customers want you to be successful, and every time one of their friends, relatives, or acquaintances purchases something from you, it reinforces the original customer's initial decision.

Devote an entire sales meeting to generating referrals. It's that important and like everything else, it takes practice and is a learned skill.

In order to keep that referral spigot flowing like a fire hydrant, you must have a plan. Use this three-point plan to train your salespeople to be referral magnets!

- **Be referable:** This may sound simple and even silly, but it goes back to not asking for a referral before you've actually done something worth being referred for. Just because someone bought from your company is not reason enough to ask for a referral.

  Let the customer experience your product, service, and the service level of the individual salesperson. That salesperson is the only thing the competition can't duplicate! Inspire your sales team to rise above the competition and ensure they provide exemplary customer service. If they do that, the referrals will come.

- **Give referrals:** The best way I know to plant the referral seed in a customer's mind is to refer someone to him.

  You cannot control whether the referral buys or not; that's not your job. You just need to get the two together in the first place!

  If you provide a referral, it is perfectly acceptable standard practice to contact the customer and let him know. Something along the lines of, "Hey Martin, I referred another client to you today. I told him you'd take good care of him."

  Yes, it's just that simple! Now, the client is thinking of referrals even if the person you referred never buys.

- **Ask properly:** There is a right way and a wrong way to ask for referrals. Train your people to use this sentence I learned years ago when asking for a referral: "Who do you know that I should be talking to?"

  I didn't ask "if" they knew someone, because that can lead to a negative response. I simply asked "who" they knew. You are much more likely to get a favorable response and a referral from the customer when asking in this manner. Train your people to use it every time.

Keep up with referrals. Log them, track them, and measure them. And when a referral becomes a customer, make sure your people thank the original customer.

Now you may be saying, "Butch, that all sounds great, but if I do all that stuff, when do I have time to manage?" Well, my friend, that *is* managing. When you have a sales force properly trained in the entire sales process, can present your product or service, ask for the sale, overcome objections, provide tremendous customer service, and continue to build their business with a strong referral base, you become a great sales manager — and your job is so much easier.

Knowing the Product

In order to be successful, your sales team needs to know what they're selling and how it benefits potential customers. Product knowledge is an essential element and another key piece in the puzzle of assembling your sales superstar.

You may have a representative who's the greatest salesperson who ever walked the face of the Earth — someone who can sell anything at any time. But, if he doesn't know how the product works, isn't familiar with the ins and outs, and can't convey how the features of it benefit their prospects, the greatest salesperson on the planet will sell nothing. Or, if he does, you'll have one of the worst customer experiences of your life because your salesperson made up a bunch of stuff to close the sale and there's no way your company can ever live up to those promises.

Spend as much time on product knowledge as you do on actual sales skills. In today's world your product, your competition's product, and the market all change at a rapid pace. You must always keep your team on the front line of product knowledge.

Knowing the necessary info

Training your team on your products and services is not a matter of handing them a stack of materials and telling them, "Read this stuff." (However, that's a very popular method and one you should hope your competition is employing.)

If you have an informed, enlightened customer, nothing turns him off quicker than a salesperson trying to fake knowledge about the product. The customer can smell an unknowledgeable salesperson coming a mile away.

Although your people should know many, many things, they *must* know at least these things:

- Actual product capabilities
- What the product won't do
- Terms of the manufacturer's warranty, guarantee, and any related information
- Key product codes and terms associated with them
- Your own internal policies on returns, credits, refunds, and so on
- Average time from order to delivery
- Where to go to find answers they don't know

The last point — where to go to get answers — is the most important. Depending on what you sell and how detailed and precise it is, there's no way for someone to know everything. In fact, I train people to tell the prospect, "I am not going to tell you I know everything, but I do know where to go to get the answer so you and I both know the truth!"

Never tolerate guessing from your salespeople. When they don't know the answer to a customer's question, insist that they get back to the customer with the truth rather than assuming something or making up an answer that sounds good. And, it's okay if a salesperson doesn't know the answer to a question the first time he's asked, but if he doesn't know it the next time a prospective customer asks about that specific feature, it's his own fault!

With even the cell phone in your pocket able to do probably 20 times more than you know it can do, you need to understand that your people aren't going to know everything — they must know a lot — but not everything. Let them know it's perfectly acceptable to ask for help. It certainly beats making something up and lying to a customer.

Using manufacturer's and vendor's support

Whatever your business, chances are you represent a manufacturer or supplier of the product or a vendor of the product or service. These people's job is to ensure your sales team has the most up-to-date product knowledge — because it's their product!

Invite your supplier or vendor to speak to your team annually to keep them fresh on the latest and greatest with the products and services you represent. Ask your vendor for a list of features and benefits for the product or service. They spend thousands of dollars on producing materials, and although these may not be slick printed brochures like in the good old days, they probably have just what you're looking for on their website. Clothing manufacturers still have trunk shows to provide retail salespeople with product knowledge. Take advantage of every benefit available.

Having dealt with many major manufacturers, I can assure you they love a sales manager who wants to know what's going on and who holds their sales team to a high standard when it comes to learning about the product or service. You receive almost preferential treatment from them if you show the slightest bit of interest in keeping your team at the forefront of the market.

Many manufacturers conduct their own schools or classes on their products. You can send new salespeople and others who want an update. It's worth almost any expense you could incur to ensure your team is well versed in what they're selling — without it, you've really got nothing. In retail, they will hold these concurrent with the annual market where new lines and items are unveiled.

These manufacturers are there to teach and train your people how to sell their product or latest versions or styles. Make sure you have the latest web portals, newsletters, email distribution, and so on when it comes to products and services. There are constant improvements and changes being made, and if your team is the first in the market with the information, it's just one more strike in your favor against your competitor.

Although your salespeople can't know everything about the product, the manufacturer's representatives can. Many times they're walking experts on what the product can do, can't do, will do, won't do, and so forth. It's their job to know it backward and forward. Use them. A lot.

Be aware of manufacturers who could also potentially sell to your customers directly — without you. You certainly don't want to be inviting them along on too many sales calls.

Selling benefits, not features

Selling 101 tells you to sell benefits, not features. This is certainly nothing new. As you (and your manufacturer or vendor partner) train your people on a product or a new feature of a current product, always teach them to sell the benefit.

Train your people to remember this phrase: "Customers don't buy what it does, they buy what it does for them." This can help them sort out features from benefits in their mind as they assemble their presentation.

Can it be confusing? Sure. But, make it as simple as possible for your people.

One of the keys to selling benefits over features is that the features are the logical part of the sale and the benefits are the emotional part of it. And emotion wins that game every time.

Most people don't care that your latest X1 is made of carbon steel and was tested by NASA under two billion pounds of pressure. They couldn't care less. Oh, it sounds good, and it makes for a great television commercial, but in the end, who cares? All customers care about the fact that the X1 is made of carbon steel is that it gives them twice the capacity at half the weight, allowing them to get more done with less effort. That's the difference between a feature and a benefit.

Check your marketing materials if you produce them in house. Are you bragging too much about the features and not enough about the benefits? It's an easy trap to fall into. Heck, the whole NASA story is cool. But, cool doesn't sell. Benefits sell.

When you get your people focused on selling benefits, ask them to watch for and bring in advertisements where even major brands are doing it wrong — you see it every day. Not many mothers care about what kind of brakes her car has, but she does care about getting her kids home safely.

Put yourself in your potential customer's place. What motivates him to buy your product or service? Is it to save money? Is it a matter of quality? Is it ego or even status? Whatever it is, find out and focus on the benefits.

Making the Most of Sales Technology

Unlike many of you, I'm old enough to remember being awed by a fax machine back in the early 1980s when their use became widespread in business. "Wait, you mean I can put this in here and a copy is going to come out somewhere else?" I was amazed. My, how times have changed. I saw an exchange recently in which someone said he didn't have a fax number because of where he was. When asked, "Where are you?" he replied, "The 21st century!"

Sales technology is on a seemingly unending upward path. Devices that were flashy just a few short years ago, like the Palm Pilot (yes, I had one . . . well, okay, I had the Palm 5 and the Palm 7), seem antiquated today. Believe it or not, back in the dark ages some of us had to wear this thing on our belt that would buzz if someone called it and then we'd have to stop at a payphone (you can look those up on the Internet) and call back the person looking for us. I think they were called pagers . . . something like that.

You've probably seen the chart showing that the basic smartphone today contains everything that was in a full-page newspaper ad for Radio Shack in the early 1990s. From phone to email to GPS to credit card reader and scanner — the power you carry in your pocket is amazing.

Yes, all these fancy gadgets are nice, but never allow yourself to be so high tech you lose high touch. Technology in general and sales technology in particular is supposed to make it easier for you to service your customer, but it's not designed to remove you entirely from the process. Many people can tell you what happens when you try to allow technology to take the place of good, old-fashioned customer service. You must constantly be looking to innovate, and technology is the biggest innovation you'll face as a manager, but never let it come between you and your customer.

Some online retailers can operate without salespeople, but they are the exception rather than the rule.

There's an app . . . for that?

Chapter 20 has a list of my favorite apps — ones I believe you should use or have something similar to.

No matter what brand of smartphone you use (and I assume you're not still on the flip phone — if so, you can skip this part), stay up on the latest apps; just make sure they're making you better and more effective.

I have deleted more apps than I use. I download them thinking they can save me time and/or effort, but they became either more work or a distraction. Just because it's in the app store doesn't mean you have to have it. Be very selective about what apps you allow your salespeople to have on their phones — especially if the phones are company owned and issued.

The advent of the smartphone has helped salespeople a lot, but it has hurt productivity as well. Social networks such as Facebook and any game apps should be completely off limits. They are giant time-wasters. Even if your people aren't posting on them during their work hours (and they probably can't resist), there's a good chance they check them.

The few exceptions I make as far as social media are LinkedIn and possibly Twitter as long as they're used for business purposes.

The bottom line is that, although it looks like one, the smartphone is not a toy for a professional salesperson. If you don't have a policy for how to handle social media postings by your people and what is and isn't acceptable, talk to your Human Resources department about devising one.

A single offensive Facebook post or Tweet by one of your salespeople can do massive damage to your company. It doesn't matter that the person doesn't speak or post on behalf of your company — if the person and the comment can be connected to your company, they will be. This is one area where it's better to be safe than sorry.

Making technology work for you, not against you

It's easy to fall into the trap of working for the technology instead of the technology working for you. Email was supposed to make life easier, but if you check it 12 times an hour, I can't really believe that's a positive step.

This book isn't about being more productive, but you should focus on sales technology that makes you more productive and more efficient. Always test a new piece of technology before investing thousands (if not more) in it and rolling it out to your sales team with the promise that it's the greatest thing they've ever seen only to have it crash and burn. If that sounds like I'm speaking from experience, I am. It's not fun. Trust me.

The most valuable piece of technology you have is more than likely your CRM (customer relationship management) system unless you're in a highly computerized field. Your CRM system is the heart of your organization and when you get all the data in there (I know that's easier said than done), it can do amazing things if you let it.

Any piece of software, app, or other computer-based system should always be able to interface with your CRM system or it's a no-go. If you have to end up doing double work because the two systems can't play together, you're a prime example of the technology working against you and not for you.

If you implement a new CRM system, get very detailed information on what it does and does not interface with and check with people who are already using that system. If they've been on it longer than a few days they can tell you the horror stories if it won't run with your current software. Technology should make you better, not bitter.

Nothing replaces a sales professional

We're living in a time when you hear the term *social selling* thrown around as much as *think outside the box* was ten years ago. In theory social selling is a great thing. In practice it can be fatal if not used correctly.

Social selling is designed to use social media to reach potential prospects and make it easier to have the initial introductions and conversations without going through cold calls and so forth. (I condone the use of LinkedIn and Twitter for this purpose, but Facebook isn't a sales tool as far as I'm concerned.)

Social selling will never replace the need for face-to-face (or a reasonable facsimile) sales conversations and having a professional salesperson answer a prospect's questions and objections. No matter what you've heard.

When used correctly, social selling is a tremendous help in getting information to and eventually getting in front of qualified prospects. It's a great way to build credibility and position yourself and your company as experts in your field. But don't think for a second that you can conduct all your business electronically without the need for a sales and customer service presence.

Features are logical, benefits are emotional, and it is virtually impossible to convey emotion electronically.

Use social media for what it is: a great tool. I know people who have built a lot of business by participating in groups on LinkedIn, getting to know buyers and striking up relationships within that forum alone. That's beautiful!

If you're in a LinkedIn (or similar) forum or group you should become the "go to" person for new ideas, new products and the latest announcements. If there is news in your industry, you should be the one posting it to those social media sites. Prospective customers should come to know you as a source of information and knowledge long before you ever ask for an opportunity to sit down and visit with them.

A critical part of social selling many people forget, ignore, or don't bother to learn is that you must give before you receive. Give information, give data, give updates on your industry. Here is where many people make the fatal mistake: they ask before they give. They join some groups on LinkedIn and then run through them like a bull in a china shop asking for connections and appointments without establishing their credibility, professionalism, or knowledge.

Social selling is not just a way to mass pitch people. If you use it in that manner, it will cost you business.

As the sales manager, you must almost police how your salespeople use this still-new area of business. Yes, you want them to use it. But you want them to use it correctly.

Part III
Training and Development

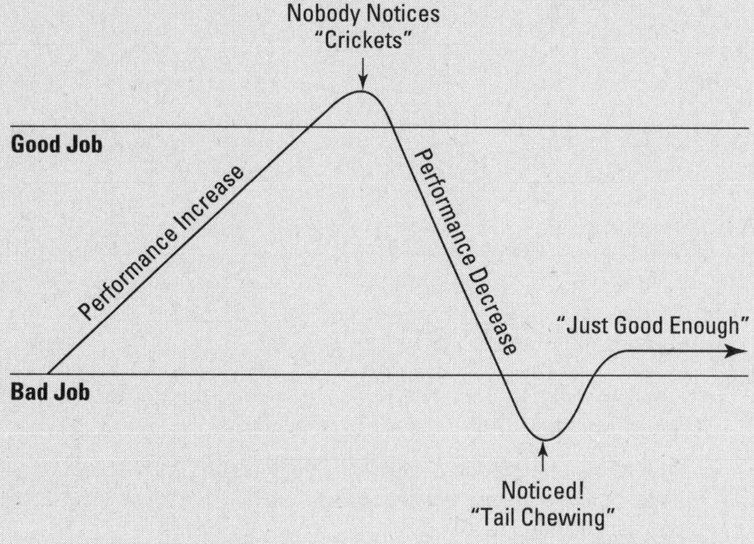

For more information about training, go to `www.dummies.com/extras/salesmanagement`.

In this part . . .

- See how to define your sales process and map out the strategy to take someone from prospect to customer.
- Realize the importance of clearly communicating your expectations for every member of your sales team and discover how to provide essential feedback.
- Understand the need for ongoing training, how to avoid burnout, and the value of an outside sales trainer.

Chapter 8

Defining Your Expectations

In This Chapter

- Writing down your expectations
- Setting up guardrails to keep your team on track
- Designing effective incentives

Your sales team is trained and ready to hit the streets. But wait: Have you told them what results you're looking for? Have you communicated with them what your expectations are for each territory or division?

In order for your team members to gauge whether they're succeeding, they need to know whether they're failing to meet, meeting, or exceeding expectations — and what, specifically, those expectations are.

In this chapter, I look at how to establish clear expectations and get everything down in writing so there are no misunderstandings about what milestones they need to be hitting to achieve the level of performance you demand — so you'll know, they'll know, and you'll know they know. And they'll know you know they know. (Okay, that's enough — this could go on all day!)

It's important in your role as a professional sales manager to lay out the ground rules, enforce them when needed, give proper guidance, and set an example.

As you read this chapter, keep in mind the best way to make your expectations clear is to lead by example. Yours is not a job in which you will succeed with the philosophy "Do as I say, not as I do." If that's your belief, as my grandmother used to say, "You've got another think coming!"

In addition to detailing your overall expectations, I also cover the importance of creating and maintaining the proper environment — one where action is happening and people expect to win.

I touch on the need to provide regular guidance — or set the guardrails, establishing and building good habits and being a leader your team can look up to.

Finally, I take a look at the world of commission programs and how to construct one that rewards the behavior you express in your expectations.

Wow. That's a lot of ground to cover in one chapter, so let's get going before we run out of room!

Defining Your Expectations in Writing

The best way to communicate your expectations — the expectations you're going to inspect — is to put them down in writing. That way there's no confusion. Everyone is on the same page and understands what's expected of her.

As you hire new salespeople, have a welcome letter for them that outlines your basic guidelines. Figure 8-1 is sample of what I've used in the past. By putting everything down in a welcome letter that you can simply copy and paste as you add new salespeople, you're always delivering a consistent message and keeping the playing field level.

In the event you inherit a sales force, you can write a similar letter as you take your new job — instead of welcoming your sales team, introduce yourself and outline the criteria by which you'll judge them and what you expect.

Communicating your expectations goes far beyond the day a new salesperson starts or your initial time in your new position. It's an ongoing communication process that should become a habit for you. Anytime something new is introduced, a new program is launched or, as I talk about in Chapter 12, you debut your annual budget or goals, put in writing what you expect of each member of your team and your team in general.

The more you communicate on the front end, the fewer problems you'll have on the back end. It's simply good business to let your sales team know what you want out of them — what you consider a good job.

Dear New Salesperson:

Congratulations! You got the job. Now the real work begins.

I'm thrilled to have you as part of our team — and it is a team. You'll be exposed to some of the most professional people you've ever been around and expected to conduct yourself in an appropriate manner at all times.

The company handbook gives you the dos and don'ts, but I like to be very upfront with new salespeople on what you should expect and what I expect.

As part of your onboarding process, you and I will sit down and establish your individual goals for your first 90 days and beyond. With that being said, I want you to know what I expect of you as a professional salesperson:

- **Be on time:** Our sales day starts at 7:30 a.m. You should either be in the office or at your first call at that time. In order to be as productive as possible, you must always make the best use of your time. If we have a sales meeting or other function scheduled, you will be expected to arrive on time, every time. If you need to plot out the route ahead of time to account for traffic, please do so before your first day.

- **Be professional:** Our customers are the reason we're in business. Your communication with them should always exemplify the highest level of professionalism. If you need help in creating letters or other communication, please ask for help.

- **Be persistent:** You only fail when you quit. Nobody on our team is a quitter. As long as you're working toward your goal, you have a chance to achieve it.

- **Be proactive:** It's far better to address an issue before it becomes a problem. If you know there's going to be a problem with an order for a customer or something that will otherwise affect her business with us, notify her and your immediate superior as soon as possible.

- **Be independent:** Use your brain as much as your brawn. I believe the phrase that has killed more business than any other is, "That's the way we've always done it." If you get that answer, please let me know. Never stop looking for ways to improve yourself, your service to your customers, and your company.

We will discuss other rules and regulations during your training and probationary period. Ask questions — even if you feel it's something you should already know. I would rather you ask today than still not know the answer six months from now.

Again, welcome aboard. I'm looking forward to working with you!

Sincerely,

Butch Bellah

Figure 8-1: A welcome letter.

You get what you inspect, not what you *expect*

As much as you'd like to give your team their marching orders and know they'd be carried out, that's just not reality. I learned a long time ago, "You get what you *inspect*, not what you expect!"

What does that mean? It means that unless you're keeping track of your employees and keeping an eye on their performance, you don't really know what you're getting.

No matter if you think your sales team is performing as you expect them to, you must inspect their work to be sure. Unless you take time to inspect, you're likely to be let down. Not necessarily because team members intentionally disregard your instructions but because of miscommunication, misunderstanding, or the development of poor habits.

Periodically either ride with or check behind each member of your department to see what she's actually doing. Understand these people are adults, and you have to trust them to a certain extent, but if they work outside the confines of your building, a lot of things can come between your expectations and their actual performance.

Keep in mind that you're not doing this to check up on them, you're doing it for their benefit! You're making sure they're using the best possible techniques and giving themselves the best chance for success. Never look at your inspection as trying to catch your team members doing something wrong. Rather, think of it as insuring they're doing something right. It will greatly change how both of you view the process.

Your inspection can include call reports, data entered into your CRM (customer relationship management) program, or any number of other checks and balances. But, the key is for you to actually take time to follow through on your end and check it. Just telling everyone to fill out a call report that you end up filing and never looking at is going to demotivate your team far more quickly than asking them to not do it at all. If you ask your salespeople to invest their time to produce any sort of data or report for you, the least you can do is look at it, absorb what you're viewing, and perhaps even comment on it.

Insisting on an environment of action

Successfully managing a group of sales professionals often is simply putting them in the best position for them to succeed and letting them do their thing. Although many bosses don't want to admit it, sometimes the best management technique is to get out of the way.

However, first you have to create an environment to make things happen for your sales team. You have to create an environment where action is expected and encouraged. And more than that, you have to let them know you expect them to be a part of this action-oriented culture.

All the good intentions in the world are worthless if you never take action. But, it's easy to get caught up in paralysis by analysis and fail to move at all, more concerned about making a misstep than taking any step. If you do anything for your salespeople to help them grow, stop this type of thinking. Encourage them to be movers, inspire them to take action and progress. If they aren't moving forward, they're falling behind.

One of the benefits of this type of environment is that when you have someone who isn't moving, she sticks out like a sore thumb. On the other hand, if you have a setting where nobody is really doing anything big, it's easy to blend in to the woodwork. Avoid this at all costs.

One of the things I always stressed to my salespeople is you can't take corrective action until you take action. If someone isn't making mistakes, I can almost guarantee you she isn't doing anything. Nobody's perfect, but it's up to you to let her know mistakes are okay. Inaction is not.

Some people want you to basically bless every move they make. If you had time to do that, you wouldn't need them, now would you? Give them the ability and responsibility to make decisions and take action.

So what do you do once you create an action-oriented environment and someone takes action that turns out to be wrong? Never criticize the act of making a decision — that's what you want your salespeople to do. Rather, sit down with the person who erred and talk through how the decision could've been made better or with more information.

Keep your people moving at all costs. When you have your entire team being action takers those few who don't buy in to this will be easily spotted — and very uncomfortable.

Working Monday and Friday

In addition to your standard expectations and creating a positive, action-oriented environment, one of the most important things you can do for your sales team is to let it be known early on that Monday and Friday are workdays. I'm continually amazed at the number of otherwise professional salespeople who have for some reason begun to work basically a three-day week. They drag in late on Monday and leave early on Friday.

The easiest way to get ahead of your competition is to work a full five-day week. It's really just that simple.

Try to start the week with some sort of interesting activity — maybe not a sales meeting, but some type of pep rally or motivational event. This can prevent a little bit of the "I dread Monday" feeling in your sales team. I've had sales managers who passed out bonus checks or SPIF (special performance incentive funds) on Mondays.

Too many times people complain about Monday, instead have them see it as the start of their moneymaking week. Something small like that can change the entire dynamic.

Monday is 20 percent of your sales week. I don't know about you, but I can't afford to let my entire team take 20 percent of their time and just throw it away. Think about that: 1/5th of your week, just gone — for nothing. It's not worth it to anyone. When you add in the half-day Friday syndrome, you're looking at 30 percent or more of your selling time being totally wasted. That undermines the whole action-oriented environment, too!

Let your competitors make Monday and Friday part of their weekend while you're out calling on their customers. The difference between an average salesperson and one who truly excels is how they use their time. I'm a firm believer that your selling hours are much too important to throw away week after week.

I've found Friday to be a great day to close sales. In fact, I've found it to be one of the best. Why? Well, for one thing, the majority of your competition has already switched onto autopilot and is literally coasting through the day. I've met some people who actually hoped they didn't get a call about a potential sale on Friday. What? Are you kidding me?

Conversely, some buyers tend to take Friday off as well. I understand that. But, that just means the ones working are ready to do business. They're professional and value their time and yours, too.

If you're a sports fan, you know that in football quarterbacks are judged many times on what they do in the fourth quarter. At the same time, baseball pays a lot of money to *closers* (interesting term, huh?) — pitchers who are brought in simply to pitch the final inning and close the game. Inspire your people to be the quarterback and the closer, Friday is your fourth quarter and ninth inning and the game is yours to win.

Setting Up the Guardrails: Providing Regular Guidance

When you think of managing a sales organization, it's a lot like setting up guardrails along an elevated road or bridge: from time-to-time your team is going to hit the rails, but it's much better than the alternative.

When it comes to your salespeople, you need to set up systems that check for poor habits or tendencies to drift off the path a bit. It's much easier to make corrections, get back to the proper way of doing things, or otherwise take corrective action while the issue is still manageable.

If you start setting up guardrails, you can alleviate some of the big problems before they become big problems. Having small checks and balances in place can help you bring your team back on point before they are too far gone.

A complete hands-off approach to managing a sales team can be devastating. By the time you find out about an issue, it's far too late to correct it. By using the guardrail approach and providing regular checkups and guidance, your ability to correct unproductive behavior is greatly enhanced.

Just like when you're driving, beware of over-correcting. If you have a salesperson tap a guardrail, don't jerk her back so far in the other direction that you do more harm than good.

I realize this is a very visual example of how to manage your team, but if you really get those guardrails set in your mind's eye, you'll be far better off in the long run. It's much better to solve a problem when it's rubbing the guardrail than when it's completely in the ditch or over the side of the cliff. There's no coming back from there.

As you outline the criteria for your team, think of where the guardrails are — they're the small indicators that something could be wrong and tell you that you need to take action now before it goes horribly wrong.

Guardrails can be reports, frequent one-on-one meetings, or even simply observing your people at work. The idea is to build a system that notifies you of issues before they blow up in your face and become major areas of concern.

Managing like a GPS system

I want you to close your eyes for a moment and envision a GPS system and see yourself putting in coordinates for a destination. No really, close them. Come on, I can see you peeking. I'll wait if I have to.

Okay, now, what did you see? What happens immediately after you put in your destination? What does the GPS system do first? It finds your current location! In order to get where you want to go, you have to know where you're starting from — just like a GPS system. There's no way to determine a route if you don't know the starting location.

As a new sales manager, your job is very similar to that of a GPS system. Anyone can tell you where they want to go, but few stop to think about where they are. Before you can take one positive move, you need to know where you're starting.

When it comes to dealing with individual salespeople, you have to know where each of them is along their career arc before you can even begin to help them get to where they want to go.

Once again using the GPS analogy: After it determines your starting point, the next thing it does is give you one simple task to perform, maybe "turn right on Elm Street." It doesn't outline the entire journey and warn you that you're going to make a U-turn 20 miles from here. All it does is move you along to the next step.

As a sales manager, think of yourself as the GPS system for the department. You have to know the entire journey in your head, but you can only make one turn at a time. You can only do what's in front of you, and no amount of worrying about future issues is going to help.

Just like the GPS system in your phone or your car, you cannot get started until you know the final destination, but you also cannot make the entire trip in one turn either. Continually focus on moving forward by asking yourself:

- Where do I want to go?
- Where am I now?
- How am I going to get from here to there?
- What's the next logical step to take?

If you use this method and train your team — especially your division managers or leaders — to think this way, you'll be miles ahead of the competition with little wasted motion.

Establishing good habits early

Since I was a little bitty salesperson, I've always been told, "It takes 21 days to establish a habit." Have you ever heard that? Recently I read somewhere it's now believed it takes 62 to 64 days to establish a habit.

Let me go on record here as saying: putting a timeframe on forming a habit is baloney. And I can prove it.

I quit smoking January 1, 2009. If I were to have a cigarette right now, I'd have a carton before you finished reading this page, then I'd have to sit down somewhere and let the nicotine high go away. I can assure you it would not take me 64 days, 21 days, or even a day to establish that habit — or at least to fall straight back into it.

Here's what I believe to be true: It takes 21 to 64 days to establish a *good* habit! But, the problem is you (and I and everyone we know) have bad habits that creep up on you daily. Before you know it, you're totally bogged down with them and not performing your best because you've gotten out of the good habits that made you successful.

Your job as a manager is to instill good habits in your people early and often. Cold calling is a habit. Asking for referrals is a habit. Investing time in personal development products or reading is a habit. Make those part of what you teach your team.

The more good habits a salesperson has, the less chance she has to let bad habits sneak up on her.

Think of a salesperson as a professional athlete. Even at the top of their game, the pros have coaches.

These coaches are just another set of eyes to watch for their mechanics and to see things from a different perspective. If a successful golfer develops a hitch in her golf swing, she may not notice it unless she sees it on video or a coach points it out to her.

Being a coach for your sales team is what your job is all about. You need to see the little bad habits or the hitches in your salespeople's mechanics and point them out early before their swing is completely gone.

When you begin to stack these management strategies on top of each other, you yourself become much better and leave less room for poor habits to invade your space.

Leading by example

"Do as I say, not as I do." That's no way to endear yourself to your team, earn their respect, or instill confidence in them. It's very poor management practice, but it happens in businesses every day.

Don't let yourself be part of that circus. Yes, you're the boss. But that doesn't give you free rein to live by your own rules.

Never put your people in a position to do something you wouldn't do or haven't done yourself. That's one of the quickest ways in the world to lose them. Never put your salespeople in a position of having to defend your actions or inaction. That's a cliff face you can seldom return from.

Whether you believe it, your salespeople are watching your every move. And, I do mean every move. You are their leader, and they want to make sure they've hitched their wagon to someone they can trust. Don't betray that trust by performing in a manner you wouldn't accept from them.

If you ask your team to be at work at 7:00 a.m., don't drag in every morning at 9:00. If you place focus on actually working a full five days a week, don't be conspicuously absent or hard to find every Friday after lunch. It's not worth it.

If you show your sales team you don't see yourself as any better than they, they will treat you as if you are. But, if you act like you're superior, they'll bring you down in a heartbeat. I've seen it happen more than once.

Lead by example. Be the first to arrive and the last to leave. Just because you're the sales manager doesn't mean you're immune to actually working. If you look at yourself in that light, you won't have to ask people to follow you — they'll do so willingly.

True leaders don't have to tell people they're the leader or the manager, their actions speak for themselves. Their personality and mannerisms speak volumes. Think of great sales managers or leaders you've known in the past. Did they have to walk around with a sign on or tell everyone they were in charge? No, they gravitated to a position of power by their actions, and those actions were the example others wanted to follow — not the example they had to follow.

Developing an Incentive Program that Works

If you inherit an existing sales team, you also inherit their compensation plan. Even though there are only three ways to pay salespeople, there are many different ways to twist and turn how you reach the end result. Your choices are:

- **Salary:** Salespeople are compensated with no regard to the sales they make or the profits they generate. They receive a predetermined base salary or hourly wage. They earn the same amount every pay period no matter what they sell.

- **Commission:** Under this plan, salespeople are paid exclusively based upon their sales or the gross profit they generate. In other words, no sales, no money.
- **Salary plus commission:** This hybrid usually pays each salesperson a base salary plus a commission based on their sales or profits.

You could make an argument for any of the above in one situation or another, but I believe it boils down to what drives salespeople in the first place: desire.

If a salesperson truly has that burning desire inside she doesn't want to be on salary because she doesn't want a ceiling on what she can earn. At the same time, being strictly commissioned can expose someone to financial issues if she falls ill or can't work for a week or two for any number of reasons.

By and large, the most successful (and wealthiest) salespeople in the world work strictly on commission — they eat what they kill. And if they don't kill, they don't eat.

A salesperson who goes to work every day worried about how she's going to pay the mortgage or buy groceries will reek of desperation. You'll know it, their coworkers will know it, and most importantly, their prospective customers will know it. It's not a good look, I promise.

Your job is to not only create a compensation and/or incentive program; but to create one that works for both you and the salesperson. What's good for you must be good for your sales team and vice versa.

The most popular compensation route is generally the salary plus commission option. If you choose this route, be prepared to set the base salary just below what someone needs in order to get by. If you set the base too high, you might as well put people on salary only because they'll have little motivation to produce. At the same time, if you set the base too low, you run the risk of the desperation I mentioned just previously.

You have to find that sweet spot where your sales team can survive but are still driven to sell, produce results, and grow.

You walk a very fine line when it comes to commissions. The salesperson must be able to change her income by increasing her sales and/or gross profit. You don't want to set the commission percentage so low that even if your salespeople move mountains it has little, if any, effect on their finances.

After you settle on a commission rate, you must decide what you're going to base the commission on. Is it on sales? Gross profit? Net profit? A good rule is to base it on what the salesperson can control.

Never hold your salespeople accountable — especially monetarily — for something they can't control. If they have no control of their gross profit, then base commission on sales. However, if they can impact your profitability, then by all means tie the commission program to that number. Give them incentive to drive your profits. Sales are great, but remember profits are what makes the world go 'round (and what will help you keep your job).

If you have to make adjustments based on territory, area, or other outside factors, make that adjustment in the base salary so everyone's commission is based on the same performance.

For example, if Jane's territory is one where everyone knows margins are significantly lower than elsewhere, perhaps you elevate her base salary a bit. In the end, you want to level the playing field, but to do that you sometimes have to prop up certain parts of it.

The hardest part of this entire process is coming up with a plan that's fair to all of your salespeople regardless of the size of their territory or the geography they work.

Changing your compensation program without causing panic

If you find yourself needing to change the compensation program, be prepared for pushback and well, sheer terror. Any time you look to change the way people are paid, their first instinct is to totally freak out and assume you're cutting their paycheck in half.

Assuming that's not the case, there are a few things you can do to lessen the blow and give yourself (and your salespeople) the best chance to make the transition successful:

- **Notify those affected well in advance.** The last thing you want to do is spring a new plan on someone with little or no notice.
- **Communicate as transparently as possible.** Your people are going to be suspicious anyway. Don't contribute to that by hiding things or being secretive.
- **Test, test, and retest before launching the new plan.** Then test it again. Nothing — and I mean nothing — undermines your authority or makes you look worse in the eyes of your people than rolling out a new commission plan only to have to roll it back up and rework it because you failed to take certain things into account. Check everything twice. Run it through every possible scenario.

- **Ramp up side-by-side.** After you're satisfied with the new process and formulas, show them to your team for a few months as you lead into the new program. In other words, if you're changing to the new plan in April, show both the new and old systems in January, February, and March to let your team see what they're currently earning and what they would've earned under the new program.
- **Listen.** During your testing and ramp up period, open your door to concerns from your team. Now is the time to address them, not after you've put everything on the table.

Nothing is more sacred to someone than her compensation. You can mess with a lot of things, but you'll never experience anything like the wrath of people who have their paycheck hijacked. No matter whether you're building an entirely new program or updating or converting an existing one, prepare your team as best you can. You probably will experience more push back when converting from an existing program. You have a group of people who are already comfortable with what they know — and good, bad, or ugly they're familiar with it.

People almost always prefer the comfort of the known than the uncertainty of the unknown. Even if the new program will benefit them, they'll be hesitant to change. Take your time and don't press.

Keeping your eye on the correct target

Focus on the correct target and you'll hit it more often than not.

Even though the most obvious number is sales dollars, don't let that close your judgment. Just because it's the easiest to see doesn't mean it's the best thing for you to focus on.

It's not how much you sell; it's how much you make. Anybody can be a *give-away artist,* someone who always has to cut prices and gives away everything at the first sign of an objection — sometimes before the objection has even been raised.

It takes no talent, skill, or ability to give away product and services. If you're going to simply sell on price, then you can hire someone for minimum wage to go out and undercut the competition.

If you keep your eye on the gross profit target, you will build a team that values the same thing you do. Again, it's not how many sales dollars you can create, it's the number of gross profit dollars you can generate.

Every other department in the company focuses strictly on sales for a couple of reasons:

- It's the only way they know how to keep score. Remember, they don't dig into the gross profit like you do, so if you have to fire an unprofitable account or make similar moves, take the time to explain your reasoning.
- Their budget is usually based on sales dollars. Each expense in their department is a percentage of sales, so that's what's important to them.

Understanding the motives and the way other departments process information can help your interdepartmental relationships a bit.

Rewarding positive results

By creating a compensation and incentive plan that works for both parties (the salesperson and the company), you reward the behavior you're seeking. It's difficult to lead a team in one direction when their motivation is taking them in another.

Most salespeople think they can sell to everybody or that at least they should be able to. Be careful not to create programs that confuse motion with progress. Just because someone is making a lot of calls, generating a lot of prospects, and making a lot of presentations doesn't mean she's making you money. That only happens when she sells something.

A busy salesperson doesn't equal a successful one. Clearly define your exception and reward only results. Don't reward wishes, hopes, and dreams.

The job's not finished until the paperwork's done, and the sale isn't complete until the product is delivered and paid for. Then and only then do you have a sale.

Being consistent

Don't change the rules in the middle of the game. Try at all costs to not change your commission or incentive program out of the blue. It's a difficult move and one that requires a lot of finesse to pull off without a complete mutiny.

I have never understood a sales manager cutting commissions because someone is making too much money. How crazy does that sound? Basically what the salesperson is being told is, "We can't afford for you to make us that much money." Really?

If the incentive program is properly set up and rewarding the correct results, there should never, ever, ever be a cap on it. You should hope someone makes a million dollars a year — that just means the company is making more than ten times that.

The last thing you want to do is choke that motivation and even demotivate your people from either picking up new business or growing their current business.

When creating your compensation plan, run it through all the crazy numbers you can. If someone increased her sales ten times are you okay with that? It's better to cover those things now than to change the program later.

Chapter 9

Ongoing Training and Helping Your Salespeople Grow

In This Chapter

- Understanding the need for continued training
- Looking at ways to provide development and training
- Organizing annual training and development events
- Availing external training opportunities and speakers
- Knowing when enough is enough: avoiding burnout

Nobody, no matter how good he is, is as good as he can be. There's always room for improvement for everyone. The most successful people in any field are constantly studying and growing, improving their skills or learning new ones.

One of the challenges sales mangers face is keeping that fire burning in their sales team. They can only listen to you so many times before it starts to go in one ear and out the other. By changing your message, you can keep their attention a bit longer, but perhaps the best way to keep your sales team engaged is to change the messenger — to bring in outside voices.

In this chapter I show you how to navigate the challenges of a sales team starting to get complacent, the value of providing annual refresher courses, and the power of an outside trainer to validate and expand on your message.

Recognizing the Value of Ongoing Training

One of the most consistent messages I've delivered throughout my career is, "If you're as good as you're going to be, life's as good as it's going to get." Think about that: If you've completely reached your full potential, your life has maxed out. You've accomplished everything you can, and the game is essentially over. There's nothing to do now but ride it out, do the same thing every day — no surprises, no challenges, no learning experiences. Does that sound like fun? Not to me, it doesn't.

Whether you sell a tangible product or intangible service, I can guarantee you that someone, somewhere, right now is trying to make it better, cheaper, faster, or to improve the process. You always have to drive this home to your sales team. Never let them get complacent. Complacency is a killer to your team's careers and potentially to your company.

Never let your team feel like they know everything or, worst of all, that they can't learn anything new or improve themselves. Keep them curious and keep them interested. Successful salespeople stay engaged and involved.

There is absolutely no evidence to show that success in any field is reserved for those who are the smartest, have the highest IQ, or score the best on their college prep tests. There is evidence, however, to suggest some of the most successful people in the world had a thirst for knowledge and invested their time (and sometimes money) in reading, attending seminars, listening to audio material, and so forth.

Successful people understand that your body may do the physical work and your brain handles the mental load, but your attitude and imagination can take you anywhere and allow you to accomplish anything you want.

You must always strive to improve your team and their skills — just to keep up with the competition, much less lead your industry. If you can have one goal, make it constant, consistent improvement.

Keeping the Fire Burning: Providing Ongoing Training and Development

The juggling act of a professional sales manager is a bit strange at times. While you're working to keep part of your team from burning out and over-committing themselves, an entirely different group needs you to constantly be prodding them along and keeping that fire stoked. One group can't put the fire out while you're doing everything you can to get it lit in the other. Strange, I know.

In order to keep that fire burning for your salespeople, you must set an example of being fired up. You don't have to be one of these over-the-top, jumping-up-and-down screamers. But, you do have to oversee a department and an environment where people want to succeed and where success is noticed, celebrated, and rewarded.

There's a fine line between too much and not enough when it comes to motivating salespeople. One of the best ways to keep than fire burning deep down inside is continuing education. Salespeople love to work toward a goal and keep score — it's what makes them good at what they do, so having professional development opportunities for them is very important.

Ongoing training and development takes on more forms than just learning new closes or updating yourself on the latest product information. One of the most difficult challenges professional sales managers face is maintaining a consistent effort from those prone to needing a little extra motivation.

Personally, I don't believe one person can motivate another. In my mind, motivation has to come from within — it has to be an internal combustion for that particular salesperson. However, what you can do is inspire — and where you want to focus your time and energy is on inspiration. I can inspire you, but you must motivate yourself.

The differences between motivation and inspiration are pretty clear:

- **Motivation:** The dictionary defines motivation as "the reason or reasons one has for acting or behaving in a certain way." It comes from the root word *motive,* and if you think about it, your sales team has to have a motive to act. They have to have a reason to do what they do. That can be as basic as the human need for food and shelter or as advanced as the desire for accolades and rewards. But, it's an internal process.
- **Inspiration:** Conversely, inspiration is defined as "the process of being mentally stimulated to do or feel something." That's external. People can be inspired by a variety of outside influences, from music when they workout to listening to inspirational speakers or watching an inspirational story or program.

As a manager, you must understand that not everyone is motivated by the same thing. Some people are motivated by money; they want to make a million dollars and that's all they can think about. But, there are others who are motivated simply by the desire to be the best and the monetary compensation is a side benefit.

To be a successful sales manager, you must understand what motivates and drives each of your salespeople. In other words, what are their motives? What are they in this for and what gets them out of bed every morning? What are their personal goals?

When you have that information then you can inspire your team to achieve their goals — but only after you know what those goals are and remember every person is different. What motivates one isn't what motivates another.

Just throwing out bonus money won't drive everyone to achievement because not everyone's motive is to obtain more money. A good sales manager finds ways to motivate his team through other areas — including them in internal training or in social activities outside the office, for example.

Modeling ways to feed your mind

As a manager, you really set the tone for how your department responds to certain things, and one of those is learning. Set the pace by continuing to improve your skills and trying to learn something new.

Challenge your representatives to find ways to feed their minds and participate in continuing educational activities by

- **Reading good books:** Your top performers are generally people who like to read and keep up with the latest in sales and your particular industry. If you find a good book, share it with your salespeople. Encourage them to be readers and to seek information.
- **Listening to podcasts or audiobooks:** If your sales team works out of their automobiles, this is a tremendous way to spend their time between calls. And, it beats listening to some negative talk radio designed to do nothing but rile them up — no matter what their political affiliations.
- **Attending seminars and webinars:** Any time you have an opportunity to send your salespeople to a good live event, take it! Nothing compares to knowledge gained in a live, interactive setting. There are also regular webinars on sales, motivation, inspiration, and more available all the time. With a little research, you can find plenty directly geared to your industry as well.
- **Participating in industry events:** If your industry or niche has a trade show, convention, or other function, get your team involved. These events usually have good speakers and/or workshops focused on your business.

If you make it a habit and set an example of looking for opportunities to improve your skills, your team will follow your lead. However, you may have to take the lead at time and create those learning opportunities — which I talk about later in this chapter.

You actually *can* teach an old dog new tricks

Contrary to the old saying, you can teach an old dog new tricks. The greatest manager I ever knew (and my mentor to this day) made a comment to me more than 20 years ago that I still remember. He said, "For my 40th birthday I want to see if I can learn something new. I'm going to learn to juggle." Juggle? What does that have to do with sales? Absolutely nothing. But, this man taught me to keep learning and never be satisfied with the way things are. He instilled in me a desire to try two things: set big, bold goals and never let myself get complacent as a person or as a manager. He taught me to never accept "good enough" and to always at least attempt new things. He would share and sometimes purchase books for other managers back before e-books were invented. He created an environment for learning and a desire to learn, improve, and innovate.

Oh, in case you're wondering: He did learn to juggle. In fact, he's quite good at it. And for his 60th birthday? He taught himself to juggle while riding a unicycle. I'm dead serious.

Accentuating the positive

Make it a practice to catch someone doing something right. I'm a firm believer that you see what you look for and if you go looking for bad performance you'll find something to criticize. However, if you go looking for the good — catching someone doing something right — then you'll find that, too. When you do, recognize it. Don't make your salespeople have to go out of their way for you to notice good performance.

You can inspire your department simply by being responsive to results, wins, and other positive actions.

As shown in Figure 9-1, most people don't know what warrants a good job — but they certainly hear about it when they do a poor job!

I believe people in general want to do a good job. It's human nature to want to do well rather than do poorly. The problem comes from management. Yes, you read that correctly: management.

If you have an employee who does a good job, and you don't recognize it, then he isn't really sure where that line is. On the other hand, if he does a bad job and gets the old tail chewing, he is well aware of where that line is drawn.

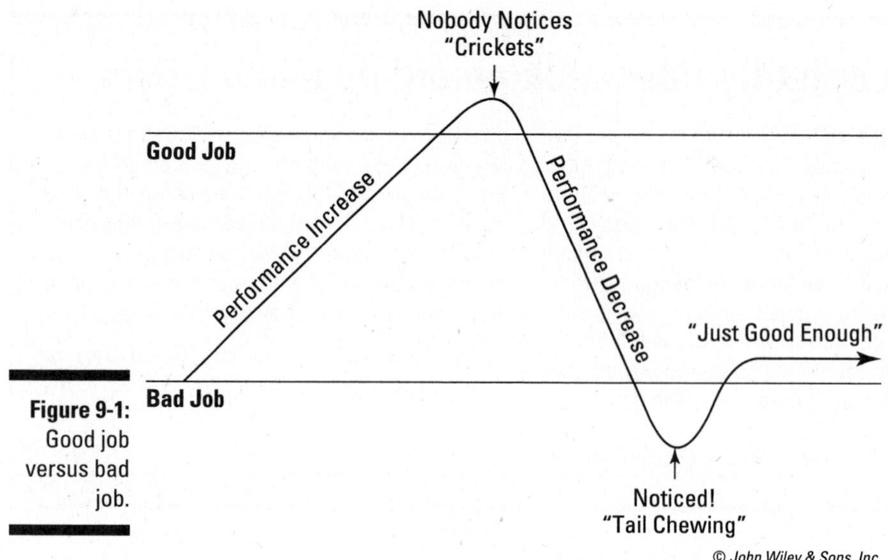

Figure 9-1: Good job versus bad job.

So, what does he do? He performs just well enough to stay above the tail-chewing line. It's not that he doesn't want to succeed; it's just that he doesn't know what that looks like.

What classifies as a good job may be different for different people. It all goes back to those goals. What one person takes for granted another has to work extremely hard for. If you have a salesperson who sells 10 units every week and he has a 15-unit week, then that performance deserves recognition just as much as the salesperson who sells 20 units every week and gets to 30 one week.

This is where being a good manager comes in. You're also a coach, counselor, and cheerleader. If it's time to cheer, then cheer loudly. In my career, I've found very few things that inspire people more than simply recognizing them for their efforts. Sometimes, "thank you" and "great job" are good enough.

Yes, it's a juggling act. You have many different styles and personalities to manage, but the one thing everyone likes is to know he's appreciated.

Scheduling regular refresher courses

Keep your team moving forward with regular refresher courses. When you lay out your annual sales meeting calendar (which I discuss in Chapter 10), don't forget to add in a few mini training days.

These refresher days are less structured, more free flowing and a bit looser than your sales meetings or other get-togethers. Put a couple of half-days on the calendar when everyone can schedule an afternoon or morning to get together and brainstorm, mastermind, and brush up on their skills.

To get the most out of your ongoing training efforts, hold these mini training sessions twice a year. This is just enough to separate them from your regular sales meetings and allow you make them a bit special.

Refresher days are important to keep everyone's attitude, enthusiasm, and processes from becoming stale. It's that semi-annual opportunity to shake things up and start anew.

The refresher may focus on product knowledge or sales skills — or you can simply open the floor and let your salespeople decide how and where the meeting goes. Too often creativity is stifled just because people are busy keeping on keeping on. Throw the rulebook out the window and invite your team to just let the ideas flow.

Any time you have a brainstorming or mastermind session, assign someone to take very, very good notes. Some of the greatest ideas, opportunities, and innovations come when you simply let your mind go unharnessed. Encourage your people to create.

Spring Training: Planning an Annual Professional Development Event

For sports fans it's an annual ritual: the weather warms, the time changes, and baseball teams report to their spring training camps in Florida and Arizona. For those who follow American football, the same thing happens in early fall when squads hit the gridiron for training camp.

For professional salespeople, spring training has a slightly different meaning — it's that annual chance to get back to the basics, uncover any bad habits you've developed, and work on improving your skills and techniques. Your spring training should be an event in and of itself — an important day that your entire company is aware of. Make it more than a meeting; make it an event.

Location, location, location: Get away from the office

Make your spring training event special and different. Your sales team should know it's not just another meeting. Find a place away from your office to host the event and get everyone away from their normal routine. If the idea is to refresh, renew, and foster creativity, the best place to do that is outside of everyone's comfort zone — somewhere they can't or don't get to go to every day.

You don't have to spend thousands of dollars and pack everything up and take everyone to Hawaii or on a cruise for a week, you just need to get away from the same four walls your team sees when you have your sales meetings and other functions. If nothing else, rent a hotel meeting room nearby — just to break up the monotony. I've had these meetings in hotel ballrooms, resorts, campgrounds, and clubhouses at a golf course — just to mention a few.

Keep the day interesting and fun by including some recreational activities with your team along with the training sessions and work.

This meeting is about getting back to the basics, and in a sense, starting over. A change of environment gives even your most senior representatives a feeling of renewal.

Don't forget to tie everything into your theme, which I talk about in the next section. Let your team know there has been some thought put into the event and it's their day.

You can make the most of your spring training by including some inspiration, new product knowledge, and all the other things discussed in this chapter in one meeting, one agenda in one afternoon.

Don't think this has to be a weeklong extravaganza. Use your salespeople's time wisely and keep the pace moving and this will soon be one day your team looks forward to every year.

You can create a committee to help with the planning and execution of this event, and if you're including other departments, invite them to be a part of the planning, too. Make it fun and informative.

This meeting should be much less formal and structured than your regular sales meetings and should include a lot of one thing: FUN!

Planning your event to ensure maximum benefit to your team

Spring training events aren't thrown together off the cuff. They are well-planned and scheduled so as to make the best use of everyone's time and to get the most out of the training. If you could see the behind-the-scenes action of sports camps, you'd see an orchestrated set of events designed for one thing: to get players into shape and work on the basics of the game.

A spring training event is the perfect activity to hold during your slow time of the year. You can take your people out of the field for a day, get everyone together, and not have it reverberate negatively through the organization.

Just like a baseball manager or a football coach is concerned about his team, you're concerned about yours. And, the management and coaching strategies used by professionals don't have to be all that different across industries:

- **Create a theme.** Create a theme for your training event and tie all your materials to it. Whether you use a current movie, a song, something in pop culture, or whatever — create a theme and then build your training around it. This helps in promoting it to your team and making it a bit more memorable.
- **Plan it out.** This is a once-a-year event so it needs to be planned carefully. Don't wait until the last minute and try to throw together something just to keep your people busy. Put a folder together (manually or digitally) and start saving ideas now for next year's event. Think what you can do to make it impactful.
- **Make it interactive.** The last thing salespeople need is to sit and listen to someone drone on and on all day long. If that's the format you set up, your average salesperson is going to lose interest very quickly. Instead, make spring training interactive and participatory. Let your teams work on projects, ideas, and role-play together. They will learn as much or more from each other than they will having someone stand in front of the room and read to them.
- **Break out of the norm.** Your spring training doesn't need to be just another sales meeting. If anything, it needs to be the exact opposite. Little things like allowing your salespeople to dress casually sets this day apart and sets the tone for an environment of fun and learning.
- **Include other departments.** This is the perfect opportunity for the people in accounting or production or purchasing to spend time with your sales team, especially if their jobs keep them from ever seeing each other in person. Let the other departments have a place on your agenda and talk about what's new in their departments. Be inclusive and invite others to participate.

- **Make attendance by every salesperson mandatory.** Plan it far enough in advance so as not to conflict with vacations or other off days. In fact, one thing to consider is to wrap up this year's event by announcing the date of next year's.

Even superstars take batting practice: Getting back to basics

You put your spring training day on the calendar and the whole gang's going to be in attendance. How do you make the best use of their time? Very simple: Go back to the basics.

Using the sports analogy again, it doesn't matter if you're a rookie or a 15-year veteran, when it comes to training camp or spring training, you start by working on the basics. The greatest athletes in the world do something salespeople should do much more of: practice. Yes, practice.

Even superstars take batting practice. In fact, that's probably the way they got to be superstars in the first place: practice, practice, practice.

Your spring training is the perfect time to hit the reset button, slow everyone down, and get back to the nuts and bolts of the sales process I talk about in Chapter 7.

The key to a successful training event is having everyone on equal footing. Your A-level salespeople are right alongside the new salespeople and the grizzled veterans who find themselves in the C-level group. (I talk about these groups in Chapter 4.) Don't let your team divide into their normal cliques. Separate them so that everyone spends time around people they may not see every day. This alone creates a tremendous learning opportunity. Did your grade school teacher make you sit boy, girl, boy, girl to keep students from breaking off into their own little chat groups? Yep, same situation here.

You may well encounter some who tell you (verbally or nonverbally) that they think working on the fundamentals of the sales process is either beneath them or not something they really need help on. The fact remains that they do need to review fundamentals — everyone does.

Spend some time working on negotiating. Role-play, let everyone learn, and have fun doing it. This is a great time to focus on closing skills, asking good qualifying questions, and other basics of the sales process.

Members of your sales team may be afraid to tell you they don't know something because they think they should already know it. Whether that's true or not, role-playing is the perfect scenario for them to learn without having to ask.

Your life is made up of habits — good and bad. And while you focus on the repetition of building good habits, problems arise because bad habits don't require any real work. They just kind of sneak up on you, and before long you're not doing things the way you had originally learned them.

Athletes refer to it as their mechanics — the basic motions they go through on every play. Periodically, their mechanics get out of whack (that's a technical term), and they don't even know it. They pick up a bad habit or two along the way and depend on someone else to watch what they're doing in order to correct it and get them back on the right path.

Your spring training day gives everyone an opportunity to take a deep breath and work on those fundamentals together. And, one of the most rewarding things is when you see your team learning from each other. You can then take a bit of pride in knowing you're creating and building an environment where everyone can improve.

Performing annual product reviews

Just as you go back to the basics of the sales process each year, do the same with your products and services, too. Don't assume everyone on your team is out selling the latest and greatest you have to offer. Invariably you discover someone out touting the benefits of version 2.0 six months after you introduced version 4.0. It happens — especially in larger organizations where the communication chain is not tight.

Your annual meeting is a good time to go through a little checklist with each representative:

- Are their samples fresh and presentable?
- Are their sales materials clean and professional?
- Do their customer-related forms (credit applications and so on) look professional?
- Can they list all the features and benefits of new products?
- What new items or products would they like to see added?

Depending on your business you're very likely to represent products or services from a manufacturer or vendor(s). This is the perfect time to bring in representatives from those companies to talk to your team. Let them unveil their latest information to ensure that your salespeople are armed with the data and knowledge they need. Communicate with your vendors well in advance as many manufacturers have money to spend on these sorts of promotional/educational meetings, and if it's not used — it's lost. Use it.

Break up the department into groups who don't normally associate. If you have different divisions present, mix them all up. Your sales representative in Division 1 usually learns from their manager and takes on that manager's style, verbiage, and habits. Let them see another version. The manager in Division 2 may use a few words differently or any number of things from which they can benefit. Again, the key is to create an atmosphere of openness, sharing and learning.

Looking at the latest in technology and social media

A key piece of your annual meeting or spring training session is exploring the latest technology releases and social media platforms. I put the list of ten apps I love in Chapter 20, but what smartphone or web-based apps are your people using? Which ones should they be using?

If your team employs any sort of device in the field, your spring training day is the perfect time to make sure everyone is running the latest version of the software.

If you've had it for any length of time, your CRM (customer relations management) system has probably gone through a few updates and revisions. Your annual get-together is a great time to refresh and reinforce the need for the system and how to get the most out of it. Take the time to explain the entire system to them, teach them what it does, what it means, and the value it brings to your company.

If you simply require them to plug in data, the system is going to fail. Why? Because your salespeople aren't going to put in the effort and data it takes for the CRM system you invested all those dollars in to be successful. Your salespeople shouldn't think of keeping the CRM system updated as unnecessary work. If you make it easy for them, and they can see how it benefits them, then you get a good idea of what's working and what's not.

Social selling has become more and more prominent over the past several years, and salespeople are spending more and more time using it as a lead source and as an introductory mechanism. If you're old school and don't believe in using that "fancy Internet thingy," you're living in the dark ages. You aren't going to be able to effectively help your team until you become familiar with all the tools they use.

If you don't have a social media policy in your company handbook, get with your human resources department and create one immediately. In today's world it's simply good business to outline what your company expects and won't tolerate when it comes to using these public platforms.

The problem comes in because, as a manager, it's a bit difficult now to see who's working and who's playing on the Internet. Looking at someone typing away on his smartphone, you can't tell if he's communicating with a lead he found and is nurturing through LinkedIn or setting the lineup for his fantasy football team.

The best thing you can do is help your team create a good social media program and show them how to make it work for them, not against them.

I don't think social selling will ever replace what I call b2b sales — belly-to-belly sales. (B2b also refers to business-to-business sales, but in my book, it's my definition that counts.) The Internet, social media, and social networking are tremendous tools for finding and nurturing leads, but for the most part sales always come down to a professional salesperson. Sure, sites such as `www.amazon.com` can deliver content or product without the interaction of a salesperson, but many products and services require an expert salesperson to handle the process.

Thinking they don't need the Internet, social media, and so forth has proven very costly for many companies. Use electronic technology to your benefit; discover ways it can make your job easier, and have it help you deliver a more valuable product to your customer. Don't let it replace you, let it restore you, reinvigorate you, and renew your creative juices.

Bringing in an Outside Trainer

An integral part of the ongoing training and development of your team is introducing them to new ideas, new strategies, and new techniques. The problem arises when all those new ideas have to come from one person: you!

No matter how charismatic you are, your sales team is eventually going to get tired of listening to you. I hate to break this to you, but they don't enjoy hearing you talk nearly as much as you do. (I know, it was shocking to me too!) It's not that they don't respect you or like you, it's simply the fact that there comes a time when you need let them see another face and hear another voice.

At least once a year, bring in someone to speak to your salespeople. Whether the speaker is from within your industry isn't important. If you sell cars, your guest doesn't have to be someone with years of automotive sales experience, he just needs to be someone who can inspire your team and bring in a fresh perspective.

Benefiting from an outside voice

Your method and style of training and the information you have to share is shaped by your experiences. Whether those experiences are from your own sales background or through books you've read, seminars you've attended, or whatever, they're all tinted by the lenses you wear. They have your flavor to them.

If you've scheduled, managed, and overseen more than a year's worth of regular sales meetings, there probably isn't anything new you can say to inspire or educate your people. They've heard your stories and know your style. Think of it as watching a movie; they've seen this one and now they want to see something new.

In order to have the most well rounded sales team in the field, you need to make sure that they're exposed to as many learning opportunities as possible. And all those opportunities can't come from you. By introducing an outside sales trainer or speaker, you not only break up the monotony of hearing the same voice, but you also expose your team to an entirely new set of life experiences, views, skills, and techniques.

When you decide to bring in another trainer, make sure he isn't going to simply parrot what you've been saying. Get someone whose background is different from yours.

Don't let your ego get in the way of getting the best outside trainer or speaker you can afford. Never be afraid to bring in someone who's more experienced than you. Look at this as an opportunity to learn something new yourself. If you introduce someone to your team and then undermine them by letting their resume hurt your ego, you're wasting your time and money.

In fact, you should relish the chance to find someone who can make your salespeople better — that's your job. As a sales manager, nobody ever said you had to be the best, smartest, most experienced salesperson to ever put on a pair of shoes.

Your job as a sales manager is to do everything within your power to make your salespeople successful. And sometimes that means giving them the opportunity to learn from someone else.

Finding the right trainer

There's no hard and fast rule that a guest speaker or trainer has to be from within your own industry. In fact, sometimes it's best if he isn't. You want to find someone whose message can resonate with your sales team and bring value to your meeting whatever his background.

First, determine what type of person you're looking for:

- **Speaker:** Someone who comes in simply to inspire your sales team. He can deliver a speech and probably take questions and interact but can't necessarily discuss or work on sales skills.
- **A trainer:** A trainer doesn't necessarily have to focus on sales. Perhaps you want to bring someone in to work with your team on business etiquette, social media, or just business in general. Many good trainers can help your team immensely without ever discussing sales.
- **Sales trainer:** This person comes to talk sales. You task him with educating, enlightening, and building your sales team through his methods, experience, or techniques. Again, he doesn't have to be industry specific, but he can focus on everything from prospecting to asking for the sale.

After you determine what you're looking for, you have to find the right person. So, how do you do that? Well, I'm glad you asked:

- **Peer groups:** The best way to select a guest speaker or trainer is through a referral from someone who has heard him before. If you have a peer group, ask around and see if anyone has someone he's heard and would recommend.
- **Industry contacts:** If your industry has a state or national association, there's a good chance it's had speakers or trainers in the past, so ask. But, don't just ask whom it hired, ask who had the best feedback from attendees. Find out whom that organization would invite back to speak again.

- **Social media:** Most sales trainers and speakers have a good social media presence. LinkedIn is a tremendous way to find a speaker. If you want someone from within your particular field, search the groups on LinkedIn and look for someone who's involved there. At the same time, a quick Internet search can provide you with a lot of leads as well.
- **Speakers' bureau:** Most larger cities have a speakers' bureau that can provide you with a list of qualified candidates. They generally have websites where you can look up information, read testimonials, and even watch video clips of possible candidates.
- **Authors:** Your budget determines whether this is a legitimate source, but authors you enjoy reading sometimes are available to speak to your sales team, too. Most have contact information in their books, or you can find them online or through their publishers.

After you assemble a short list of people you'd like to consider as your guest, do your homework and check references and talk to past clients.

The best trainers and speakers won't be available if you call them a month ahead of time. Plan your speaker two to three months in advance. This gives you flexibility and can get you a better price — especially if you're paying for transportation and/or accommodations.

Know what you are expecting of your guest speaker and let him know up front what you'd like him to do. Is he coming in to simply deliver an inspirational speech, do you want him to discuss specific sales skills, or are you looking for something as detailed as a sales workshop? Whatever they are, make sure your needs are clear. Just because someone is a great speaker doesn't mean he can put on a workshop or hold your team's attention for a whole morning.

If you're looking for an outside sales trainer, check personal resumes. Look at jobs candidates have done in the past, what they've sold, and what qualifies them to be an expert. Unfortunately, I've seen many sales trainers who have never sold anything but their sales training. Personally, I always want someone who has walked the walk and doesn't just talk the talk.

After you decide on your guest, you execute a contract and probably have to pay half the fee at the time of the booking. If your speaker has a book or other materials he's authored, you can negotiate to have copies available for every one of your salespeople at the end of the event.

One final note to remember when booking an outside speaker or sales trainer: You get what you pay for. If someone's fee is half that of everyone else you're looking at or considering, there may be a reason why. If you're going to only do this once a year, budget for it and spend the money to get a quality speaker or trainer. A $5,000 speaker/trainer show that really brings the goods is much better for your organization, your salespeople, and your event than a $1,500 one who leaves everyone asking, "What the heck was that?"

Delivering a consistent message

One of the most important aspects of hiring an outside trainer or speaker is to make sure the message he's delivering to your people is consistent with what you've taught them. Although it's important to give your salespeople a fresh perspective, a different voice, and a new way of attacking their jobs, the basis of what you've built shouldn't be compromised.

This doesn't mean you have to have someone come in and simply regurgitate your words with a different accent. There are plenty of sales techniques, skills, and even full workshops that can benefit your team.

Introducing an outside trainer or speaker to your team should serve to highlight and reinforce the things you go over day in and day out. Though his message may be completely different from yours, it needs to be complementary and not contradictory.

Spend some time before the event outlining areas you feel your team needs work. Is it in prospecting? Setting appointments? Phone skills? Follow-up skills? Whatever it is, talk to your trainer and let him know. Most can customize their training for you and your organization or industry.

If your company has certain requirements or even things you prohibit, make sure you discuss them with your trainer prior to the event. There's nothing worse than having someone you paid a lot of money to walk out the door and you needing to turn to everyone and say, "Forget everything you just heard!"

Unless you've seen it for yourself and know beyond a shadow of a doubt that it's applicable to your specific need, avoid sales trainers who teach their own system. If their system hasn't been tested and proven in your particular field, you certainly don't want to be the guinea pig.

At the conclusion of your event, have handouts for your salespeople and ask them to grade the sales trainer. Ask them to evaluate a range of issues: Did they enjoy it? Was it beneficial? What did they like, dislike, and so on? Let them submit feedback forms anonymously so you get good feedback. Use the evaluations when you start looking for your guest the next year to know what your team responds positively to.

Finally, if you've done all your homework ahead of time, you know the speaker or trainer is going to deliver what you're looking for, so you can sit back, relax, and enjoy this part of your spring training. Hey, you might learn something, too.

When Less Is Actually More: Avoiding Burnout among Team Members

There's a fine line between being driven and being driven crazy. You can't operate at your best if you're mentally fried (that's a medical term).

Many times your top performers possess a drive that is almost insatiable. They're so driven and laser focused that they fail to take care of themselves — until they crash. Everyone needs time away, time to recharge the batteries and just relax. But, the ones who need it the most are generally the ones least likely to take it. They don't want to miss anything, or they don't feel as if they can turn their territory or accounts over to anyone else while they get in a few days of rest.

There's an odd paradox found in top producers: When they're at work they feel guilty about not spending time with their families; yet, when they take time off, they feel guilty that they're not working. It leads to a never-ending cycle and they end up working themselves until their health breaks down. It's just not good for anyone.

As a professional sales manager, you want your team members to perform at their best, but they can't do it if they work themselves to the breaking point. You have to let them know that rest and relaxation are both part of the prescription for success.

I've seen people go for several years without taking a vacation because they felt nobody else could handle their business for them. If you ever find that to be the case with a member of your team, insist — yes, insist — that he take some time off. I am the first person in line to learn and participate in ongoing training, but part of managing your team is knowing when to say when. Make whatever arrangements are necessary to have your over-worker's accounts covered while he gets away.

If people don't take breaks, they're setting themselves up for a textbook case of (cue the scary music) burnout!

Burnout occurs when someone works himself beyond a healthy state. Physically, mentally, emotionally — he's just out of gas. He's used up all his reserves, his tanks are empty, and his battery is dead.

Burnout is actually rather common in certain industries, but it can and does take a heavy toll on the employee and ultimately those around him.

The best way to deal with burnout is to avoid it in the first place. Instead of being reactive and waiting until one of your people is already there, be proactive and help keep everyone from ending up burned out.

As a manager, you need to be aware of what it takes to meet your requirements. If you ask your salespeople to make a certain number of calls per day, be sure it's not only physically, but also mentally and emotionally possible. For example, assume a salesperson is spending his day calling on and soliciting new business. Even though he can physically make eight to ten calls per day, mentally it's almost impossible to make that many new calls each day. Because you have to be "on" and have your energy at such a high level when calling on new accounts, the best you can do is make five or six new calls a day. Now, you can make more calls, but those prospects are basically wasted because you don't have the necessary energy and enthusiasm as you did for the first half-dozen calls.

Understand the physical, mental, and emotional toll sales and the sales process has on your people and ensure your expectations aren't overly aggressive. Helping them develop good, sound habits in their scheduling and quotas can go a long way to avoiding burnout.

Another thing you, as a sales manager, can do is to make sure you allow plenty of time for projects you assign to your team. If they're doing their regular job and you add an entirely new set of tasks to that, be aware that something is going to suffer. I know we're in an age of trying to get more out of less, but you can ride a good horse to death. Let team members help establish timelines and deadlines for additional projects or allow them to ask for help with part of the process.

Burnt out employees are a real problem today. Some believe more than 80 percent of the workforce suffers from it. I imagine sales professionals are at the high end of the spectrum. The job is stressful enough. Do what you can to help manage that and foster an environment where your people can be successful without putting their health at risk.

Burnout is nothing more than a fancy name for stress. That's really what it comes down to is being overly stressed. Nobody can be on all the time — it's just not possible no matter what his personality type. Even that happy-go-lucky Type A personality needs some downtime every now and then.

A few things that personally help me avoid burnout and keep me mentally sharp are

- **Unplugging:** Every so often I have to force myself to unplug and get away from the computer, cellphone, iPad, and so forth. It can be frightening initially until you realize that the world isn't going to end if you're away from your favorite device for a day.
- **Having a creative outlet:** If you have a salesperson struggling with burnout or you see the classic symptoms, suggest a creative hobby. As silly as it sounds, something like drawing or jigsaw puzzles gives you time to let your brain have fun and still work. Most salespeople can't turn their brains off, so the trick is to give it something else to do.
- **Taking a short get away:** I'm not an avid outdoorsman, but I still manage to take a day occasionally and get back to nature. I'll take a walk, sit on a park bench, or just go sit in the backyard and watch the clouds. If you see signs of burnout, the best cure is usually outside.
- **Playing with a pet:** When I really want to relax, unwind, and de-stress, I have two puppies at my house who just love for me to play with them. You may find that humorous, but take some time with a pet and not only do you recharge your batteries, but you put a lot of things in perspective, too.

Notice none of these involved traveling. If your salespeople travel, the last thing you need to do is coach them on taking a trip. They see the inside of the car, hotel, and/or airplane enough.

Chapter 10

Creating and Running an Effective Sales Meeting

In This Chapter

- Scheduling your sales meetings
- Understanding the goals of the meetings
- Knowing what mistakes to avoid
- Looking at how to keep them wanting more

Sales meetings are an integral part of your department. They're your opportunity to offer continuing education, work on sales skills, introduce new items from vendors, and generally disseminate information to your salespeople.

Meetings can be a key cog in the wheel that drives your department if you put a little time and effort into their creation and execution.

Contrary to popular belief, meetings aren't just opportunities for the out-of-town salespeople to clear out the bar at the Holiday Inn with their group karaoke version of "Achy Breaky Heart." Although sharing good times is certainly part of the experience, it's not the purpose of the meeting.

The main goal of a meeting, whether it's a sales meeting or any other type, is to create value while using everyone's time effectively. When you plan your calendar and your individual meetings, if you make that your primary goal, your salespeople will benefit, you'll benefit, and the company's money will be well spent.

Plenty of research out there points to how much productivity is lost because of needless meetings, so please don't read into this that you should meet just to have a meeting.

When planning a sales meeting, start with what you want it to look like when you're done and work back from there. It will make the development much easier.

Developing a Sales Meeting Calendar

No matter what month you're in, you can put together a sales meeting calendar for the balance of this year and start next year with one in hand.

When I talk about a calendar I mean an actual calendar, one you can (and do) publish for your team so they can plan around it. But, before you can create a calendar, you need to create a *sales meeting planner* — a tool you can use to make sure every sales meeting hits all the areas you want for your people.

Put together a template to help you build your meeting and then use that template for every meeting. You can fill it in as you plan each meeting. This helps you establish a set meeting flow and assists you in making sure you have everything you need for every meeting.

The sample meeting template in Figure 10-1 shows the key elements of a meeting. The one essential is the main topic — you build your entire meeting around this is one thing.

You may also include a secondary topic, a couple of vendor spots, and some new items.

If you represent a product that introduces its spring line in February, you know that's going on the calendar then. You can use it to plan ahead. If a vendor or supplier wants to be a part of your meeting, you can schedule it in advance, as well.

You may have just one new item and one vendor for a meeting, and that's fine. If you have a great main topic and don't want to take away from it with a secondary topic, that's okay, too.

Sales Meeting Planner 2015

	January	February	March	April	May	June	July	August	September	October	November	December
Main Topic												
Secondary Topic												
Vendor												
Vendor												
New Item												
New Item												
New Item												
Promotion												
Promotion												
Lunch Provider												
Sales Training												
Guest												

Figure 10-1: A sales meeting planner template.

If you have lunch, you can even schedule lunch providers, the sales training topic, and any guests you have.

Get with Human Resources and even your legal department before planning your meetings for the year. You may be required to go over certain benefits or safety items periodically and you can pencil them in on your chart.

Using the template allows you to schedule speakers and topics so that you don't double up or have conflicting products or services in the same meeting.

Your sales meeting planner is simply a "fill in the blanks" system to make sure you cover valid, important, and relevant topics each meeting. Using it gives your meetings a sense of consistency and professionalism. It's nothing more than a tool to help you plan, promote, and execute the best meeting possible. A template is simply a planning tool to make sure you hit the high points and don't leave anything out you know you want to include.

When designing your own sales meeting planner, you can adjust the topics to fit your particular criteria and needs, but the format should remain essentially the same. The idea is to give yourself a single go-to document to see what you need to schedule or other gaps to be filled for upcoming meetings. Do you need to invite a guest or select a vendor? You can know at a moment's notice if you have a spot open if a vendor or manufacturer requests to attend.

In designing your planner, think about the topics you cover in a normal meeting and leave yourself room for special items, promotions, or seasonal items that affect your standard meeting agenda.

When you complete your template, simply start filling in the blanks. If you have a vendor partner who wants to introduce a new item in September, you can go ahead and get that in your planner today. On the other hand, if you look at next month and see a gaping hole, you know you need to fill that quickly.

Your sales meeting is designed to improve the performance of your sales team. If that's the case, you should give it the time and attention it deserves. The more time you spend planning and putting the meeting together the better it will be and the more your people will take from it.

Never just show up to a sales meeting and wing it and hope everyone has a good time. Your salespeople aren't there just to have a good time and see everyone else. A sales meeting isn't designed to be like a family reunion. Although your sales team can certainly enjoy it, they're at the meeting to become better representatives of your company and the products and services you sell. Don't lose sight of why you're having these meetings in the first place.

Deciding how often to meet

After you create your calendar it's time to decide how often to meet. Oh, you'll have some salespeople who think you should meet about as often as Halley's comet appears, but you're going to put on meetings they look forward to (or at least that's the idea).

Determining the frequency of your meetings really comes down to two factors:

- **Geography:** How difficult is it to get your entire team together in one location? If some members of your team have to drive six hours it's hard to justify a weekly meeting.

  If everyone is working out of the same office or central location, weekly meetings may be appropriate while less frequency is better for teams who are spread out a bit more.

- **Content:** Never meet to just have a meeting. If you have enough content and material to have a meeting, then have a meeting. Don't huddle everyone up to just sit around and stare at each other.

Think of it this way, if you drive for a half-day and enjoy an amazing, educational, motivational meeting it's one thing. By the same token, a trip across town to a worthless, waste of time meeting can drive you nuts. The distance and the content are directly proportionate and determine the success of your meeting.

Even if you have to meet via Skype or other video conferencing system, meet with your team no less than once per quarter. In sales, absence does not make the heart grow fonder. For the average salesperson, absence creates undo anxiety at times. The way salespeople are wired, a lot of them have an anxiety of not hearing from the home office. They don't generally feel that no news is good news. A lot of times they think the exact opposite.

Depending on the size of your sales organization you may want to get team members involved in the frequency decision.

One other thing to consider if you have separate divisions or territories is to have the salespeople in each area have a regular meeting covering the same or similar information. As the sales manager, you should make regular appearances at each.

You can get the entire team together less frequently and your salespeople can still receive the same level of commitment from you and the company.

If you hold separate division sales meetings, work with those managers to make sure they hold professional meetings. Ultimately you're responsible for what information is sent down to each individual salesperson — make sure their direct managers have the same commitment and ability to put on a professional meeting.

Choosing when to meet

Do you schedule sales meetings during the weekday or have them on the weekend? That's the big question!

After you determine how often you'll bring everyone together, it's time to tackle perhaps your hardest decision when it comes to sales meetings: when are you going to meet? And it's not as easy as just picking a day. If you operate in a retail environment where someone has to be manning the floor, you may have to have two meetings so everyone gets involved.

The day and time you choose may depend on your meeting frequency. If you're meeting weekly the meetings are likely to be shorter than monthly meetings. Having a short, weekday meeting doesn't take your entire team out of the field for a long time.

But, if you meet quarterly and your meeting is going to last half a day, it's hard to justify pulling an entire sales team out of the field for that much time. In doing so, you're basically taking all those sales hours and throwing them away and giving your competition free run of your market. I never liked to hold quarterly meetings on a weekday. I don't think it's too much to ask for someone to give up a Saturday once per quarter. Especially if they feel it is time well spent.

However, if your meeting weekly, you can't very well ask everyone to give up a day off to have a sales meeting each weekend. In that case, you have to work it into your weekday schedule.

First I tackle the weekday meeting conundrum. When and what day? I've seen them all from Monday morning through Friday afternoon. Though each day and time has its pros and cons, I was recently introduced to a new idea by a friend and vice president of a large media organization I did some sales training for. He holds his meetings on Tuesday morning at 8:15 a.m. When I asked about it he explained that he requires his salespeople to be in front of a prospect or customer first thing Monday morning and wants everyone working on Friday. You can bet he makes sure his sales people are where they're supposed to be on Monday morning.

The 8:15 meeting time accommodates his workforce, the majority of whom have children they have to take to school or daycare. An 8:00 a.m. meet time was difficult, but 8:15 worked fine. Now, that's how you listen to your people!

This may be one of the best arguments I've heard for a particular day and time. He's got his entire sales force out working the market to start the week and to end the week. He's making the best use of everyone's time. In addition, he's accommodating the needs of his team to meet family obligations as well. Tuesday morning is safe and works for them.

I'll admit, I liked early Monday morning meetings so I could ensure my people were up and out — but if they're in the office for a meeting, they aren't out calling on prospects. After hearing his idea, I was thoroughly convinced it made more sense than my argument for Monday mornings. And, I'd been making that argument for years!

When selecting your day and time, think about the availability of prospects. I know of another company that has its sales meetings on Friday afternoon. They found their buyers almost impossible to reach on Friday afternoons because many of them switched onto autopilot and coasted toward the weekend. Since that's the case, they found a way to work around it.

Don't just arbitrarily pick a day. Put some thought into what makes the most sense for you, your team and your market.

If you meet less frequently — say monthly or even quarterly — your meeting naturally lasts longer than a weekly one because you have a month's or quarter's worth of information to cover. With that in mind, I can't see giving my competition free reign over the entire market. In these instances, I would suggest a Saturday morning meeting. Depending on travel time, your team can come in Friday evening, participate in the meeting early Saturday morning, and return home afterward.

If you ask your sales team to give up a day off, you better have a very high quality meeting lined up for them. No fluff — all stuff!

Weekly meetings should be kept to an hour or less — any more than that and you're just wasting time. However, if you meet on the monthly or quarterly basis, you can easily fill half a day (8:00 a.m. to noon) or something similar.

As long as you provide valuable content that makes your team better, no meeting is wasted. But the minute it breaks into something less useful than that you need to blow the whistle, ring the bell — do whatever you've got to do to turn them loose.

Deciding what to talk about

Each sales meeting should be a well-planned event. Don't wing it and hope something good comes of it. It won't.

I always tried to include a variety of information at my meetings and keep the meeting flowing from one subject to another to hold everyone's attention. If you rattle on and on about the same subject, you're going to have to wake everyone up when it's over.

When you put your sales meeting planner together (refer to Figure 10-1), you can select what topics you want to cover, what items or services you want to highlight, and whether to work on prospecting skills or whatever the case may be.

Using your planner in advance allows you to tie your training and/or product and service discussions to the seasons. For example, if you're in the soft drink business your topic and focus right before summer is drastically different than your wintertime meeting.

Ask your sales team what they want you to cover in an upcoming meeting. Are there issues they're having they'd like to see addressed? Are there products and services they'd like more training on? Is there a certain vendor or other partner that would benefit them seeing and being able to talk to? Get their input. After all, the meeting is for them!

You can even let team members submit ideas anonymously. Someone may be embarrassed to say she needs help with prospecting or open-ended questions or whatever the case may be.

If one person is having a problem and vocalizes it, I can assure you she speaks for several others who didn't have the nerve to bring it up but are facing the same challenges.

Keep your meeting professional but fun. And yes, that is possible. Not everything has to be so buttoned down corporate. There's a difference between making a meeting enjoyable and having it be a free-for-all. It's okay and even encouraged for everyone to have a good time, but you must maintain a sense of decorum and professionalism. There's no place for someone playing around when it wastes others' valuable time.

People learn and retain more when they are enjoying their environment and surroundings. But, set the boundaries early on professionalism.

If you have your meeting on a monthly basis, review the previous month's sales, celebrate the wins, and talk about ways to improve.

Don't get into the habit of making the entire meeting a lecture instead of a conversation.

Encourage your people to participate and when possible create opportunities within the meeting for breakout sessions that let them work together as teams. Be sure to split them up so that people are teamed with those they don't normally work with. For example, if you have four divisions, have one person from each division represented on a team. Allow them to develop working relationships they wouldn't have had the opportunity to otherwise.

Publishing the calendar well in advance

You've put together a planner and decided when to meet. Now it's time to publish your calendar for everyone to see. After you decide on the frequency and day and time for your meetings, a simple list will do. The example in Table 10-1 shows a meeting on the first Saturday of every month in the conference room. Or, perhaps you want to move the meeting around and are going to hold it in different locations; you can list that on your meeting schedule, too.

Table 10-1 2015 Sales Meetings

Date	*Time*	*Location*
January 3, 2015	8:00 a.m.–noon	Conference room
February 7, 2015	8:00 a.m.–noon	Conference room
March 7, 2015	8:00 a.m.–noon	Conference room
April 4, 2015	8:00 a.m.–noon	Conference room
May 2, 2015	8:00 a.m.–noon	Conference room
June 6, 2015	8:00 a.m.–noon	Conference room
July 11, 2015 (Second week of July due to Independence Day)	8:00 a.m.–noon	Conference room
August 1, 2015	8:00 a.m.–noon	Conference room
September 5, 2015	8:00 a.m.–noon	Conference room
October 3, 2015	8:00 a.m.–noon	Conference room
November 7, 2015	8:00 a.m.–noon	Conference room
December 12, 2015 (Second week of December to coincide with company Christmas celebration)	8:00 a.m.–noon	Conference room

Meeting to plan the next planning meeting

I once had a customer who was in meetings from the time he walked in his door every morning until the time he left the office in the evening. I'd call in the morning, "He's in a meeting."

Try again just before lunch, "He's in a meeting."

After lunch, early afternoon, and just before closing time, the answer was like a broken record. I used actually keep up with the days and times I would call and though I never did the math, I would guess his week was comprised of meetings 90% of the time.

And he wasn't dodging my calls. His day was literally filled with meetings.

What in the world they can be meeting about for that much time? Is there really that much to talk about? There were times I felt inferior because I *wasn't* meeting that much. I thought maybe I was doing something wrong.

How productive can that really be?

We joked that he was having a planning meeting to plan the next planning meeting.

Note that two dates had conflicts and couldn't adhere to the normal schedule. Know that ahead of time and what you're going to do about it. Sales meetings should be mandatory!

If you publish your sales meeting schedule at the beginning of the year, there's no excuse for a vacation conflict. Everyone has ample time to plan her entire year around her sales meetings. You're asking for 12 days a year — that's it. I don't think it's over the line to expect everyone to set aside those days to commit to her job — especially if you put the effort into making the meetings as valuable as possible.

Check and double-check before publishing your calendar. If you're not going to let people take vacation on those dates and require mandatory attendance, it's a bit unprofessional for you to go back later and change the date because you forgot something. After you publish this calendar, only an act of God or natural disaster should change it. It's that important.

Conducting a Sales Meeting

Some ground rules make a good sales meeting.

By effectively using your sales meeting planner (see the preceding section), you can produce a consistent agenda for your meeting in no more than five or ten minutes. Although you send out the schedule of meetings for the year, wait to hand out the agenda at the meeting.

If you post that the meeting will start at 8:00 a.m., close the door at 7:59. 8:00 a.m. does not mean 8:01 or 8:05. If you do nothing else, you should always — always — start and end your meetings on time. As the sales manager, you're the keeper of the clock. You have to keep the meeting on track and keep people from hijacking it and taking it off in a direction you didn't intend.

If you have someone trying to get into the weeds on a topic, stop her, write down a quick note about her concern, and invite her to visit with you personally after the meeting. Don't waste the meeting time.

If you have eight items on the agenda and every one of them runs five to ten minutes long, you're going to be about an hour late getting your people out of there. And it happens so fast you never know it. Watch the clock and stay on point.

A pet peeve of mine is people not respecting the speaker. Whether it's me, one of the salespeople, a vendor, or guest, or whoever has the floor, everyone needs to pay attention to that person. It's a matter of respect. You should demand it of your people — again, not for you but for anyone who is speaking.

Depending on the size of your sales team, if they break off into their own little groups and start the chitchat at the table, before long nobody is paying attention to anything going on at the front of the room. One final note in preparing your agenda is to assign a time to every topic, activity, and element of the meeting. You spend most of your time with your sales meeting planner on this task. The rest of the work is done for you if you developed a useful sales meeting planner.

If you have a vendor or a guest and allot her 30 minutes, let her know that 30 minutes doesn't mean 31. If she needs you to notify her when she has five minutes left, give her the wave or thumbs up or whatever it takes to get her attention and keep her on time.

Making the best use of everyone's time

One of, if not *the,* most important factors in a successful sales meeting is to make the best use of everyone's time. If you have people who travel a long way to get there, respect the fact that when the meeting's over, they still have a long way to go to get back home.

While starting and ending on schedule is critical, the things that happen between those two times are what determines the value of the meeting. By having an agenda and sticking to it, you're well ahead of the game, but there's more to a good meeting than just being on time.

In order to best utilize everyone's time I suggest the following be a part of how you run every one of your meetings:

- **Have one main topic:** If you try to cover too much ground in one meeting, you end up not covering any of it well. What is the focus of this meeting? What do you want your team to learn? Try to tie as much of the meeting to that one topic as possible.

  If you must have a secondary topic, make it very short. Don't steal the thunder of the main theme or topic.
- **Take other discussions offline:** Don't let anyone dictate the content or the direction of the meeting. If someone has a point you feel is important and warrants further discussion, take it offline. Don't let it take you away from your main goal.

You're basically feeding your sales team with a sales meeting. You're feeding them knowledge, information, facts, figures, product knowledge, and sales skills among other bits and pieces.

It's important to give your sales team enough to satisfy their hunger and make it worth their time, while being careful not to overfeed them. If you stuff them full, two things are going to happen: they'll get sick on you and they won't want to eat what you're serving again!

Two questions to always ask literally and figuratively:

- **What's working that we need to do more of?** What are your people having success with? What do you need to double down on and focus more efforts toward that will produce more positive results?
- **What's not working that we need to do less of?** Never get married to an idea or a strategy so much that you cannot change. Never. Know when to say "when" and move on.

Regular sales meetings are a great place to address these two questions and to foster growth, prevent stagnation, and encourage creativity. Get your people involved in developing the solution — not just implementing a solution someone else has come up with.

When I say, "ask these questions," I mean ask them. And then listen to what your sales team tells you. I can't count the times that management thinks they know what's happening in the field and is completely off base. Even worse is when management makes decisions based on what the home office thinks the customer wants when nobody bothers to actually ask the customer.

Sales meetings should be a two-way sharing of information: from you to your salespeople and back up the chain from them, as well. That's the only way you'll truly have effective communication.

If a question is ever answered with "because we've always done it that way" and that's the only reason, stop immediately.

The entire purpose of the meeting is to consistently and constantly improve your sales team's performance — nothing more and nothing less. Although you can get into hundreds of topics at these meetings, ultimately it comes down to determining what you want your sales team to learn, what you want them to do, and the results you want to see afterward.

Keeping the meeting interesting

One of the challenges you face is keeping your sales meetings interesting. Simply holding your team's attention can be trying and doing it for an extended period of time is even more difficult.

There's a method to how you should structure your meeting. I talk about ending on a high note in a bit, and you also want to come out of the gate with a bang.

Let everyone know the meeting has started — kick it off with a scream, not a whimper. Now, I don't mean you have to stand on the table and shout at the top of your lungs, but you need a kick start to the event — get everyone's blood flowing and wake her up — especially if you're meeting in the morning.

No matter how interesting the topic is, people's attention begins to wander after about 45 minutes. Not even the most dynamic speaker, funniest comedian, or most entertaining raconteur can keep people focused longer than that. It's just how humans are wired.

When you lay out the agenda, keep each subject area or topic to 30 to 45 minutes at most. This keeps the pace of the meeting moving and keeps your audience from being bored as well.

As I touch on in Chapter 9, another thing to keep in mind is that your sales team gets tired of hearing you talk. I know it's hard to believe, but they do. Even with that lovely, velvety voice of yours! If you're going to be the speaker in one of the segments or cover one of the topics, do little more than emcee the rest of the meeting. Introduce the vendor or guest and then get out of the way. It's not all about you. (You read that in Dr. Phil's voice, didn't you?)

Schedule regular breaks throughout the meeting if it's going to last more than an hour. As an example, if you're hosting a four-hour monthly meeting your agenda could look similar to the one in Table 10-2.

Table 10-2 January 3, 2015 Sales Meeting Agenda

Welcome/Introductions/Review Agenda	8:00–8:05
Main Topic	8:05–8:40
Secondary Topic	8:40–9:00
Vendor	9:00–9:30
Break	9:30–9:45
New Item Introductions	9:45–10:15
Promotions	10:15–10:30
Guest/Discussion	10:30–10:45
Break	10:45–11:00
Sales Training	11:00–11:45
Q&A/Close	11:45–12:00
Lunch	12:00

This agenda shows a pattern of content, content, content, break repeated twice during the meeting. With these regular breaks, you develop a nice flow, people aren't squirming to use the restroom, and their attention is drawn more to where you want it to be. I like to start with my main topic first — it's the meat of the meeting. You have as much of everyone's attention as you're going to get right at the beginning — don't waste it. Cover the main topic of your meeting first.

Note that the table shows a secondary topic and a spot for a vendor. This can be a supplier or a representative from your manufacturer if you have one. If not, you can use this time for a discussion of a sales-related skill.

If you're the person introducing the new item at 9:45, get someone from purchasing or even a division sales manager to discuss the promotions at 10:15. You want to break up the monotony of one topic or one voice frequently.

If you're doing the sales training yourself, you don't need to be the voice right before it — you really want to capture your team's attention and I always liked a break before the training part of the meeting.

If you think of the sales meeting as an orchestrated event instead of just another sales meeting, it becomes much more interesting and creates much more value for your sales team.

Using vendor and manufacturer support

There's a good chance your company represents or sells products for a manufacturer, vendor, or multiple vendors. If that's the case, you certainly want to take advantage of everything those partners have to offer in the way of making your meeting the best it can be. From sending representatives to introduce new products and services to offering SPIF (Special Performance Incentive Fund) monies, they can and should play a large part in your sales meetings.

When you make out your initial sales meeting calendar, notify all your major manufacturer and vendor partners. Let them know if they have new items or other promotional opportunities they need to schedule with you as soon as possible.

Most large manufacturers have their launches and promotional calendar planned before you're even thinking about your meeting calendar, so your contact should know when she needs to be involved in your meeting, down to the specific month.

It's a good idea to have the vendor submit its information prior to the meeting so you can approve it. You want to make sure it's not off-topic or something you don't want introduced. I've told vendors we weren't going to promote a new item and have them show it to the sales department anyway. That backdoor tactic doesn't work well twice.

Although budgets have been drastically cut in recent years, many companies have money allotted specifically to promote and push their products. They may not be able to participate and fund other programs, but expenses directly tied to selling more of their goods are generally still in their budget. Take advantage of it.

If you don't ask, you don't get. If you never ask your vendors or manufacturers to fund a lunch at the meeting or provide money for an incentive or bonus program, you never get any monies. Hey, what's the worst thing that can happen if you ask?

A lot of the dollars manufacturers and vendors used to throw around are gone, so don't just go to them with your hand out. If you can find a way to create value for them, many times they can find a way to pay for it. Too many companies and brands were paying a lot of money for nothing in years past — now you have to bring value to the table. Look at what you can do for them to make their participation valuable and meaningful for them.

Treat getting to speak and appear at your sales meeting as something special for your vendors and manufacturing partners. You have a team of people your partners want to be in front of. Yes, it can benefit both of you, but you need to see it as an opportunity to have them help underwrite part of the meeting or provide something of value.

Avoiding the Pitfalls: What Not to Do

I cover a lot of the *do's* to make for a great sales meeting in the preceding sections, but what about the *don'ts?* I'd be remiss if I didn't at least touch on a few of the things to stay away from.

Avoid the things in this section like the plague. These aren't good for anyone.

Your sales meeting should be almost sacred ground. You're there for an honorable purpose: to improve the knowledge and skills of your sales team. And, therefore some things just aren't welcome.

It's absolutely acceptable to publish a brief sales meeting rules and regulations outlining what you expect. You can make it fun, but get your point across as in Figure 10-2.

To All Members of the Sales Department:

Our Sales Meetings are an important part of the ongoing growth of you and our company. Therefore, I want to make sure you understand the rules surrounding the meetings. This isn't all-inclusive and when in doubt about whether something is acceptable, simply ask yourself, "Is this going to make the meeting better or worse?" If it's better, add it. If not, keep it to yourself until after the meeting.

The meetings are officially designated by the Department of Agriculture (or by me, I can't remember which) as a Negativity Free Zone. There will be no negativity allowed. In addition the following rules apply to everyone:

- Be on time!
- Respect the person who has the floor.
- Be on time!
- Keep personal chatter to a minimum.
- Be on time.
- Check your ego at the door.
- Be on time!
- Arrive EXPECTING to learn something and you will.

In addition to the above, I ask that you BE ON TIME! If you adhere to these guidelines, you and everyone else will have a much more productive meeting.

Thank you!

P.S. Remember to be on time!

Figure 10-2: Sample meeting rules and regulations.

Don't let it become the complaint department

Don't let negativity take root at all in your meeting. You must snuff it out at the first sign. Now, I'm not saying you need to stick your head in the sand and ignore real issues, but I am saying there is a time and place for everything. And your sales meeting is not the time to crank up every complaint in the book. I've had times where I felt like I was standing in front of a firing squad.

Now, does this mean you cannot talk about problems during the meeting? Absolutely not! In fact, you should address issues, but keep the conversation positive.

You will have certain salespeople who are problem finders. They seem to thrive on pointing out what's wrong, what others have messed up, and what isn't working. Oddly, these people never have a solution, just a problem. This is the type conversation to avoid.

Don't lose control of the meeting

I was conducting a sales meeting several years ago when a group of the salespeople thought they would basically ambush me with concerns about their commission program. It was obvious later that it was an orchestrated event by a couple of disgruntled employees who unfortunately talked a few others into falling on their swords as well.

It didn't end well.

As I always did, I invited them to talk offline privately because the item wasn't on the agenda and I wanted to respect the time of the other 30-plus people. I wasn't trying to ignore them or put them off, I just didn't believe that meeting was the time or place to talk about their personal issues with compensation.

A couple of them disagreed and it quickly derailed into raised voices and an emotional outburst by one young lady who shouted at me and started to walk toward the door. As I was telling her, "Don't walk out of this meeting! Don't walk out of this meeting," she walked out of the meeting.

Bad move. I went to work Monday morning. She didn't.

The moral of the story is I lost control of the meeting and, it got ugly. Once it did there was no way to bring it back. You can't un-hear or un-see some things. It should've never gotten that far in the first place. I did a poor job of handling it and ultimately it ruined the meeting, wasted a lot of people's time, and cost one person her job.

And, it didn't have to happen. I should've done a better job at laying out the meeting ground rules: If you have a personal issue, we'll talk about it personally. Don't use the meeting for grandstanding or showing off because it's not going to go well for you.

However, if you have an issue that you and your team can discuss in a positive, professional manner and work through potential solutions, it most certainly has a place in your meeting.

One of the ways to head off efforts to go negative is to require people to have a potential solution when they bring a problem to the floor. This will stop a lot of those who simply look for things to complain about. They generally don't want to do that much work to look at the positive, they just want to b . . . well, you know.

This isn't the time for criticism

Just as you ask your salespeople to be positive, make sure you do the same.

Your sales meeting isn't the time to criticize or call someone out for something she did or did not do. There's nothing to be gained by it — in fact, many times it makes you look small because I can assure you the rest of the sales team will sympathize with the criticized person.

If you have sales results to announce or display, you don't need to hide anything, even if numbers are down. You can still focus on the positive.

You'll never build a strong salesperson by tearing her down in front of others. Contrary to what some may believe, that doesn't build character. It makes you look like a very unprofessional manager.

Praise publicly; criticize privately. If you need to discuss someone's shortfalls and areas she needs to improve upon, do that alone when it's just the two of you in your office. Don't do it in front of the entire group.

If you really want to create a strong team, find something good to say about everyone. You don't have to go down the list like you're Santa Claus reading off every little good boy and girl. But, make it a point to build people up and realize that the best place to do that is among their peers.

Amazingly, when you find something to compliment people for and brag on, you get more of that behavior naturally. For example, if you really have to stretch to recognize Bob for his prospecting skills, Bob will become better at prospecting. If he thinks that's your perception of him, nine times out of ten, he'll live up to that. By the same token, if you criticize Bob because he failed to make the required number of calls, he'll repeat that behavior as well — or he'll quit.

Your job is to build a better, stronger, more talented sales team. One way to do that is through positive, public feedback and guidance.

Leave 'Em Wanting More

I had the good fortune to be able to do stand-up comedy professionally for almost ten years as a young man. I never did it for a living, I got to do it because I loved it and I got pretty good at it — to the point where I had to decide whether I wanted to do it for a living or not. With three young children at home at the time, I chose to stick with the day job. I think I made the right decision.

I was also lucky enough to work for a man (my mentor to this day) who encouraged me to expand my comedy repertoire and do as many gigs as I possibly could. He saw it as tremendous public speaking training.

In addition to being addictively fun, it was truly the best sales training I ever got. If you think a crowd is in a comedy club to laugh, you're wrong. Many of them are there — arms crossed, head cocked to the side with that "Okay, big boy, make me laugh" look on their faces.

It was a challenge every time I stepped on stage. Was I going to win them over or were they going to eat me alive? Thankfully, more often than not I won the contest.

I learned to think on my feet. I learned amazing ways to use voice inflection to drive home points and to tell stories and truly get people hanging on every single word. Writing out every single joke long hand (this was before everyone had laptops and tablets), I learned the value of scripting and making a presentation planned not canned.

In a set that lasted 45 minutes to an hour, I would have literally 99.9 percent of my routine memorized to a T. Nothing was an accident — even when the crowd thought, "He's so quick how he just thinks of those things!"

Nope. I've been doing that same line every night, and I'll do it tomorrow night in Des Moines. That's the secret of a great comedy set and a great sales presentation.

But, the single most valuable lesson I ever learned is this: Always leave them wanting more. No matter how great it's going, how much they love you, never wear out your welcome.

At 45 minutes they think I'm the funniest thing they've ever heard. At an hour and five minutes they're thinking, "Geez, is he ever going to hush?"

Which do you think is better to be their last thought? When it's time to wrap up the meeting. Wrap it up and get it over with. Live to fight another day.

Including motivation and inspiration

Every sales meeting should have some sort of motivation and inspiration aspect. Not necessarily as a line item on the agenda — although that's okay if you can have a guest speaker from time to time. Just make sure you don't miss the opportunity to focus on attitude and to help your people keep that fire burning.

The great part about including inspiration and motivation as part of your sales meeting is that they tend to spread like wildfire. It's much easier to get a group of people excited than just one. You're going to have a hard time getting an individual fired up with any speech, but you put a group of people together and enthusiasm begins to feed on itself.

There are numerous great motivational audio and video products if you want to set aside some time at your meeting. Even you allot just 15 minutes or so, select a piece in advance that fits the theme or main topic of your meeting.

It's easy to spend the entire meeting dealing with business. But, don't get so busy with the business that you forget one of the cornerstones of what makes a salesperson succeed — motivation.

Recognizing performance

Your regular sales meeting is the perfect time for performance recognition, announcing contest results, and so forth. Not only do the people who are receiving the accolades find out, but they get to find out in front of their peers.

Handing out awards at a sales meeting can motivate not only the person being recognized, but also those who aren't. Many times you'll have salespeople thinking to themselves, "That's going to be me next month." You win on both ends. You've got the best of both worlds.

If you're issuing or passing out bonus monies, be mindful of people's privacy unless the monies have all been made public beforehand.

Keep your eyes and ears open for other things to recognize during your sales meeting to build company pride and inspiration.

A few years ago I had a delivery driver who literally drove up on a car on fire on the highway and broke a window out of the car to pull people out. It was a truly heroic experience. This obviously got recognized in front of his peers, but I invited him to the sales meeting and shared the story with the sales team. Standing ovation and goose bumps. It was an amazing moment to see the sales team take so much pride in what another employee had done.

Building the suspense with awards

I managed a sales force once and we passed out promotional monies during each sales meeting. These dollars were well known and public beforehand, but nobody knew how much they'd earned or how much another person earned.

I created a lot of suspense and fun by having the envelopes stacked in ascending order so that I passed out the smallest amount first meaning the longer someone had to wait, the more money she knew she was going to get.

I'd announce it something like this: "Finishing the month earning $74.85 . . . Congratulations TANISHA!"

At that point everyone else knew they made more than $74.85. As the numbers grew larger and someone's name hadn't been called, it became pretty intense and a lot of fun.

It got to the point to where I'd call out the amount and people would say, "not me, not me" because they wanted theirs to be higher. It was a lot of fun for everyone involved and a great way to add some recognition to what would've been simply sticking an envelope in their company mailbox.

Be creative. Have fun and find a way to build some suspense and friendly competition!

Take off the blinders — there are opportunities to recognize outstanding performance everywhere if you just look!

Ending on a high note

Think of your sales meeting as one big sales presentation. You start with a bang, take your people on an educational ride, get them emotionally involved, and now it's time to wrap it up.

Just as you would do when asking for the sale, you need to end on a high note. You want to crescendo, not fizzle out. As songwriter Neil Young says, "It's better to burn out than to fade away."

The other thing the comedy career taught me is to finish with the big close. You see performers save their best song for the last one of the set or even for their encore. There's a reason for that.

You want the last impression to be a positive one. When you get your salespeople all jazzed up — that's the time to turn them loose. Don't get them all revved up and then slam on the brakes!

Plan to end your meeting with some positive high note — whether that's an announcement of some sort or the achievement of a goal your team has been working on.

Part IV

Sales Meetings and Key Performance Indicators

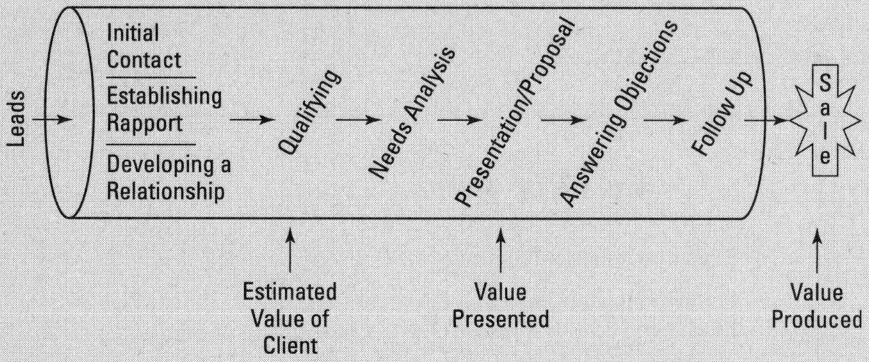

For more tips on running effective sales meetings, go to `www.dummies.com/extras/salesmanagement`.

In this part . . .

- Develop a sales meeting calendar that works for you.
- Uncover the most important key performance indicators (KPIs) for you and how to measure and manage them.
- See whether a customer relationship management (CRM) system is right for your organization and how to make one work to its maximum effectiveness.
- Discover ways to create healthy competition, celebrate wins, and recognize your true top performers.

Chapter 11

Measuring What Matters: Key Performance Indicators

In This Chapter

- Establishing your key performance indicators
- Understanding what other matrices to measure
- Looking at the ultimate performance indicator
- Using a CRM program to track data

As a general rule, salespeople are competitive by nature and need to know how they're performing. Many times the answer to that question depends on whether they're selling anything. But you can and should use many other measurable matrices to increase the performance of your team. This chapter looks at ways you can measure how your salespeople are doing.

Key performance indicators (KPIs) are — just as the name suggests — the key things you should be measuring (and managing) for each salesperson. You can use KPIs as benchmarks to determine the actual performance of an individual salesperson, territory, or division.

Don't subscribe to the theory that sales is "just a numbers game." Many other factors indicate how successful a salesperson is. Just like the old saying that you can put a monkey at a typewriter and he'll eventually type a word, you can throw anyone out there and with enough cold calls he'll probably sell something. But, in the meantime you've upset a lot of people, burned a lot of potentially good prospects, and sullied the name of your company. Not really a good plan, is it?

The alternative is to have some KPIs in place to allow you to see how each member of your sales team is doing and where in the process someone may need help, assistance, or more training.

For example, if you have a salesperson who has lots of prospects but no sales, the problem isn't prospecting — it's obviously something he's doing or not doing between those two steps in the process. But, if you don't measure a few of those things, you really have no idea *why* he isn't selling anything — all you know is that he isn't.

Your job as sales manager is not only to put these measurements in place but also to follow through and view the data. Keep up with it regularly and give your salespeople feedback on what you're seeing — good and bad.

If you initiate a KPI program and then don't follow up, your people will figure that out in a heartbeat, and you'll have wasted the entire program. It's not about what they put in; it's about what you do with the data. Use it to help them be better, not just to give them busywork. Make sense? Well, let's dive in!

The Big Three KPIs

There are potentially hundreds of KPIs you can measure for your sales team, but there are three that every manager must measure. No matter what business you're in, no matter what product or service you market and sell, a good sales manager always keeps up with and knows the following:

- The number of new contacts each salesperson is making
- The number of presentations each salesperson is making
- Each salesperson's sales

If you look at the so-called big three KPIs — contacts, presentations, and sales — you get a very good idea of how each member of your team is performing compared to the others. In fact, you have hard, fast numbers you can use to improve your team.

These are the obvious KPIs and the three I touch on first, but there are others. Think of the words, "performance indicators." What performance in your team do you want to measure?

Your goal is to find out what elements of the sales process you can measure to determine the effectiveness of your sales team. Nothing is off limits, but I focus on some you should constantly be watching.

The data you gather should be entered into some sort of customer relationship management system (CRM) or you won't have a consistent way to track it. (I talk about CRM systems in "Using CRM Software" later in the chapter.) Handwritten notes, call reports, and so forth are fine for on-the-spot contact, but the information and the progress of the sales process must be logged in order for you to properly manage it.

The KPIs you establish for your team shouldn't be kept a secret. Let your people know the criteria by which they are judged. Once they get in the habit of entering the data in the CRM system, and you use the information to give them the right feedback and help, it's one of the most positive interactions you'll have as a sales manager.

Don't be too quick to judge. Not everything is as it appears on the surface. Let the data speak for itself, but when the numbers do tell the tale, respond and take action.

Tracking contacts

The most basic question about contacts you need to answer is very simple: "How many new contacts is each salesperson making — weekly and monthly?" Success in sales starts with making contact with another human being, and if your sales team (or a specific salesperson) isn't making new contacts, eventually your new business will dry up.

If a salesperson is struggling, it's not because of what he's doing today — it's because of what he *didn't* do in the past.

Whether you require each salesperson to make a certain number of new contacts each week or each month is up to you, but this is an area you must police and hold your team accountable in.

There's no way for salespeople to grow their business if they aren't introducing themselves to new people constantly and consistently.

Visualize a grocery store full of people. In my world, every one of those people is a *suspect.* They could eventually be a *prospect,* but I don't know enough about them to make that determination yet. How do I find out? I make contact.

Figure 11-1 illustrates how the process works from suspect to prospect.

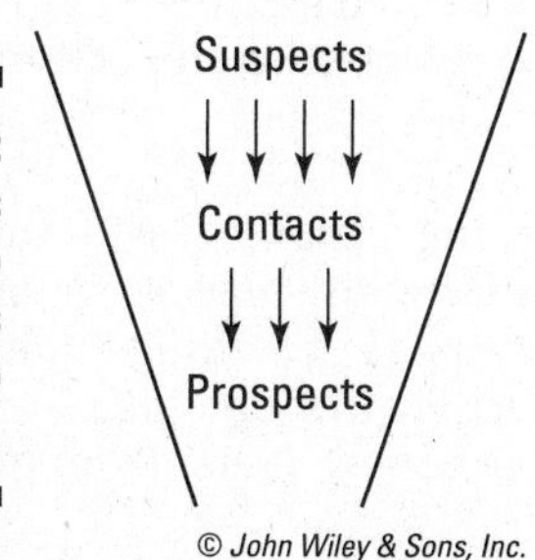

Figure 11-1: Suspects lead to contacts who lead to prospects.

The key to having your sales team make contact is to not be picky and try to determine which suspects could be prospects. Have them just start meeting people! Tell them to introduce themselves, tell what they do, give out their contact information, then ask, "What do you do?"

If your people try to find out as much as possible about the people they come into contact with, they will be much better off and more successful than just going in trying to tell contacts as much about themselves as possible. Listening skills are very important here.

One of the things I teach salespeople is to make a habit of generating new contacts. Make X number every week. Now, the operative words here are *habit* and *every week.* You have some get all fired up and go out and make 75 new contacts in a couple weeks, then not do anything for 90 days.

That doesn't work. The idea is to keep a steady supply of new contacts coming in at all times. Will they all be prospects? Absolutely not! But, you have to start somewhere.

Granted, if you're selling a high ticket, luxury item, five contacts a month may be good, but in retail direct sales you may need to average several hundred contacts. Whatever the number is for you, get your salespeople into the habit of making new ones regularly.

Tracking presentations

How many actual presentations is each of your salespeople able to make? It's important to know this number because this is the first indication of where there might be a problem in his sales process — and the first chance for you to determine what part of the process he needs help on.

If you require your salespeople to make a certain number of presentations every week or month, this number should be readily available to everyone. But, what are you going to do with the information?

For example, Marisol and Javier both make the same number of contacts in a given time period. However, Marisol is making twice as many presentations as Javier.

You have the first indication that Javier is having a problem with building relationships, qualifying, or properly assessing the prospects needs and wants — the early parts of the sales process. He's making enough contacts, but he's not able to get them any further through his pipeline for some reason. Whatever it is, something is keeping Javier from making presentations.

This is where you become sales manager extraordinaire (cue the super hero music)! Now you can work with Javier on those steps of the process in order to improve his ability in the presentation stage of the sales process.

Your salespeople input the data — probably into your CRM (which I talk about later in the chapter) — and you use that data to look at what they're doing and how you can help each of them. Without this data, you're really only guessing why Javier's sales aren't up to par with Marisol's.

Javier probably doesn't even know he has an issue — that's the great thing about KPIs. Javier may be thinking he's rocking and rolling, yet when you compare his numbers against the team's average or another salesperson, you, and more importantly he, can see his performance is not up to standard.

Without these key performance indicators at certain stations along the sales process, you'd have no idea where to help Javier and he wouldn't know he has an issue in the first place.

What would've probably happened without KPIs was Javier would've had every excuse under the sun as to why Marisol was outselling him — the weather, the government, he's been sick; she's funnier, smarter, whatever. I've heard them all.

Until you know where the injury is, you can't put a bandage on it!

Tracking sales

Everybody knows his sales numbers, doesn't he? In fact, many organizations only track this KPI. Their attitude to so forget all that other stuff, it doesn't mean anything — sales are all that matter. To which I say, "Really?"

Going back to the example of Marisol and Javier, both are making the same (or similar) number of contacts, taking those contacts through the steps to the sale, and making the same number of presentations. However, Marisol is selling 25 units a month and Javier is only selling 15. Under the old "sales are all that matter" banner, the sales manager would just chew Javier out and tell him to get out and see more people, work harder, or put in more hours.

But, is that really the problem? Does Javier really need to be calling on more people and making more presentations? Hardly. In fact, the more he makes, the more likely he is to burn up a prospect someone in your organization could've sold.

Just because someone isn't putting sales on the board, doesn't mean he isn't working. Assuming he is can be fatal.

Unless you're taking the correct KPIs, you have no idea where Javier is struggling. It's like being lost. You're on the wrong road and being told to drive faster. Well, you're just going to get to the wrong place sooner! It's not about how fast you drive or about how hard Javier works, the process is broken and you need the relevant information on how to help him fix it.

You are the sales manager, and your job is to manage this process. Focus on where Javier is missing the boat and help him correct it. Again, unless you have the data and use it, you're spinning your wheels. What should you do with Javier in this particular case? Well, you know he's getting to make presentations. But, are his presentations strong? Do they highlight the benefits instead of the features? Is he presenting your products and services enthusiastically? You only know this by observing him in action. (I talk about presentation skills in Chapter 7.)

If his presentation skills aren't the problem, you need to consider what else could it be. Perhaps he's not comfortable or strong enough with asking for the sale? Maybe he's struggling to overcome objections, or perhaps he's rushing that process and making the buyer uncomfortable. Whatever it is, you must find it and work with him.

None of those things gets better by having Javier make more calls.

Just because a salesperson is falling short of his goals, it doesn't mean he isn't working. Although lack of effort could certainly be the cause of the problem, that issue will show up in the number of new contacts. But until you start planting these measuring sticks along the way, you'll never know for sure.

Picture a horse race. All the horses are loaded into the gate and the bell rings and the gates open. Every horse is even at that point. A couple of horses jump out to the lead and you hear their time called out at the quarter-pole (a quarter of a mile into the race). These early leaders lead for a while until another horse starts moving up on the outside to run with the leaders at the half-mile pole. And out of nowhere comes a horse who has been sitting back waiting his turn and letting every other horse get burned out while he cruises to the win at the finish line. Those quarter-poles and half-mile poles are KPIs!

Everyone on your team starts side-by-side in that gate. Some may be good starters and don't have a finishing kick, while others may be very methodical and take their time and finish ahead of everyone else.

Managing your sales team is a lot like watching a horse race. But, with your KPIs, you know who your starters and finishers are and how to work with all of them to ultimately improve each of their performances.

Looking at other Measurable Matrices

The sales process has a lot of moving parts and they all must work in concert with each other. It's like dialing a phone number — if you get one digit out of place or don't use it, you're never going to get connected.

Every one of the KPIs I talk about is designed to give you a set of guardrails along the track of the sale so that at any point if the sale becomes derailed — if for some reason the prospect doesn't progress to the next step — you can find out why.

There are probably hundreds of things you can measure to make some sort of educated determination on how your sales team is doing. If you're not careful, though, measuring too many KPIs can become an administrative nightmare. The idea is not to create more work; it's to create good data that allows you to make the best business decision.

Don't create things to measure just to have things to measure. Make sure you're gleaning good data from them. We are all in data overload, and the last thing you need to do is to create more useless data. It's a time-waster for everyone involved. It's not about being viewed as cutting edge or super intelligent or slicker than everyone else. It's not about being impressive; it's about being efficient.

You certainly measure the big three KPIs — contacts, presentations, and sales — but now I dig a little deeper into some other things I suggest you monitor. Some of these may be critical to your business and others may be totally inconsequential. That's okay. Use what you can to build the best database you can for measuring your sales team's performance.

The whole reason you have key performance indicators is to find out where a specific team member is weak or needs work. The more good data you can gather, the easier it is to make those decisions.

Making outbound calls

If your sales team is charged with making outbound calls on prospects, you certainly need to be tracking this as one of your KPIs. It's as important as making contacts for sales teams who generate prospects from cold calls.

When you start looking at how to measure outgoing calls, I suggest the following:

- **When calls are made:** Track the time of the call and the result. You'll quickly find there are good, better, and best times to make those calls. Track everything you can and then train your people in the best practices.

- **Who calls are made to:** Not every prospect responds to phone calls the same as they do to in-person cold calls. If you see a pattern developing in a certain market area or a potential set of prospects, adjust accordingly. For example, no matter what you're selling, you're never going go get a doctor or a dentist on the phone. This could hold true for other market segments, as well. But, you won't know unless you track it.
- **What's said in the call:** I've beat my "write a sales script" drum plenty of times, but it makes so much sense here. If one person is having ten times more success making outbound calls, record what that person is saying and train the rest of your people to say the same thing — in their own words.

  Try to make the sales conversation planned, not canned. Monitor your team and make sure they don't sound like a robo-caller!

If you begin to track these three parts of outbound calls it won't take long before you start to see patterns developing. Those patterns are the KPIs you're looking for and how you can raise the bar for everyone.

Of course, in certain scenarios outbound calling conflicts with the marketing department process, but if it's applicable for your sales process spend some time to track, check, and improve the system.

Circling through sales cycle time

Sales cycle time is simply establishing a timeline to go along with your sales cycle, a process I cover in Chapter 7. Your cycle time could be days, weeks, or months. The point isn't how long your cycle time is, the point is to assign a time value to each step and to communicate that to your sales team.

No matter how long you think your sales cycle should take, reality is sometimes drastically different.

Using sales cycle time as a key performance indicator gives you some really good feedback to work with. It can answer the following questions:

- **How long does the average sale take?** Until you gather this data from everyone on your team, you're really just guessing. Track the progress from the time the lead goes into the system until that contact comes out as a customer and determine what your average time is currently.
- **Is someone way ahead of the average?** If so, what's that salesperson doing?

  Having the quickest sales cycle time isn't always a good thing. If one of your salespeople is rushing the process or skipping steps, he may be shortening the cycle only to pay for it later with unhappy customers, returns, cancellations, or other issues.

However, if a team member is onto some positive, timesaving step, capture it so it can be replicated.

- **Who's slower than average?** Identify anyone in your sales force whose average sales cycle is noticeably longer than the others. This may indicate several issues: are they working too many prospects? If so, they could be taking too long to get back to people they are already working with which could ultimately cost them sales.

In your role as sales manager, you're always searching for acceptable (notice that word) ways to shorten the sales cycle. Don't do it at the expense of customer service or proper sales techniques, but look to see whether there's something to be done. Is the credit department holding up the sale because it takes them longer than it should to approve terms for a new account? Is the transportation department taking too long to give your salesperson information on routing, delivery, or other aspects needed?

When you know what your average sales cycle time is, immediately go to work to see how much of that time is spent waiting on other departments. Many times you can change the process and have two processes working at once. For example, instead of waiting for credit to be approved to set up the account with transportation, perhaps you can get a preliminary delivery schedule based on credit being approved.

You're always looking to become more efficient. And when your KPIs are all based on time, you may uncover some tremendous opportunities for improvement when you map the entire process out from start to finish. Don't leave anything out.

Weighing average sales volume

If every member of your team is selling virtually the same thing to the same type of prospect, there shouldn't be a large swing in *average sales volume.*

In determining your average sales volume, throw out any that would alter your numbers. For example, if one salesperson has a large corporate account or some other factor skews your numbers, throw it out before you determine your average.

You can gather other KPIs from your CRM system, but average sales volume comes straight off your desk. You look at how many sales each team member made and the total sales dollars.

If two salespeople have larger than normal differences, look at potential causes for these deviations from the norm. Ask why one is selling higher-ticket items than the other? Is it the type prospect they're calling on? Is it the market they work? What is it?

Many times you find some salespeople who are much more comfortable selling the lower-dollar items than asking the customer to purchase the more expensive version or brands of what you sell.

Another possible scenario is that people tend to sell what they're familiar with. If they know and understand the lower-dollar item more than the higher priced one, that's the one they're more apt to sell.

Whatever the case, average sales volume is good, useful information for you to use to better train, educate, and manage your sales team. Hey, you're called the sales manager for a reason!

Keep an eye out for a salesperson who's quick to give discounts or lower prices in order to close a sale. If his average sales volume is lower than normal, it's one of the first things you should investigate. Perhaps you need to work with him on his negotiating skills. His habit could be costing both of you money!

Checking closing percentage

Some may wonder why closing percentage isn't part of the big three KPIs mentioned in the first section. In another time and place, I would be one of them. But, I've learned that closing percentage is just another KPI.

The best way to figure closing percentage is to take the number of sales and divide it by the number of presentations.

Just like every other KPI, closing percentage is designed to provide you with some insight on where your salesperson is either strong or someplace he needs help.

Don't get too caught up in what someone's closing percentage (also referred to as *closing ratio*) is or isn't. I discuss how to manage it, but don't give it more weight than others just because of its name. If your job is to increase sales, you certainly have to monitor this, but no more than any of the other KPIs discussed in this chapter.

A high closing percentage doesn't necessarily equal success. If a salesperson is making just two presentations a month and closing one, he has a 50 percent closing percentage, which is outstanding! If that were the only thing he was judged on, he'd be considered a superstar. Yet, he made only one sale that month. Is that all you want?

Everyone wants to be a better closer, but that only matters if you get the prospect to that point in the process.

If one salesperson, call him Sean, is making twice as many presentations as Bridget, but closing only half as much, Sean has a noticeable issues in asking for the sale and overcoming objections.

Have your sales team tell you what they feel is a good closing percentage. Find out what they think they should be closing. Is it one out of three? One out of ten? Whatever it is, compare what they tell you to the actual numbers. The results could be surprising.

Unless they track the numbers themselves, most salespeople think their closing percentage is higher than it actually is. They tend to discount certain presentations or throw out certain data that doesn't favor them. Don't let this happen.

A professional salesperson will never become truly the best he can be until he can look in the mirror and know he did not do his job if the prospect doesn't buy after a presentation.

Now, let me back up that bold statement. If I do my job at every step along the way — build a relationship and good rapport, qualify the prospect, ask good questions, uncover the customer's needs, find a way to solve his problem, make a great presentation, overcome any objections, and so on — If I do everything and the customer doesn't buy, it's my fault, all the way.

Before you shout, "What if they can't afford it?" If that's the case, then I didn't really do a very good job of qualifying, did I? I should've found out there was going to be a money problem long before I ever got that deep into the sales process.

Don't let your sales team play the blame game every time they don't close a sale.

Using CRM Software

Not too many years ago, good customer relationship management (CRM) systems were priced out of range of many small-to-medium size companies. Unfortunately, the ones that were affordable left a lot to be desired. To this day, some people view CRM systems in a less-than-favorable light. If you fall into that camp, it's time to give them another chance. In fact, you have to. Business today is moving at such a pace that you must have a centralized system of some sort to keep up with everyone's leads, contacts, prospects, customers, and data. A filing cabinet and your memory bank won't cut it anymore.

Another problem is that the term CRM was thrown around as a buzzword so much a few years ago that some people totally ignored what it was originally designed to do: help you manage your relationship with your customer.

That function has been expanded now to include leads, prospects, and other data, and the purpose of a CRM system is simply to help you better take care of your customers by centralizing the data associated with all of them.

I'm not a fan of any one particular system, although several have distinguished themselves and become industry leaders. I strongly recommend that if you don't have a CRM system yet, don't go for the cheapest one. This is definitely an area where you get what you pay for.

As with anything you bring to your sales team, they must embrace it. Take time to make sure they're properly trained on how to enter data and how to get the data they need in order to best service their customers. Have you ever heard, "garbage in, garbage out"? Well, it's certainly true with CRM systems.

As the sales manager, you're responsible for the accuracy of the data in your CRM. If you suspect someone is corrupting your data by falsifying reports, address the problem immediately. Perhaps the easiest way to ensure accurate data is to have a sales assistant or administrator input the data or at least check behind the salesperson. Have a policy in place to cover issues regarding falsifying data or abusing the system. Periodically do a random check of each salesperson's contacts, presentations, and other data he puts into the system.

Perhaps the biggest hurdle is getting some of your senior representatives to embrace the technology. Yes, I know they've done just fine all these years without something like this — I've heard all that before. But, you're going to have to drag them kicking and screaming into the new millennium. The train is leaving the station and they have to get on board!

Managing the data

If you're new to your position or just implementing a CRM system, keep in mind one thing: Just because it will produce a report doesn't mean you need that report.

If you're not careful, you can spend your entire day under a mound of reports and by the time you finish reading them, the next day's are ready to print.

I've heard data like this called "perfectly accurate, perfectly useless." Think about that. The data is accurate, but has no value to you or, even worse, it takes you away from things you should be doing.

Don't get caught in the "perfectly accurate, perfectly useless" trap. Every report or piece of data extracted from your CRM should be held to that lens to make sure it has value to you. Make a list of what you want out of the system first rather than seeing what all is in the system you can get out. After you have the information from your initial list, then go back and see if there's anything you really need — yes, *need,* not want — that the system can produce.

So, what is it you want from this thing we call CRM? How about customer profitability analysis, including:

- Item profitability analysis
- Individual salesperson sales data
- Individual salesperson profitability data
- Customer history
- Customer buying habits
- Seasonal changes in business
- Salesperson's sales process activity

This is a good place to start. If you can get that data out on a consistent basis and use it to make good decisions, you'll be ahead of most people.

If you get your salespeople and customer service representatives to input all this data and then select these reports to give you feedback, be prepared to act on it. This system is not designed just to give you something to read each morning; it's created to give you actionable data that allows you to make good business decisions.

Each lead entered into the system should be classified and labeled or tagged. My preferences are:

- **Hot:** Should close in a relatively short period of time. This prospect is ready to buy.
- **Warm:** A great prospect, but a little work has to be done. This lead still has the ability to become a customer quickly.
- **Lukewarm:** This one could go either way, but it is worth pursuing and putting in the effort. It's going to take some time, but still a potential future customer.
- **Cool:** Cool leads aren't going to be closed in the near future. It's worth staying in touch and working with this prospect, but they are not at the top of the list.

- **Cold:** This prospect may have just signed a two-year contract with a competitor or something similar. They're worth keeping in your system, but there's really nothing you can do for them at this time.
- **Dead:** This one wouldn't buy from you if you were the last person on Earth. Okay, maybe that's an exaggeration, but you get the idea. These are leads being serviced by their brother-in-law or in similar situations that make your selling to them virtually impossible.

If you aren't prepared to take action on what you find, don't waste the time or money to install the system in the first place.

CRM is a tool, not a salesperson

The biggest mistake you with a CRM system is not in not knowing what it is, it's in not knowing what it is not. No CRM system is the salesperson. It's simply another tool in the toolbox to help everyone take better care of his customers.

The depth of the knowledge or information in a CRM system is directly related to how much you give it.

But, don't expect it to replace your salesperson at any point in the process. I realize there are some very advanced systems on the market and all their capabilities of auto responders and email automation, but none of those things happen in a vacuum. Your salesperson should either be involved or at least be aware.

If you employ a system that automates some email responses, always have it copy the correct salesperson so the salesperson knows what his customers are being told. If the customer were to call, the salesperson should immediately know what that customer is referring to. This is where the system really shines — when the customer thinks, "Wow! These people have really got it together!"

If a customer calls and the salesperson wasn't copied about the online interaction, the conversation goes something like this:

> **Customer:** "I really appreciate you following up and I'd like to ask you about something in your email."
>
> **Salesperson:** "What email?"
>
> **Customer:** "Uh, the one *you* sent me."
>
> **Salesperson:** "Oh, hang on. Our system does that automatically."

Don't laugh. I've seen it happen.

Now in one instance you look like a well-run company, concerned with your customers and looking out for their best interests. In the other situation? Well, you kind of look like a dummy (pardon the pun).

Use your system to support your sales team, not replace them. The more they learn about it, what it will do, and how to use it, the better experience your customers will have with it, too.

You installed (and paid good money) for this system in order to have a better understanding of your customers and their business, the products and services each customer is purchasing, and the profitability of customers and individual products or services. Don't lose sight of that.

Successfully implementing or using a CRM system to its fullest potential requires you not only know what it is, but what it isn't. A CRM system has never sold a single item or closed a single deal — don't let anyone tell you otherwise. Your CRM system is there simply to give you data to allow your salespeople to close more sales and keep their current customers happier — nothing more, nothing less.

Reviewing each salesperson's pipeline

If you could have all your salespeople place their working deals on your desk, would you? It would allow you to look through a massive stack of manila folders to see where each salesperson is with each prospect: what's been done, when it was done, and where the deal is going next. Would you want to see all this? Perhaps.

Instead of doing that, perhaps the most effective and valuable data a CRM provides is for you to be able to see each salesperson's pipeline. You can view the progress (or lack of progress) on each of the deals he's working at a glance.

In order for you to make good decisions, your sales team needs to enter their leads, tag them as Hot, Warm, or whatever (see "Managing the data" earlier in this chapter), and set a potential sales value for the deal. The deal value is flexible and can and should change as the salesperson learns more about the prospect and his actual situation.

In Figure 11-2, notice that the sales process looks just like a pipeline — what goes in one end should come out the other. The more time you spend at the start of the process, the easier it is to have results (sales) produced at the end.

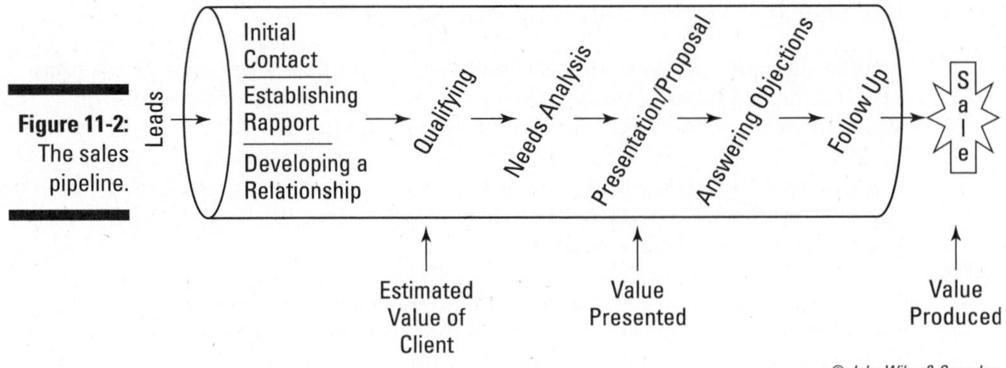

Figure 11-2: The sales pipeline.

By having access to pipeline reports, you can sit at your desk and see where each salesperson is with each deal.

Every point in the sales process is like playing a game of catch: Either you (or your salesperson) have the ball or the prospect does. Pipeline reports let you see whose turn is it to throw it back and move the sale to the next step. Are you waiting for the prospect to provide you with materials or information in order to assemble the final presentation? Is the salesperson working on the presentation? What's the anticipated value of the ultimate sale?

Again, this is where being a manager comes into play. You can help each person manage this process by having good, accurate information available at every step.

The accuracy of the data is only as good as what's put into the system. If your salesperson enters the lead and then never updates the status, there's really no reason to use the system at all.

Let your team know you need them to enter data not just so you can see how many deals they have in their pipelines, but so that you know exactly where each deal stands and see whether there's something you can do to help move it forward. After all, that's what you're there for: to help them grow their business!

Once you begin to review the status of these deals, your sales team will become much more responsive — knowing you're keeping up with how their progress. They know that if they enter a Hot lead and fail to move it to the next step, you're going to be asking questions.

Use your pipeline reports to compare your salespeople's progress through each step, their sales cycle times, and the size of the deals they work. Let CRM software make your job easier!

Setting your system to trigger notifications

Most, if not all CRM systems allow you to set triggers to email you when a certain activity takes place. For example, if Marisol enters a lead for ABC Company and tags it as *Hot,* you can have the system send you an email in a few days to follow up with Marisol about ABC Company.

If you have more than one salesperson, you cannot possibly remember everything each of them has working. These triggers allow you to stay on top of the business by letting the technology do all the heavy lifting.

By the same token, if a lead is marked *Cold,* perhaps you set a trigger for 90 days out so that you can email Marisol and call the prospect yourself to offer new information, the latest product pricing, or something else to possibly unstick the lead.

Looking at the Ultimate Performance Indicator

In earlier sections I talk about the big three KPIs — contacts, presentations and sales. Then I addressed the importance of outbound calls, sales cycle time, average sales volume, and closing percentage. And, you may have a laundry list of other key performance indicators you choose to track in your business.

Now it's time to talk about the ultimate performance indicator. This one is above all others — in fact, without this none of the others matter. What is it? Profits.

The ultimate measure of an individual salesperson, a territory, region, or your entire department is whether you're generating enough profit to cover the company's expenses. If you're not, the number of contacts and the average sales volume really don't matter much, do they?

If you're not comfortable reading monthly operating statements, take some time to learn today! It boils down to this: Are you able to manage your department to generate the required profit dollars without exceeding the expenses allowed?

Depending on your industry, your salespeople may have no pricing flexibility or all the room in the world. It simply depends on how your system runs. Whatever it is, if a salesperson has to do anything at all below your agreed-upon lowest price, it should be approved by you or someone in management.

The numbers don't lie

When you start judging your salespeople by the profits they generate, there's no room to be subjective. It's not a situation of whether they're working hard, working enough prospects, or any other criteria. The bottom lines is whether they're paying for themselves and generating enough profit dollars to cover the costs to employ them.

You must look at gross profit dollars, not percentage. It doesn't really matter if a salesperson is making a 50 percent profit if that only amounts to three dollars. You can't put percentages in the bank, only dollars.

The numbers don't lie. Your monthly statements are the ultimate test for a salesperson's value — and once you look at them in this manner, you may find yourself a bit surprised.

The top salesperson isn't always the top salesperson

I inherited a sales team several years ago in which the top salesperson was well ahead of everyone else in terms of sales volume. If the rest of the team was doing X, he was doing that plus 50 percent. For some reason, his sales percentage stood head-and-shoulders above the rest of the five-person team.

What was it that made him so much better than everyone else, I wondered? He was clearly doing something they weren't, and I wanted to find out what it was . . . and quickly!

The sales team's monthly sales looked something like this:

- Salesperson A: $150,000
- Salesperson B: $100,000
- Salesperson C: $100,000
- Salesperson D: $95,000
- Salesperson E: $75,000

That's quite a disparity from top to bottom! But, things aren't always as they seem.

As I began to dig into the sales dollars and gross profit produced by those sales, it became painfully obvious why the so-called superstar was outselling everyone else! He wasn't selling, he was simply cutting prices in order to move product. His sales dollars were amazing, but his gross-profit dollars were dismal. If judged only by the sales dollars he generated, he looked like the greatest thing since sliced bread, but of the five salespeople, his gross-profit dollars were fourth out of the five! *Fourth!*

Interestingly, the salesperson producing the most gross profit dollars — not percentage but dollars — was Salesperson D! With a third less sales, this representative was putting more money in the bank for the company each month. Yet, he wasn't recognized in any way as being anything special. In fact, I was told he was on the verge of getting fired if he didn't get his sales up prior to my arrival!

Who's really producing the profit for the company? It's not always the person selling the most — don't get blinded by flashy sales numbers or new accounts. Look at how much they generate in profit dollars.

Another thing to watch for is churn and burn. Is a salesperson generating new business but losing his current clientele? If so, he's costing you money! When you figure all the costs of bringing a new account into your company, you need to make sure a new customer remains a customer and isn't just a one-off. The only business that pays is the business that stays!

Not all sales are good sales

When you begin to look at each salesperson, each customer, and each product or service through the profitability lens, you know that not all sales are good sales and not all customers are good customers.

There are times when you have to make the decision to fire a customer if he isn't profitable for your company. There are times when your bottom line would improve if you weren't doing business with a certain customer or if you choose to not make a certain sale.

The problem arises from the fact that since birth we're taught to sell, sell, sell, sell. We're not very good at turning a customer loose. But, sometimes that's the best thing.

I know it sounds strange and it's even stranger when you have to make that call, but if you stay in sales management long enough, you will.

Sales is the only department in the company that contributes to profitability — everything else is an expense. By the same token, every customer you have and every product or service you distribute has to be profitable.

Granted there are situations where certain customers are sold at a lower than desirable margin in order to increase your buying power — therefore, making every other customer more profitable, but that's not what I'm talking about here.

I'm talking about the customers you do business with day after day. Are they pulling their weight? Are they covering the expenses it takes to service them?

Have a profitability worksheet designed to run some numbers on potential new customers prior to ever bringing them onboard or making a sale. Calculate what it will cost to service them. Are there special requirements from other departments that will increase the expense of doing business with the account?

This pre-sale evaluation can save you a lot of time and money and allow you to make more sound financial decisions on pricing for new customers, especially if you have a prospect asking for price concession.

Regularly review items and/or services you provide. Are they profitable? Are they paying for themselves? Just because you can, doesn't mean you should.

Chapter 12

Assessing Performance: Keeping Score and Celebrating Wins

In This Chapter

- Looking at sales forecasts, budgets, and goals
- Creating an environment of effective competition
- Building and maintaining confidence through praise

As a sales manager, you have to decide how you're going to keep score — the methods you'll use to determine how your team is performing, — and find creative ways to push them to achieve even more.

In this chapter I jump into sales forecasting, budgeting, creating commission programs, and more. You may be more comfortable out in the field or dealing with the sales aspect of your job than with assessing your sales team. However, as sales manager, you have to take care of this side of the business, as well.

If you're like most sales managers, dealing with the numbers probably isn't the part that comes naturally to you, but it's a part you must embrace, take seriously, and perform to the best of your ability. If you're not good at the detail work (hey, I'm as bad as anyone), this is one area you're going to have to bite the bullet and push through.

You'll never look at the weatherperson on television the same again after working on your first sales forecast. You'll never look at revenue and expenses the same after your first budget, and you don't even want me to tell you what happens if you foul up a commission program. Just look up "drawn and quartered" on the Internet.

Crunching the numbers may be a necessary evil, but it is necessary. In addition to establishing benchmarks, you must also use programs wisely to create enthusiasm, reward the right behavior, and incentivize your team accordingly.

This chapter delves into the world of sales contests, employee recognition, celebrating the wins, and lamenting the losses. It's all a part of the job — and there is a way to make it fun and interesting to everyone involved.

Have at least a working knowledge of basic accounting principles and know how to read an income statement and a balance sheet. If you need a basic course, talk to your employer about helping you gain some knowledge in this critical area.

Talking about the Money: Sales Forecasts, Budgets, and Goals

Interestingly, money is a subject many people want to talk about but few are comfortable talking about. As a manager you're the person who creates forecasts, sets budgets and goals (and there is a difference between the two), builds commission programs, and otherwise manages how your team is compensated. That's a lot of responsibility.

No matter what program you create or adjust, always test it against some real numbers before rolling it out to your sales team or putting it into effect. Nothing looks worse or costs you credibility quicker than announcing a big program only to have to backtrack because you didn't go through all the possible scenarios.

So what's the difference between a sales forecast, a sales budget, and a sales goal? The forecast should be as accurate as you can possibly be. The budget should set a target a bit lower than you anticipate (you want to exceed budget, not be chasing it all year), and a sales goal should aim high and make your team stretch.

In some larger organizations you may be required to meet with upper management to flesh out the sales budget and forecasts. If so, participate — get your opinions and feelings in because you're the person who's going to have to stand up each month and each quarter and answer for the performance against the budget or forecast.

In other words, the forecast is what you feel is going to happen, the budget is what you would accept happening, and the goal is what you hope happens.

Figure 12-1 is a good representation of how goals compare to budget and forecasts.

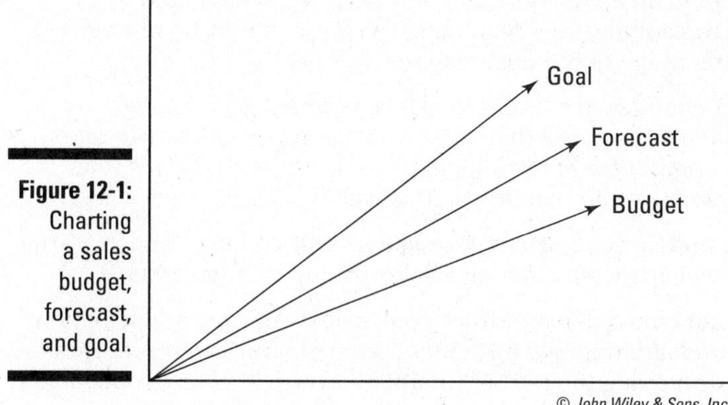

Figure 12-1: Charting a sales budget, forecast, and goal.

You can tweak many processes with salespeople, but tread very lightly when working with their money. One small misstep can cost you a seasoned representative (or more) with no chance to make it up, so be very careful — check and double-check before implementing new programs.

Forecasting the future

In your position as sales manager you will be asked from time-to-time to produce a sales forecast for the coming year or financial period. Even though a forecast is all subjective, the more accurately you can predict your future sales the more valuable the information is to others making decisions within your company.

It's not a coincidence that it's referred to as forecasting because it's like predicting the weather — you rely on past history, current data, and future assumptions to arrive at your forecast figure.

Many tools can help you more accurately forecast your future sales, but a lot of forecasting comes down to knowing your company, your product, and your market. When preparing a sales forecast start by asking yourself several questions:

- **Where are we today?** What are your current sales compared to the prior year (or financial period)? You must know where you're starting in order to provide even an educated guess at where you're going.
- **What market changes are likely to affect your sales?** What outside forces could cause a sales increase or decrease based on your geographic market or the market segment you're servicing? If you sell

to homeowners in an area where 250 new homes are expected to be completed in the coming year, you need to factor that into your equation. What percentage of the business will you get?

- **What product changes are likely to affect your sales?** Is there a new model being introduced that gives you a competitive advantage? Or, perhaps a competitor is introducing a new model that gives it an advantage — you need to plan for that as well.
- **What pricing policies can affect your sales?** Will you experience a price increase that will artificially increase sales or impact purchases?
- **What personnel changes may affect your sales?** Are you adding a new territory or consolidating two into one? Is one of your top representatives retiring or moving to another position? How will your people affect your future sales?
- **What regulations affect your sales?** Are tax changes or other government regulations set to either go into effect or expire within your forecast period? Will they be positive or negative for your industry?
- **What other changes are on the horizon?** Are you going to add or lose a significant customer that will impact sales volume? What other factors — inside and outside your control — are likely to have an impact on your sales during the coming year?

Take time to consider all these factors and more. Anything that could possibly affect your sales, your sales team, your market, your company, or your product should be taken into account. It's tedious and sometimes mind-numbing work, but it has to be done — and the forecast needs to be as accurate as you can possibly get it.

Take each month separately and calculate the number of sales days within that particular month. If you know what volume you expect from your salesperson, you can then calculate average sales per day. Then simply multiply that by the number of sales days in the month. Figure 12-2 shows a sample monthly forecast for an imaginary company.

Sales Forecast

	Jan	Feb	Mar	Apr	May	Jun	Jul	Aug	Sep	Oct	Nov	Dec	Total
Jose Dominquez	$ 25,000.00	$ 25,000.00	$ 32,500.00	$ 32,500.00	$ 35,000.00	$ 40,000.00	$ 50,000.00	$ 50,000.00	$ 40,000.00	$ 35,000.00	$ 35,000.00	$ 30,000.00	$ 430,000.00
John Smith	$ 35,000.00	$ 27,500.00	$ 40,000.00	$ 40,000.00	$ 40,000.00	$ 50,000.00	$ 65,000.00	$ 70,000.00	$ 60,000.00	$ 50,000.00	$ 45,000.00	$ 45,000.00	$ 567,500.00
Makayla Washington	$ 35,000.00	$ 30,000.00	$ 35,000.00	$ 45,000.00	$ 50,000.00	$ 60,000.00	$ 70,000.00	$ 75,000.00	$ 70,000.00	$ 65,000.00	$ 65,000.00	$ 55,000.00	$ 655,000.00
Bobby Joe Thomas	$ 20,000.00	$ 17,500.00	$ 20,000.00	$ 20,000.00	$ 25,000.00	$ 25,000.00	$ 30,000.00	$ 30,000.00	$ 30,000.00	$ 27,500.00	$ 25,000.00	$ 25,000.00	$ 295,000.00
Jasmine Pinkley	$ 55,000.00	$ 50,000.00	$ 55,000.00	$ 60,000.00	$ 65,000.00	$ 75,000.00	$ 80,000.00	$ 80,000.00	$ 75,000.00	$ 75,000.00	$ 70,000.00	$ 65,000.00	$ 805,000.00
Northern Division	$170,000.00	$150,000.00	$182,500.00	$197,500.00	$215,000.00	$250,000.00	$295,000.00	$305,000.00	$275,000.00	$252,500.00	$240,000.00	$220,000.00	$2,752,500.00
Ernesto Gonzalez	$ 50,000.00	$ 40,000.00	$ 40,000.00	$ 45,000.00	$ 55,000.00	$ 60,000.00	$ 60,000.00	$ 65,000.00	$ 65,000.00	$ 55,000.00	$ 50,000.00	$ 50,000.00	$ 635,000.00
Sol Russo	$ 65,000.00	$ 60,000.00	$ 67,500.00	$ 70,000.00	$ 72,500.00	$ 75,000.00	$ 80,000.00	$ 80,000.00	$ 70,000.00	$ 70,000.00	$ 65,000.00	$ 65,000.00	$ 840,000.00
Liam Jacobsen	$ 75,000.00	$ 70,000.00	$ 75,000.00	$ 85,000.00	$ 85,000.00	$ 90,000.00	$ 90,000.00	$100,000.00	$ 95,000.00	$ 90,000.00	$ 87,500.00	$ 85,000.00	$1,027,500.00
Anna McKinney	$ 45,000.00	$ 40,000.00	$ 50,000.00	$ 55,000.00	$ 65,000.00	$ 75,000.00	$ 75,000.00	$ 80,000.00	$ 75,000.00	$ 70,000.00	$ 60,000.00	$ 55,000.00	$ 745,000.00
Southern Division	$235,000.00	$210,000.00	$232,500.00	$255,000.00	$277,500.00	$300,000.00	$305,000.00	$325,000.00	$305,000.00	$285,000.00	$262,500.00	$255,000.00	$3,247,500.00
Company Total	$405,000.00	$360,000.00	$415,000.00	$452,500.00	$492,500.00	$550,000.00	$600,000.00	$630,000.00	$580,000.00	$537,500.00	$502,500.00	$475,000.00	$6,000,000.00

Figure 12-2: A sample monthly sales forecast.

You need to consider all these things and more when creating a professional sales forecast. Begin with each salesperson's sales each month and put the time and energy into accurately forecasting their production.

If your business is seasonal, you must factor that in, as well.

Building your budget

Just as you must live on a budget in your personal life, your business requires the same attention. At home you deal with income and outgo, while at work you deal with revenue and expenses.

As the leader of the sales department, it's your job to not only create the revenue for the entire company but also to manage the expenses for your department.

When creating your sales budget, underestimate your sales and overestimate your expenses. Not by a large margin, but a realistic amount that allows you to come in under budget on the expense side and exceed your budgeted sales amount.

Be prepared to put your negotiating hat on during the budgeting process. Nobody is going to just accept your numbers at face value. Be ready to support your data and justify your projections.

The rest of the company's department heads probably use your sales number to budget their expenses. So, you have to be within reason but you don't want to get this confused with your sales goal.

The budgeting process is one that takes time, focus, and energy. Don't rush through it just to provide a number. Analyze the data available and just as you do with your sales forecast, break everything down on a monthly basis.

Unlike in forecasting, when working on a budgeting process you need to address the expenses of the sales department. From sales payroll to vehicle expenses and everything in between, you need to establish the amount of money allotted monthly to each.

Budgeting is an area where you want to set your number and then give yourself a little room for unexpected changes. Don't create a budget that simply looks great on paper but is an unrealistic target you'll be falling short of every month. Again, take into account seasonality, new products, new territories, the addition of new salespeople, and other issues you anticipate in the coming year.

If you underestimate sales and overestimate expenses, you'll be surprised at how often you need that little buffer you provided.

If your division managers, regional managers, or others are responsible for their own group of salespeople, involve them in the process of creating the budget. They not only learn how the process works, they'll be more involved in the monthly examination of the numbers and take ownership of the budget as well.

When dealing with your expenses, figure them as a percentage of sales. For example, if you budget sales for the month at $500,000 and your automobile expense at $5,000, your vehicle expense is effectively 1 percent of your sales. Therefore, the next month if you budget sales at $750,000, budget your automobile expense at $7,500 (1%).

By calculating expenses as a percentage of sales, you never budget for a free sale. No sale is free. Every sale carries a cost all the way through your system and setting it up this way from the start is the best way to ensure you account for it correctly. Are there some economies of scale? Sure, the more you sell the lower the cost per sale, but you never get to a free sale.

Every other department wants you to set your sales budget as high as possible because the others set their expenses as a percentage of sales. Hold your ground. They won't be the ones who have to suffer the consequences every month when you fall short of budget. You — and only you — should set the budgeted sales dollars.

Goal setting for success

Now it's time to dig in and really take a look at how to establish your sales goals. Now's the time when you shoot for the moon, go for the gusto, and all those other tired old clichés.

As a manager, require each of your salespeople to turn in her sales goals for the coming year. I am a firm believer in having those goals in writing. They're much more powerful and everyone knows where she stands at all times if goals are written down. You can also encourage each member of your team to write down her own personal goals.

You're probably familiar with the S.M.A.R.T. acronym for goals. There are a few different versions, but the one I subscribe to is:

- **Specific:** Be as specific as possible. What do you want to do and when do you want to do it by?
- **Measurable:** Make your goal something you can actually measure your progress on. "I want to get better" doesn't give you a very good measuring stick. "I want to increase my sales by 20 percent" is measureable.

- **Attainable:** Simply, make your goal something you can accomplish. A vacation home on the moon isn't achievable; a vacation home in Maui may be.
- **Realistic:** Make sure you can achieve your goal in the time you're allowing yourself. You can lose 50 pounds — that's attainable — but realistically you can't do it in two weeks.
- **Time-bound:** Set a deadline for when you want to achieve your goal. Give yourself a due date.

As your team works through its goals, make sure each goal meets the S.M.A.R.T. criteria. This makes you think about each goal in detail and drill down to the core of what you're truly trying to attain. For example, someone can write "I want to increase my sales." That's way too vague. Have her set a specific number. Something like, "I want to increase my sales by $100,000."

Now back into it. Have her figure out how many contacts she has to make to generate the required number of sales at the required closing percentage to yield those results.

I am continuously amazed at the number of salespeople I meet and work with who don't have their goals committed to writing. And, I honestly don't know why. It's not like it's hard work or difficult to do. You simply have to take time to do it.

If your people don't have their goals in writing, do yourself a favor: Ask them to try it. Humor you. Write down four or five short-term goals — yes, write them down and get in the habit of reading them daily.

I've heard every excuse as to why someone doesn't have time to look at or read her goals each day, and I don't buy it. Make time. It's not brain surgery — don't make it harder than it is. Don't accept excuses.

Goals are a curious thing. Those who set them, write them down, and read them regularly swear by them. Those who don't, don't think they work. Odd how that works, isn't it?

When you have each salesperson's individual goals, create a master sales goal for the organization. Run it through the same S.M.A.R.T. test you required of your team. Then review it with your group. Get their agreement and convince them to believe in the number. If you set a goal for them, they're much less likely to buy in and believe the goal is achievable than if you let them participate in the process.

Drill down to the basics. That is where you find success and where you find the achievement of your goals. Keep asking yourself, "What have I got to do to accomplish that?" and it will take you deeper and deeper toward the actual goal you need to focus on.

The best place in the world to keep your goals

If your salespeople work from their vehicles, I have the best place in the world for them to keep their goals. Yes, I think they should post them on their bathroom mirrors, but I came up with this little trick many years ago:

Have them take the goals they've written down (hint, hint) and print them on a piece of plain paper. Then fold that paper in half long way and place that paper into a clear plastic sleeve.

Then clip, tape, or otherwise affix it to the underside of the sun visor in their car. Put it on the side that's hidden when the visor is folded up.

Then every time they get in the car, have them flip that visor down and read their goals. Wow! What a concept! If they work from their automobile, they'll be reading their goals several times a day.

But, here's the great part: when they come out of one of those appointments where the prospect or customer has just beaten them to a pulp (and it happens to all of us), there's only one other time that it's better to read those goals. Only one other time they will ever get nearly the affect out of this little habit. When? How about when they've just closed the biggest deal of their year or perhaps even their career and they're literally walking on air! Then they get back to that car and flip that visor down and read those goals. Their next prospect is already sold. That prospect doesn't stand a chance.

Teach your sales team to write and think of their goals in terms of "I will" instead of "I want." It doesn't matter what you "want," it only matters what you "will" do.

When the master goal is established, post it for all to see. Then track your progress individually and as a group monthly. Keep your sales team's eyes on the prize. Even though they may get detoured, don't let them get derailed. Just because they're behind their goal in March doesn't mean they can't be crushing it by June. It's a matter of continuous focus and belief in the goal you're working toward.

Have your team create their own (they take ownership) individual goals — add those all together for a team goal and test it against the S.M.A.R.T. acronym and then post it loud and proud.

For example, if you have five team members and each of their individual goals totals $200,000 in sales — getting to $200,000 is now your team goal. It has to pass the same test their individual goals do, but now they're part of something larger.

Just as in sports, it's great to win an individual award, but the championship is what everyone is playing for.

Post the team goal in a place they can't help but see it. When you have your entire team pulling in the same direction, the energy created is hard to deny.

Avoiding Complacency: Competition Is Good!

Complacency is the leading killer among sales teams; it steals enthusiasm, crushes motivation and otherwise saps the energy of your salespeople. Avoid it at all costs. Instead, create a little friendly competition and have your sales team stretch.

The best way to avoid complacency is to continually inspire your people and give them incentive to progress, grow, and innovate. Never let them get stale.

Most salespeople are already competitive — it's one of the most common traits among the truly great sales leaders — so it doesn't take much to stoke that fire. If you dangle the carrot, the good ones respond very quickly. They want to win. They need to win. It's in their blood.

The great thing is competitiveness is contagious. If you can light that spark in a few of your people, most of the others usually catch on. Nobody wants to lose — and if they do, they probably aren't going to be around for the next sales contest.

I've had some people tell me they didn't want their people competing against each other. Forget that! You most definitely want them competing, but as much as they are on different sides, they're on these same team.

Ultimately, your sales department must operate as one. But, within that department very few things drive sales better than a good, competitive team with each member having a burning desire to succeed. Be careful not to let the competition sabotage the overall good of the team.

Show them the numbers

One of the great debates among sales managers and leaders of sales teams is how much information to share with the people on the front line. The theory is that if they knew what gross profit actually was, they'd give it all away in price concessions if they have some influence over price. I'm not sure I buy that.

Personally, I've always liked to share as much information as possible with my sales team. I want them to know where they stand and where the company stands. I've just never liked the cloak of secrecy surrounding profitability — it just never made sense to me.

If professional salespeople are properly trained and compensated based on gross profit, they have a vested interest in not cutting prices. If you train them to build value, hold their ground, and actually believe their product or service is worth what you're asking for it, amazing things will happen.

If you don't show them the numbers, I can almost guarantee you the numbers your salespeople make up in their mind will be far worse than what you're trying to keep them from seeing. If you're not disclosing profitability because you're making 20 percent gross profit, they think you're making 50 percent.

In my years as a sales manager and as VP of sales, my mentor used to share the numbers with everyone — good, bad, or indifferent. When asked why he said, "Well, I don't want to be the only one worried about them."

You know salespeople like to win. If you show them what the score is, they will help you win, but if you keep that information concealed they really have no way of knowing how well they're doing other than what you tell them. When salespeople have some skin the game, their attitude about price cuts changes dramatically.

I once heard it described as bowling behind a curtain. Think about that for a moment: you've got a curtain in front of some bowling pins and you ask your sales team to roll the ball down the alley. Now, they can't see the results, but they hear some pins fall. You look back behind the curtain and say, "Not bad, but you can do better! You can do better. C'mon! Go get 'em!"

"Uh . . .what do I do?"

"Move a little to the right."

As silly as that sounds, that's exactly how many sales teams are managed. I've trained sales teams who had to go to their manager to get every price and had no latitude to do anything with a client. In my opinion, that's not managing, that's micromanaging.

I've seen some organizations where the sales team really never knew how well they were doing. They got the old, "Not bad, but you can do better!"

This kind of game gets old very quickly to professional salespeople. They not only want to know how they are performing, but they need to know!

Share the good and the bad. When you do, take the time to explain the difference between gross profit and net profit and let them know just because you made 20 percent on the sale doesn't mean the company is taking that to the bottom line.

It's not what you make; it's what you keep

For almost 16 years I was in an industry that worked on extremely thin margins, and we shared the financial information with the entire staff. Additionally, we shared each salesperson's gross and net profit with them. There were no secrets. Everyone knew where they stood and the management team knew where the company stood.

While we were doing hundreds of millions of dollars in sales volume, we were netting less than one percent on the bottom line. More than once, I used a dollar's worth of change to show the sales team or new salespeople how we actually had less than a penny left over out of every sale.

I started with the dollar then took away 93 cents for the cost of goods, then added in the cost of utilities, transportation, payroll, benefits, and on and on and on.

Ultimately, I would end up needing to break a penny.

It was a dramatic way to emphasize the point that every gross profit point counts but also the critical need to control expenses.

Step through a set of sample financials with them and let them guess how much the company actually nets at the end of the month. Their assumptions again will be much higher than the reality, and the truth could be eye opening and very beneficial.

Obviously, your salespeople need to know that the information you choose to share with them is confidential. If they ever betray that trust, you have to deal with it in a way you see fit, but for me it was always an offense that included termination, depending on the circumstances.

Promote sales contests

Keeping score and celebrating wins helps to keep your salespeople focused on growing their sales and gross profit.

One of my favorite ways to do that is through periodic sales contests. This is not something you can do constantly because it will lose its effectiveness, but properly planned and executed, a sales contest is a great way to keep your team engaged and focused.

I always tried to run one contest per quarter for a few weeks or even for a month. It seemed to be just often enough to keep everyone interested and not water down the real goal.

Mission possible

In the mid 1990's while I was vice president of sales for a large food distributor, within a few weeks of each other our two largest customers notified us that they'd chosen not to renew their contracts with us. They both gave us the required six months notice in the summer that they'd be leaving at the end of the year. These two customers accounted for over 40 percent of our sales volume.

After the initial panic wore off, I created a sales contest called Mission Possible.

I brought in five division sales managers and unveiled the plan. We would pull out all the stops and go after every single account we could with the goal of replacing the business by the time they left. My goal was that on January 1 of the following year our volume would be where it was in July before the two customers left.

I had a local sign company create a huge 4-x-8-foot dry erase board, complete with Mission Possible on it and all five divisions. We tracked every single new account and had goals for each salesperson within each division. It was all hands on deck.

Amazingly, with the help of a lot of great people, tremendous division sales managers, and a committed team backing the sales department, we did it. When January 1 rolled around, we had not only replaced the volume, but we'd won it with more profitable business and diversified away from our dependence on two large clients.

So, how did we do it? I believe it came down to having the right people, but also in sharing the information with them, having a place where they could keep score, and sharing the information with everyone.

Everyone on the sales team knew what her individual mission was — it became a rallying cry. I'm not sure I've ever been prouder of a group of people in my life. It was an amazing sense of accomplishment and proved to everyone that we could do it.

The best part? The growth didn't stop on January 1 — we kept growing . . . and growing . . . and growing. And, what could have been a devastating blow to our company turned out to be our greatest blessing simply because we set a goal, tracked it, and got everyone to buy in.

It's not a bad idea to plan an annual calendar in advance, but you should also be prepared to put a program in place at a moment's notice if needed.

Creating the contest is the easy part — getting your team to buy in is another story. Let them be a part of the process. Find out what they want out of it and make sure you are all working for the same goal. The results could be surprising.

If you work with and represent manufacturers, get them involved in your contest. They sometimes have money budgeted for SPIF (Special Performance Incentive Fund) programs to drive the sale of their product. After all, you're selling their product — let them help you promote it.

If you manage a paint store, have the paint manufacturer help with an in-house promotion. Why do you think restaurants periodically have the wait staff strongly suggest you try a dessert — there's a good chance there's some type of bonus on the line.

Deciding whether to name a salesperson of the month

For many years, I, like a lot of people, had a salesperson of the month award. And for many of those years, it was the same people over and over and over again. No matter how I structured it, the same people rose to the top.

Although that's good on one hand, it can be bad on another. It was almost like a race; I only had one winner and a bunch of other people who felt like they lost. Even if they had a great month, they weren't able to celebrate or be acknowledged for it.

I suggest that having a salesperson of the month can be a bit detrimental to morale if you aren't careful. What's meant to be a motivating factor can be a demotivating one. One person is happy and the rest are left out.

I think there's a better way.

First let me say, I believe in recognizing performance. If you don't, you tend to keep getting less productivity and poorer performance as time goes on. But, in singling out one person you can sometimes run into problems. That one person wasn't the only one who had a great month, was she?

Instead of having an award only one person can receive, create a program that recognizes everyone who exceeds their sales or profitability goal by 10 percent. Or create a president's round table you use to recognize and reward, not just one salesperson, but anyone who qualifies for it.

Setting up a program to reward those who exceed their goal also levels the playing field for different territories or geographic inconsistencies.

Every month recognize those who achieved above and beyond what was expected of them — now you can have multiple winners.

One of the things I learned a long time ago is when you have an award like this, share it with the employee's family. Even though you may make a presentation at work, take time to mail something to her home address, whether it's a copy of the certificate, a note of congratulations, or just a thank-you card. People love to be recognized in front of spouses and children. Let the family in on it and they'll be pushing for your salesperson to continue to achieve this lofty level of success.

Even with other awards, I also recognized a Salesperson of the Year at our annual company function. But, I took everyone who qualified more than a certain number of times for the monthly award and let the sales team vote anonymously on who they wanted to represent them as Salesperson of the Year.

I went to the local company that produced class rings for high school and college students and had a ring made (women got to choose a ring or a pendant). The ring had the company logo embedded in the stone and the *Salesperson of the Year* around the setting along with the winner's name and the year.

The response was overwhelming. I probably spent less than $500 on the ring, but the reward seemed to be worth thousands. It was prestigious and not something everyone had.

Those rings were worn with pride because they not only signaled consistent achievement above their goals but the respect of their fellow salespeople, too.

When you create programs like this, you're well ahead of your competition in not only obtaining but maintaining top talent!

Make it fun!

A key ingredient in successfully implementing sales contests, programs, and promotions is to keep it fun. There's nothing in this world wrong with enjoying your job. In fact, if you're not, maybe you should do something else.

This isn't a dress rehearsal. This is the only life you're going to get so you might as well enjoy it.

As a manager, you set the tone for your people. If you have a good time, they'll have a good time and see that it's okay to be pleasant and enjoy what they do. It doesn't have to be so serious all the time. Lighten up. Relax and enjoy the job.

Build your contests and incentives around holidays or events and let your salespeople really take ownership and get into the spirit of competition. Put together sales teams of people who don't normally work together and count their total sales toward the score or contest — give them a reason to foster new and stronger relationships with each other.

When setting up contests and competitive programs always remind your department that everyone ultimately is on the same team. Create an environment where people are sincerely happy for each other's success and not trying to succeed at another's expense.

When people are having fun, I can assure you they will sell a lot more than when they are just dragging around waiting on Friday to get here.

Delivering Effective Praise

As a manager, you have to be conscious of the fact that praise is as important as criticism — sometimes more important. Too many times a manager's only feedback to employees is negative — what they did wrong. It's time to change that.

Most people want to do a good job. Call me naïve, but I believe there's something ingrained in most of the world that pulls people toward the good instead of the bad. However, the problem comes in when employees, associates, salespeople, and others don't know what constitutes a good job.

You often fail to acknowledge when people do a good job — every manager does. But, you're probably very quick to let someone know when she's doing — or is close to doing — a bad job (or underperforming). So, human nature takes over and the employee ends up doing just enough to stay above that bad-job line.

What a waste — a waste of her talent, time, energy, and ultimately your company's productivity and profits.

Just as you let people know when they're performing substandard work, tell *everyone* about doing extraordinary work. Be the bell ringer and shout it from the mountaintops. Criticize when necessary, but praise when it's deserved. You'll be amazed at the results.

Recognizing your superstars

In addition to sales contests, incentive programs, annual rewards, and other recognitions, the fact remains that you must always recognize your top performers. Whatever criteria you choose to judge them by is irrelevant; you have to let them know their efforts have not gone unnoticed.

Great salespeople have great egos and those egos have to be stroked periodically. Not daily, but regularly. I honestly believe most people want to do a good job at whatever they do, but your true superstars are performing at that level for a reason. They don't settle for less.

Regardless of whether you have a contest or incentive program running, stay in close contact with your sales leaders. As I discuss in Chapter 4, these A students thrive on your feedback.

Include the elite performers in some of your decision making — get their input and opinions and honestly listen to them. Let them be a part of the process. Sometimes that's all they need is to know you recognize their achievements.

If you have a salesperson who is consistently leading your department in every critical category, it's easy to take that person for granted. Just like a great customer, never let a great salesperson feel unappreciated or underappreciated. A regular casual lunch or just calling to ask her opinion on something can go a long way in very subtly saying, "I know you're an exceptional part of the team and I appreciate what you do."

Celebrating the wins

"The squeaky wheel gets the oil." For sales managers that old saying usually means the problems and the lost customers are where you focus your time and attention and that you miss out on the good stuff. It's an easy trap to fall into.

You need to celebrate the wins. When a salesperson lands a new account — send out a mass email, a text message, or another form of a virtual high five. Get everyone in on the action!

You want your team all cheering for each other — win as a team and lose as a team. But, spend more time celebrating the wins than lamenting the losses.

You get what you focus on. If you spend all your time looking at the negative, you'll get more negative to look at. At the same time, if you learn to take time to celebrate the wins, those wins come quicker and more often.

Winning is contagious. When you start celebrating the wins, you'll have more people winning — not just more wins. More members of your team will want to be recognized and cheered. It's a really fun cycle to be a part of and watch grow.

Everyone wants to get on the celebration train. No one wants to be left out. If you're sending out a mass text congratulating Marita, don't you think Javier's ego wants to play, too? Absolutely! People love to be a part of a winning team. There's a camaraderie there unlike any other, and it feeds right into the ego of most professional salespeople.

If you have a salesperson who's struggling, you may have to stretch a little to celebrate her. It may take a bit of work to find something to celebrate, but it's there and those struggling probably need that public acknowledgement the most.

Realizing that it's not always about the money

Different people are motivated by different things, as I discuss in Chapter 9. It's not always about the money. In fact, money is seldom as good as something you have to put some thought into.

Like a birthday gift for your spouse, using cash as an incentive is a bit of a cop-out. It's too easy. Heck, anybody can just give away money. Well, okay not anybody, but you get the idea.

I always liked to try to come up with ideas and incentives people either wouldn't or couldn't come up with on their own. Instead of just throwing money at them, get creative! Instead of $1,000 cash, think about how your team would respond to some of these:

- **Two front-row tickets to a sold-out concert.** They're not as hard to get as you'd think. Many ticket brokers have great seats for the right price.
- **An overnight stay in a presidential suite.** Go big! Find the most exclusive hotel in your area and book its most expensive suite — complete with all the trimmings!
- **A private helicopter tour of the city.** Hey, don't be afraid to get crazy! Be creative.
- **A seven-course dinner for two in a private dining room in the finest restaurant in town.** Wow!

Think about the difference between these and cash. People spend money and don't really remember what they spent it on. But, with a unique and personal reward, you're making memories! You're putting your people in situations they'll never forget.

If at all possible, include a spouse or loved one in the program. A dinner for two or concert for two is much more meaningful than sending someone alone.

The trick to making the prize something that really moves the needle is to come up with ideas and items the recipient wouldn't buy for herself. Would she spend $1,000 on one dinner? Probably not. But, what a great prize to win! And, she (and her spouse) will remember those moments long after the money would be gone.

Never destroy their confidence

I can't stress enough that all sales contests, incentives, and programs are supposed to be fun. They're designed to ignite your team, keep them engaged, break the monotony of the everyday humdrum of the job, and reward those who achieve their goals and otherwise excel.

At no time should a reward demotivate someone. Be very careful about the wording, the design and the execution of the programs. Just because you have winners doesn't mean you have losers. A salesperson's psyche is a fragile thing. You spend enough time keeping your team pumped up without creating problems for yourself with ill-chosen language. So, as you roll out your awards programs, take a little time to double-check everything and make sure there isn't a way the wording could be misconstrued. It's not worth it.

Most people want to win. They want to succeed and have fun doing it. Be the type leader others want to work with and for. Create an atmosphere and environment where your sales team can enjoy themselves and be a part of something special. You'll be amazed at the results.

Chapter 13

Addressing Poor Performance: Counseling and Critiquing Effectively

In This Chapter

- Getting to the root of a performance problem
- Assessing performance effectively and regularly
- Knowing when (and how) to issue written warnings

In this chapter I take you through the ups and downs of being a real sales manager. Okay, maybe not so many ups as downs. Any time you have to address someone's performance, it's a tension-filled situation. If the performance is poor, it only exacerbates it.

The truth is a salesperson's performance isn't going to improve by having you close your eyes to it, ignore it, and hoping it will get better. Hope is not a management strategy. Turning a blind eye not only makes things worse, it indicates to the rest of your sales team that you aren't really interested. And you never want that!

Identifying the Cause of Poor Performance

If someone on your team isn't producing the desired results, you have to treat them just as you've trained them to handle a prospect:

- **Ask questions:** Never assume you know why someone isn't living up to expectations. Ask questions. Find out what's going on that could be hampering your team member's performance.

- **Uncover the problem:** Just as you would with a prospect, you have to find the pain before you can offer a solution. Something is keeping your salesperson from achieving their goals and objections; what is it?
- **Provide a solution:** Your job is to assess the situation and offer a way to solve the problem. After you find out what's keeping your salesperson from producing, you need to be prepared to offer a solution that works for both of you.

The only way you're really going to find out what's going on is to talk to someone face-to-face. Don't depend on the grapevine or what you think is happening. Ask open-ended questions such as, "We both know you're not reaching your stated goals and objectives, what's keeping you from succeeding?"

Many times, someone underperforming doesn't know exactly what's wrong — if he did, he'd correct it himself. By asking questions about what he's doing, how he's doing it and maybe even observing him in action, you can discover where he's drifted off track.

Don't be quick just to dispense punishment or criticism until you talk to the person. Sometimes life creeps in and distracts even your top performers from producing in a manner you both know they're capable of.

Don't jump to conclusions

Many years ago I had a salesperson who was consistently one of my top two or three sellers every month. And then something happened.

Over a period of four or five months, his production dropped significantly. He fell into some terribly bad habits of being late with reports, had a few complaints from customers, and a few other otherwise minor offenses. But, when they all stacked on top of each other, they were a real cause for concern. Something was going on and I had no idea what it was.

I would ask, and get the "No, I'm okay. Just struggling right now" type answers. The old, "don't worry about me" stuff. It was as if he'd quit his job. He stopped communicating and really withdrew from me and his coworkers.

After watching his performance fall for several months, I called him in prepared to give the old, "shape up or ship out" talk. And, I didn't want to. Just a few months before he'd been one of my top people.

When he arrived at my office, I had the performance review written and ready to go over and put in his file. Not five minutes into the meeting he began to tear up — which was way out of character. After what seemed like an hour (it was probably only a minute or two), he struggled to tell me that his wife had been diagnosed with a terminal cancer and he was providing round-the-clock care for her himself.

I was stunned. I never thought that perhaps there was something going on outside the work world that could be the issue. I had looked at call reports, sales numbers, and so forth, but forgot to look at the person behind them.

He went on to tell me his wife's health was rapidly declining, and he was just a basket case. He wasn't eating right, couldn't sleep, and was totally lost.

There were more than a few tears shed by both of us. He hadn't known how to ask for help — and didn't really know what kind of help to ask for.

Well, I did. I assigned one of our merchandisers to handle his sales route three days a week — he wanted to continue to work and call on his main customers — and allowed him to spend time with his wife.

I wish this story had a happy ending, but it doesn't. What you need to take from it is that behind the numbers are people. People who have lives outside of work — people who are fathers, mothers, husbands, wives, sons, and daughters. In my haste to run my department, I failed to see the obvious: Something was going on in his life that was taking away from his work.

I've tried to never be guilty of that again.

Never forget there are human beings behind all these numbers you look at every day. And those people have lives outside the four walls of your company.

I'm not naive enough to believe we can solve everyone's personal problems, but when you have someone who needs help, offer it if you can — but you've got to be aware he needs it. Never lose sight of your people.

You don't have to wait for someone's annual review to address a problem. Don't think that the only time you can counsel your team or offer constructive criticism is during one time of year. If the need arises, respond to it. But, if you do, make a note of that consultation when you do your annual review so you have it on record as well.

Giving Regular Performance Reviews

Instead of waiting for something to go wrong or something bad to happen before you talk to your employees, provide and perform regular evaluations and performance reviews. If you don't have an employee performance form get one.

Your human resources department (HR) can help you find a form that covers all the areas important to you and your company. Make sure it's all-inclusive and allows for plenty of written feedback. You don't want to just hand someone a report card with no feedback behind it.

Take the time to familiarize yourself with the entire performance review documentation. Understand what you're going to be discussing with your team members.

Put forth the effort and thought to complete each review document professionally. Don't just run through each one checking boxes, just to say you filled it out and move on to the next one. All your people deserve for you to take the time to properly assess their production and performance and have you help create ways for them to improve.

I recommend holding a scheduled performance review either every six months or once a year at the least. The more feedback you can give your team, the easier it is to use those guardrails discussed in Chapter 8.

When you commit to doing performance reviews, stick to your schedule. This goes a long way to your credibility as a manager. Don't roll them out with a lot of fanfare one time and then never do it again. If you use reviews as a tool to provide guidance and direction to your team, you need to do it on a regular basis.

It's okay to think of your review or assessment as a report card, but you have to sit down with each person to go over it. You're not grading your people as much as you are guiding them. It's not something you need to fill out and just leave a copy in their company mailbox. Set aside a day to spend at least an hour with each person and go over each review in depth. Believe it or not, your salespeople want to know how they're doing. They want to hear what you have to say. Don't be afraid to tell them.

A performance review isn't the time to give everyone a blue ribbon just for playing. You have to approach this with professionalism and an unbiased look at how each person is performing in each area you measure. You aren't performing the review to pat everyone on the back; you're doing it to give your staffers actual feedback on what they're doing well and what areas need improvement. And everyone has at least one area that needs improvement.

Know what to review

You should be prepared to review:

- **Sales numbers:** Whatever numbers you track, be it sales dollars, gross profit, closing percentage, or whatever, be prepared to have up-to-date, actual numbers to review.
- **Specific performance:** If you have a specific target or goal for a team member, this is the time to address his progress or lack thereof.
- **Overall performance:** This isn't as subjective as you may think. Look at how well each team member is performing in all the measurable key performance indicators you have established. (Head to Chapter 11 for more on key performance indicators.)

Be very careful about discussing or critiquing anything to do with attitude or other subjective issues that cannot be quantified. You're there to address performance and performance-related issues only. There could be some legal issues here, as well. Check with your human resources department before getting into anything other than numbers and criteria you can back up.

Be prepared to hear every excuse in the book. Sadly, many salespeople spend more time making excuses than making sales. At some point you have to direct the focus to the solution and to the consequences of continued poor performance.

Be honest

Priority number one when doing performance reviews is to be honest. It's not going to do you or the salesperson any good if you sugarcoat the bad parts and play up the good parts just because you want to avoid confrontation.

You're not doing your employees or yourself any good if you make every review just a glowing report of how they're the greatest thing since sliced bread. In fact, they're going to be suspicious of everything you say because they know — trust me, they know — there are areas they need to work on.

You can't worry about your employees liking what you have to say. If you're truly honest, they'll appreciate it whether it's what they wanted to hear or not. Anyone worth his salt wants good, honest feedback because that's the only way he can really improve.

Understand the anxiety your team members feel coming into the review. It's a very stressful situation for them, so do everything possible to make it as easy as possible even when the discussion focuses more on subpar performance than on high performance.

It's a struggle at times to walk the tightrope between praise and criticism, but when you have to be critical, remember: criticize the action, not the actor. Simply be honest and tactful. It's called being a professional. This is when you take on more of advisor and counselor role in your demeanor, actions, and language.

In *Performance Appraisals and Phrases For Dummies*, author Ken Lloyd shares some great suggestions on how to reframe a conversation by using the proper verbiage. For example, Lloyd suggests:

- **Quality and quantity of work:** Accuracy, productivity, thoroughness, and goal attainment
- **Communication and interpersonal skills:** Teamwork, cooperation, listening, persuasion, and empathy

- **Leadership:** Accessibility, responsiveness, decisiveness, collaboration, and delegating
- **Self-development and growth:** Learning, advancement, education, skill building, and career planning

There are several others, but these are great for addressing salespeople and mid-level division or territory managers.

Words matter. Even though you're going to give your employee a copy of their performance review, they'll remember the words you use more than anything. Give your words some thought and be careful with them.

Be helpful

One of best things you can do when providing a performance review is to view it for what it is: an opportunity for you to assist the salesperson to improve his performance. Your job isn't just to point out all the issues or problems, but to have a discussion about your concerns about areas where improvement is needed and to either work with the salesperson to improve or offer a solution to a problem.

The goal of the review is not to find fault, but to improve performance. Offer solutions when team members may not have one and work with them to grow and get better at their areas of deficiency.

Anyone can be a critic. Be a resource your people can depend on to offer assistance, counsel, and advice. You're in your position as a sales manager for a reason — put your experience to work in helping others improve and grow.

When you write the review, be as specific as possible and stay away from vague statements like, "you need to work harder" or "you're not putting enough effort into it." Give your people something to work with. It's much better if your feedback is along the lines of, "Your weekly calls average 22 and our goal for you is 30. How can we get that number up?"

Don't let yourself focus strictly on "what have you done for me lately" during an annual review — or even a bi-annual review. It's not about the past month or two; it's about the entire review period. As you gather your data, keep in mind that you're looking at the review period as a whole and not simply pulling out a small sample size to make your assessment and judgments.

Your end game should be to come up with a plan for each team member to improve in each area you deem them to be deficient. If there's one thing you want them to leave with, it's an idea of how they can improve. You do them no good if their only takeaway is what they're doing wrong with no thought or idea on how to correct it or improve their performance.

In Chapter 11, I talk about the importance of having key performance indicators (KPIs). Include all the data you collect in the key performance indicators. If they're indicators of performance, then it only makes sense they be addressed in the performance review.

It looks very bad if you told your team they're being assessed by certain criteria all year only to have their review and use a totally different set of data. That's unfair and unprofessional.

If you keep KPIs in mind, you'll have a much more productive review — your team members will come away better equipped to tackle the challenges of their jobs and hopefully have an improved performance review at the next sitting.

Listen to their concerns

The process of handling the performance review is as important as the review itself. When it's time to meet individually with your people, make sure you allot plenty of time so as not to rush the process. You should have a quiet, uninterrupted environment where you can sit down with each team member and the two of you can talk openly and honestly.

Before starting the review, take a moment to let the team member know why you're performing it: not to criticize, but to highlight things he's doing well and to explore ways he can improve in other areas. Don't assume he knows the reason for the review.

You're sharing a performance review, not a report card. Don't just give an employee two stars for this, three stars there, and five stars for that, then shake his hand and move on to the next person.

Ideally you have detailed notes written for each area you plan to discuss with each team member. If so, give the person a copy of the review early in the meeting. Allow him time to read it to himself. (Please don't sit there and just read it to him — I can't tell you how unprofessional that looks.)

When your team member has had time to look over his review, read it, and digest it, let him talk. Perhaps ask what his take is on your assessment. Then listen. Don't talk. Listen. Let him give you his thoughts.

You should know the form backward and forward and be able to grasp the areas he discusses without having to keep looking down at your notes. It's important to maintain eye contact, treat your employee professionally, and hear him out.

Just like your sales meeting, this is meant to be a discussion and dialogue, not a lecture. Use your ears as much or more than your mouth.

Also, this is meant to look forward and not just backward. You're not simply talking about what he did in the past, but what he needs to do in the future. Spend time talking about ways for him to achieve his objectives, not just pointing out that he missed them last time.

If someone vehemently disagrees with an assessment, never, ever let the conversation dissolve into an argument or a shouting match. Maintain proper decorum and talk through it professionally.

Your team members won't agree with everything you say about their performance, so expect to hear them disagree with some of the things you've written. After they give you their thoughts, begin the discussion on how you arrived at your assessment and let it be conversational. Their input is important — it can give you insight as to why some of their numbers aren't up to snuff — or why you feel they need work in some areas.

I've had situations in which people expressed things at their review that let me know they weren't really paying attention to the guardrails and regular communication we were having. They were just waiting to get their review to see how they were doing.

Always get input from the person on the implementation of an improvement plan. If it comes from him it's workable — if it comes from you, he may well see it as a directive — even if the numbers are the same. Crazy, I know.

Provide your team members with plenty of time to talk. Don't rush them or cut them off. This is their review and they have a say in how it goes. But, always try to end on a positive note. Find something they're doing right.

I once had a sales manager tell me performance reviews were like playing golf. No matter how bad the round had been, the only thing you remember is the one good shot you hit. There's a lot of truth in that. Don't kill your team member's spirit. Be honest, be helpful, be specific, but be professional. Send him off with a smile and a pat on the back.

Putting It in Writing: When to Issue a Written Warning

You should be managing your team and their performance every day — not just when it's time to do performance reviews. Don't look at the performance review as your one chance to talk to team members and either praise positive behavior or critique and analyze negative patterns. Monitoring performance is an ongoing process that happens daily.

Ongoing feedback — both positive and negative — is evident in the interactions and conversations you have with your people when you're actually managing and promoting the results you want and assisting your salespeople in getting out of the bad habits that produce the results you don't. By providing regular feedback you prevent them from straying too far off track before receiving input. If you wait until they're too far gone for help, you haven't done your job.

Make it a point to talk to every person on your sales team on a regular basis, if for no other reason than to find out what's happening in their world. Don't get stuck in the office. My biggest issue with sales managers is that they sometimes get so caught up in their own world they forget to actually get out in the field periodically. You need to see how things are for yourself so that you don't lose sight of what's happening with your sales teams.

Will upper management put demands on your time? Yes. Manage it well and communicate with your team even when you can't be physically present.

Communication with your team should be a given. And, that communication should be regular, consistent feedback on their performance. You need to have a relationship in which they can come to you or you go to them to discuss issues and solve problems while those problems are still solvable. Don't wait until the molehill becomes a mountain.

In Chapter 8 I talk about the importance of putting your expectations in writing. In the event those expectations aren't met, you need to get that in writing as well. You need to decide what offenses constitute a written warning and make them known. Don't find yourself in the situation of issuing a written warning for something you'd give no notification was subject to a written warning.

Open the curtains and let your people see what's going on. Don't assume they know what behavior is and isn't acceptable.

Your policy should be in writing so everyone is treated the same, and you have protection in the event of legal issues. I am not a lawyer (and don't play one on TV) so consult your human resources or legal department if you have questions specific to your situation, company, or state.

I always post the bad list of offenses and generally deal with them with:

- First offense: Verbal warning
- Second offense: Written warning
- Third offense: Written warning and discipline up to and including termination

Obviously, some situations circumvent this process and lead to immediate dismissal. But, if you're not firing someone immediately, write down the behavior and what you did about it.

If you have to issue a verbal warning to someone, document that in writing immediately. Include the warning issued and the date and put it in his personnel file. That way, if you need to issue a written warning, you have proof you started with the first level.

Ultimately, giving warnings is all about consistency (that and covering your tail personally and corporately). Follow the same procedure for every person every time. No matter whether it's your top salesperson or the guy who's barely hanging onto his job, if the behavior warrants a written reprimand, it has to happen. Period. You have to be consistent. And, whenever possible, have the person sign the document. If he refuses, make a note in his file that he refused to sign.

In today's lawsuit-happy environment, you can never be too careful, so document everything, and save every email and all correspondence. You never know when they will be needed.

Your HR department almost assuredly has an employee handbook that outlines everything from use of company property to sexual harassment. If you feel the need to go further and develop your own departmental addendum with issues that specifically address the sales department, seek help from HR or the legal department prior to publishing sales-specific standards.

After you publish company or sales department standards, you cannot change them without publishing an update. You can't give just a verbal notice if you decide to change the rules or the punishment after you set precedent in writing. Once you put it in writing, anything you do regarding that should be in writing. That way, there's no question about when a written warning is needed and justified. It's not a subjective matter and one where you have any gray area to decide whether you should or shouldn't.

When you have to issue a warning in writing, always follow it up — in writing — with what you want the salesperson to do to correct the problem. Just like in your regular performance reviews, don't just point out the problem without offering a solution. Your written warning shouldn't be, "You did this wrong so I'm writing you up!" Any warning should include three pieces of information:

- The issue involved
- The date and details of the verbal warming issued previously
- What the salesperson needs to do to correct the problem

If the offense is serious enough, also include that a future occurrence will result in discipline up to and including termination (if that's the case).

If someone has done something wrong three times, it shouldn't be a surprise to him to receive a pink slip.

Be specific

When you must dole out disciplinary action and put together a written warning, be as specific as possible. Even if you and the salesperson both know exactly what happened, you need to spell it out so that an outside party who knows nothing about the situation could read the warning a year later and be able to understand exactly what prompted your actions. Being vague is not only poor management practice, but could leave you exposed should any issues arise in the future — and not just with this employee.

If you need to issue a performance warning, follow these steps:

1. **Do your due diligence.**

   Never respond to accusations of others without doing your own investigation, talking to those involved, and arriving at your own decision. If the offense is serious enough to warrant an official warning, it's serious enough for you to put in the time to get to the bottom of it before reacting in a manner that may come back to haunt you.

2. **Meet as soon as possible.**

   After you complete your investigation, meet with the employee immediately. Don't wait. These things are never fun, but they get less enjoyable the longer you wait. Everyone involved deserves to have the situation rectified as soon as possible.

3. **Provide specific details of the offense.**

   For the sake of discussion, say one of your salespeople has an attendance issue. You need to know the dates he was late or didn't come to work. You can't go with just, "You've been out a lot lately." Be overly specific, if anything. If you know he arrived at 8:27 for an 8:15 sales meeting, don't just say, "You were late," include the time he arrived, the date, and so forth. You cannot have too many details on the offense.

4. **List the names of others involved.**

   If the violation affected or included others, list everyone's name and how each figured into the act. If someone else was also disciplined, include that information. In a case with a victim (and I hate to use that term), get a statement from the injured party regarding the infraction and include it in all materials and reports. If some victims are anonymous, keep their names from the offending employee but make victims' names part of a private file kept only by the human resources department.

5. **Provide specific feedback.**

   Your proposed solution should not read, "Start getting here on time." Rather, provide specific direction to your employee about how you expect him to perform and what behavior you expect in the future. If you're giving him a certain amount of time to correct a deficiency, note the due date for observable correction and detail how and when you and the employee will come back together to review whether appropriate action has been taken and the issue has been corrected.

6. **List specific consequences.**

   You see the pattern developing: Be specific. If the next step is automatic termination, say so. If the next offense will result in a suspension, put that in writing.

Nobody likes to talk about legal issues, but they're a real part of the business world today. You need to familiarize yourself with your company's policy so that you don't expose your organization to litigation because of how you handle a personnel situation. In some instances, you can be held personally responsible in addition to your organization. To say this matter is an important one is an understatement.

Ask how you can help

After you issue a warning, ask the salesperson, "How can I help you solve this?" or "How can I help prevent another conversation like this?"

As a manager, Part of your job is to find out what you can do to prevent this behavior in the future. Is it more education? More frequent discussion? Simply making the employee aware of policies he should already know? Whatever it is, it's your job to try to keep this employee from receiving a second or third strike. Ultimately, everyone is responsible for his own actions, but as a manager you shoulder some of that responsibility.

Ask questions and listen. It's called *counseling* and *critiquing* for a reason. You must do both. You have to be the person who admonishes, but you also have to be the resource who helps an erring team member take corrective action or change his habits or behaviors.

After going through the written warning, always give the employee an opportunity to share his side of the story. Have an open conversation about how he sees the situation. His view may be exactly the same or totally different. Whatever the case, he deserves the opportunity to share his views.

After he has his say, allow him to add whatever comments he'd like to the written warning. He may agree, disagree, or be somewhere in between, but let him get his story on the record. His information is as important, if not more so, than yours.

Encourage him to open up and include his side of the story in the narrative. Make this a part of the permanent file and give the employee a copy of everything (except anything with anonymous persons on it). If you have to, create a separate document that's an exact copy but blacks out or redacts the names of those who wish to remain anonymous.

Use this opportunity just like a performance review to create a dialogue on how you and the salesperson can better his performance and correct whatever action brought you to this point in the first place.

Don't look at this as simply an opportunity to slap someone on the wrist or write him up; use it as a coaching opportunity — a chance for you to point out incorrect actions and behaviors and discuss what can be done to grow, progress, and improve.

Finally, after you complete the session and discuss the next steps on how both of you agree to follow up, have the employee sign the document and notify him that it becomes a permanent part of his personnel file.

Whether your company requires it or not, I always like to get a witness to the signing of the document. I don't want anyone coming back later and saying, "I had to sign it to keep my job," or anything like that.

Be fair across the board

If you remain a manager long enough, there will be times when you have to counsel some of your top performers. And, although the natural inclination is to let your top people slide or maybe give them the benefit of the doubt for a momentary lapse in judgment, apply the same rules to them as you do to everyone else.

Never put yourself in a position of favoritism. One instance of treating someone differently will call into question every evaluation, warning, and any other issue you've had with anyone else. Just be fair.

I can remember my parents telling me as a child "this is going to hurt me worse than it is you" when they had to punish me for something. Like everyone else I thought, "Yeah, right!" But, when you have to give a verbal or written warning to a top performer, you'll understand exactly what they meant.

Be firm. Stick to your guns and understand that your credibility, integrity, and ultimately your word depend on how you handle personnel situations. Treat everyone fairly but firmly, and you remove the decision-making aspect of professional reprimands. The decision is made by the employees and what they do; you just have to respond to that.

One of the hardest decisions I ever made

I once had my *top* performer — not *one* of my top performers, but *the* top performer — do something that was a terminable offense. I had just been promoted into my position, and to make matters worse, the salesperson was probably 15 years older than I and had more time with the company than I did.

But, what he did was wrong, and there was simply no way to look the other way. I knew, he knew, and unfortunately others knew it as well.

Even though nobody ever said anything, I'm sure the general consensus was, "Let's see how he handles *this* one!" I agonized over the potential of losing my top salesperson just mere months on the job. At the same time, there was little question about what ultimately had to be done.

I called him into my office after thoroughly investigating the situation and allowed him to present his side of the case. He didn't deny it, he just felt he had a reason to do it — that it wasn't done with malice, but out of trying to help a customer. Still, wrong is wrong.

After what seemed like an eternity, I told him I had no choice but to let him go. Amazingly, he understood. He knew the position I was in and took it about as well as anyone could.

I was physically ill. It was the first time I had ever fired anyone, and this was my top salesperson walking out the door to boot. But, he said something to me I'll never forget. He said, "Hey, it's my fault for putting you in this position. You did what you had to do, and I respect that."

Though it did little at the time to make me feel better, I look back on it and see that as much as I struggled with it, I couldn't take responsibility for his actions. Those were his, and he had to deal with the consequences. The sales were secondary to my integrity and that of the company.

Afterward, the rest of the sales team had almost a newfound respect for me. Though I didn't share any of the details, they knew what I'd gone through and how tough it was. Those who remained on my team made me stronger because of it and thankfully he landed on his feet as well.

No matter what someone does, you cannot take it personally. As hard as it is, it was a lesson I learned and am glad I did.

Part V

Now You're Managing

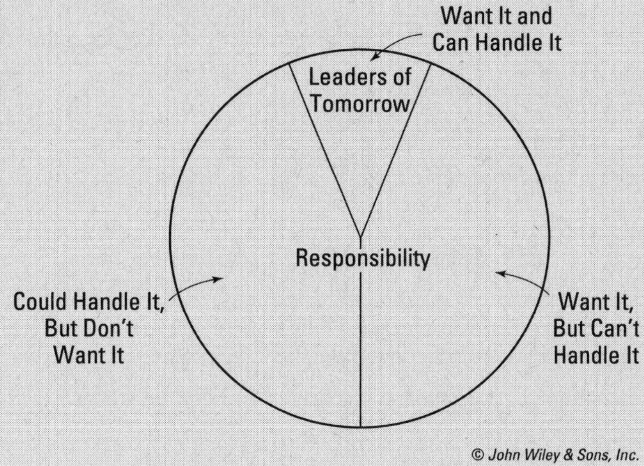

For more on handling the harder aspects of your job, go to www.dummies.com/extras/salesmanagement.

In this part . . .

- Understand how to professionally critique a salesperson's performance without destroying his confidence.
- Create an environment in your sales department where everyone can win.
- Figure out when to say goodbye and make the hard decision to terminate a salesperson. There's not only a best way to handle it, but also a best time.
- Discover the three types of salespeople in every organization and how to manage each.
- Understand and accept the idea of building yourself out of a job and how it is crucial to grow your organization.

Chapter 14

Inspiring Your Superstars: Managing Your Best People

In This Chapter

- Taking care of your top talent first
- Treating your staff fairly but not the same
- Creating a winning environment
- Giving all the attention they deserve
- Empowering your team to grow

In Chapter 4, I cover the fact that every organization has salespeople who turn out to be the peak performers — the cream of the crop, the top bananas, the A students as I like to call them.

They distinguish themselves from the rest of your team not only through their performance and the numbers they put up, but by their attitude, actions, and overall professionalism. There's no doubt about it — they're your superstars.

When managing a team, many sales managers are tempted to take their eye off the top people and focus instead on the lesser performers. It's tempting to do this because the top people are so successful and need so little attention, so they often get taken for granted and left to their own devices. It's not necessarily intentional; it's just the old "the squeaky wheel gets the grease" syndrome.

You don't mean to put your best salespeople aside or isolate them, it's just how it plays out — they always have their work done, paperwork in order, and happy customers.

If you look up from your desk, you know they're working — they're on the phone, waiting on a customer, or otherwise being productive. You don't have to stay on top of them every minute of every day.

But, these are the true leaders of your sales team. They need your attention as much as anyone, and sometimes you have to remind yourself of that. Just because they aren't doing something wrong or making a lot of noise doesn't mean they don't need a strong manager. They do.

In this chapter, I cover some ways to keep yourself engaged with your top salespeople, find out what they need, and look at ways you can be the manager they need. I also talk about ways to keep those stars growing because they hold the key to the growth of your company.

Managing from the Top Down

Too many times as a manager you find yourself managing from the bottom up rather than from the top down. You spend your time and energy on the bottom ten percent of your workforce or sales team rather than the top ten percent because they're the ones who have all the problems.

Sometimes you notice the lesser salespeople are the ones creating problems in the first place. Then you have to help them sort out what they've done and how to best solve it. It's easy to feel you need to spend all your time with these employees. All the while, your leaders are rocking along taking care of business.

But I want to suggest that you turn that around and refocus as much (or more) on the people who are really the movers and shakers of the department.

Now, I firmly believe that everyone needs help. I'm not in any way suggesting you ignore anyone who isn't a superstar salesperson — everyone has to be managed and everyone needs your attention. But, you need to determine whether you're spending an inordinate amount of time with a certain segment of your team while your top sellers go unnoticed.

If your top salesperson needs you and can't get into your office because you have three other people lined up with problems they created or should've been able to handle themselves, you aren't properly managing your team. You've failed the people who deserve your time.

It's a slippery slope and a challenge to make sure you're always providing the most benefit to those who need it. But, you should ask yourself, "Is this where my time is best spent?" If that answer is not a resounding yes, then it's time to stop and analyze how you're allocating your most valuable resource: you!

If you only had one hour to spend with your sales team today, where would that time be best spent? Where could you do the most good as a manager and as a resource? Whatever the answers, that's how you should be spending your time.

If you train your salespeople to spend their time and energy wisely, shouldn't you do the same? Granted, not everyone needs the same amount of your time and attention, but don't let yourself be pulled into the vortex of doing nothing but cleaning up messes. Just as your salespeople should focus the majority of their attention on their top customers, you should focus yours on your top talent.

You'll find your best people require less of your time on a regular basis. They need less handholding, as they're generally self-motivated and the type to jump in and take care of business. However, when one of your top performers needs your attention, give it to her. She should go right to the top of your list because generally when a top performer needs help, it's for an important issue.

Offering perks to your best salespeople

I have little doubt most sales managers take care of their poor performers — they either work them up or work them out. But, you need to look at how well you take care of your best people and how much you do for them.

In Chapter 12, I discuss the idea of a president's roundtable or a club that your top performers can earn their way into. Think of things you can do for the members of this club that will drive their productivity and inspire others to want to do what it takes to join:

- **Shout it out loud:** Whatever program you create, make it public. Salespeople — especially those at the top of their game — love to be recognized publicly. Post the monthly roundtable members, or gold circle membership, or whatever you call it in a place where not only your sales team can see it but customers can see it, too.
- **Membership has its privileges:** Invite your sales leaders to a regular lunch, dinner, or other type outing open only to those who qualify. Perhaps you have an annual trip you take only your top five percent or top five salespeople on. Be creative, and make special perks stand out as something over and above because they reward performance that's over and above.
- **It's not always money:** Monetary incentives are one of the last things I suggest for you to offer this group. Your top salespeople should be making good money already, so you need to do something more — something extra.

Now that's taking care of your people

Many automobile dealers include their salesperson or salespersons of the month in their advertising campaign. If you pick up the Sunday newspaper, you find that real estate brokers do this a lot, too. It's a great way to recognize and promote their top people. But, it's gotten so common it's almost like the participation ribbons — everyone seems to get one.

One of the best examples I've ever seen in being creative with recognition was an automobile dealer who had large outdoor banners made with pictures of the top salespeople at the dealership. These banners were maybe 14 feet tall — they were huge.

Like most dealerships, there were light poles throughout the lot and these banners were affixed to the poles. Keep in mind these pictures were displayed throughout the lot in front of customers, prospective customers, and the general public just driving by.

Do you think this was a motivating factor or a sense of accomplishment for a salesperson to earn her own banner? Absolutely!

These banners were not cheap, either. The owner put some dollars into these banners. But what a great way to boost the confidence of his superstars! It's a great way to recognize them and promote his business all at the same time.

This was a triple-threat! The auto dealer got great exposure, his salespeople certainly wanted to be on one of those banners, and the customers certainly had to have an increased feeling of trust and confidence in their salesperson if her face was on a 14-foot banner!

Don't keep your top performers secret! When I talk about taking care of them, I mean doing it in a public way and letting everyone know about it.

Salespeople are driven by many different motivators, but one that runs through most of the elite is a desire to be recognized. Forget the money, the accolades, and so forth. All that's fine, and everyone likes that, but to be acknowledged publicly is a reward in and of itself. Use it to your benefit.

Not Treating Everyone the Same But Not Treating Anyone Differently

In order to really inspire your superstars to achieve more and continue to outperform the rest of your team and their competition, you need to give them special treatment. If one of your sales team puts in the effort to achieve a certain goal or attain a certain level of customer satisfaction and gets the same treatment as the person who underperforms, it's not going to take long for her to become very demotivated.

If someone's performance justifies recognition or special treatment, I am all for making a big deal of it. If a salesperson singlehandedly has the best month in company history, and you respond with a, "ho-hum, nice job," you've crushed that salesperson and demoralized her — perhaps fatally as far as your company is concerned.

Instead, make an announcement to the entire company. Recognition in the local newspaper, the company newsletter, or even a special note to all the salesperson's customers are all good acknowledgements. I'm not talking about breaking the bank, but you need to do something, anything to let that person know she's appreciated and her accomplishment was meaningful.

Don't treat anyone differently, but don't treat everyone the same. Now, that may sound like I'm talking out of both sides of my mouth. Let me stress the difference: Don't treat any one person differently, but you cannot treat everyone the same. I feel strongly about that.

Never do anything discriminatory against anyone for any reason. Everyone should have an equal opportunity to earn her way into whatever you call your elite group. And I never treat anyone poorly, I just have to give extra special care to the people who are bringing in the big deals and keeping the doors open.

When your best people distinguish themselves, by all means treat them differently, just as you treat customers differently based on their value to your company.

Another way to look at it is to think of yourself as a doctor. (And honestly, that's a lot more true than you think.) You have to diagnose the issues with each of your salespeople to discover what ails each of them and what problem you need to solve for each of them today.

Now, do you think everyone is going to have the same problem? Are you going to write the same prescription for everyone? Probably not.

Each person on your team has special needs exclusive to her. Handle her accordingly. But, when it comes to the peak performers, they deserve to be put at the top of the list.

If a top salesperson is waiting on a customer and needs you, turn your attention to her immediately. Don't let yourself be bogged down with issues that aren't as pressing or handling something that isn't as important as what one of your top sellers has in front of her. These people don't ask often, but when they do, help them and their customer!

Here comes a soapbox moment: Some people may see an inequality in treating people differently, and they're right. I don't believe in awarding participation ribbons for salespeople like they do in Little League and youth sports. The world doesn't work that way. I don't mean to sound crass and uncaring, but there's a reason we keep score, and there's a reason some people are successful and some aren't. It's that innate desire to be a winner. And it should not only be recognized, but rewarded. (Exiting soapbox.)

Look at it this way: If two people were to go to a personal trainer and begin individual workout programs, I can assure you the trainer would take in to account their current physical health, past history, injuries, and their overall abilities. Not everyone can start bench-pressing 100 pounds. But, if the trainer treated everyone the same and set the bench press at 50 pounds because that was the most the weakest person could do, how much good is that doing the strongest person? It's not doing her any good. In fact, it's hurting her.

You lose strength every day you don't push yourself harder and attempt more. Sales skills are just like a muscle — if you don't use it, it gets weak and eventually atrophies.

By not pushing your top performers and treating them as top performers, you're letting their sales muscles decline.

To push your top performers, continue to raise your expectations for them as you would anyone else. Ask them, "What do you need from me to increase your sales by X percent?" Some goals may scare even a superstar salesperson, but that's okay; in fact, that's good. All goals should be a little scary; if they aren't, they're not big enough.

As you find yourself helping your best salespeople improve, you'll begin to teach them about more than sales. You start getting them thinking about managing other salespeople and becoming a division or district manager.

You start developing skills they need to advance their careers. You aren't there just to make your people better salespeople; you're there to make them better, period.

As I cover in Chapter 16, some of these people will be your leaders of tomorrow, and now is the time to help them start finding those muscles. You may not be developing them fully, but they need to know deep-down inside they can be a leader, they can be a manager, and they can be a part of the future of your company.

If you're trying to treat everyone alike, stop. Now. You're killing the motivation for your top performers and not helping anyone else, either.

Discovering what your top players need

Alright, a segment of your sales team has earned the right — note the word *earned* — to be considered your top performers. You should align most, if not all, of your systems, reporting, and other ancillary tasks to fit their needs.

But, how do you find out what they need? How can you help them grow?

One of the things I've found about the top salespeople is that they're usually quiet, they keep to themselves, and they get the job done. They aren't necessarily prone to going around making a lot of noise and asking for help. They didn't get to the top by complaining.

So, how do you find out what you can do for them?

I use three methods to uncover ways I can be of assistance to those superstars. And remember, your job is to help your salespeople grow; they're leading the charge.

- **Ask questions:** What a novel concept, huh? Take time to ask your best salespeople how you can make them more efficient and help them build their business. Generally, they're so focused on the task at hand they need you to put them in the mode of thinking bigger.
- **Mastermind sessions:** The power of a mastermind session is invigorating and enlightening. If you've not held one before, you should. Study ways to get everyone involved and use the combined knowledge to make the entire team stronger. (See the nearby sidebar "The power of the mastermind.")

  A *mastermind session* is simply a gathering of two or more people who then harness the power of all their knowledge and experience to work toward a common goal. It is literally a meeting of the minds where you let everyone participate. Two heads truly are better than one, and three or four are phenomenal.

  Ideally, hold a mastermind session a minimum of once per quarter. Get your people involved and in tune with sharing ideas. You'll find each session is more productive than the last as people begin to open up more and share their ideas. Stress that these sessions are off limits to ridicule and comments like, "That'll never work." That kills creativity and creativity is what you want to foster.
- **Roundtables:** Not as formal as a mastermind session, I used roundtables to spitball ideas and brainstorm quickly. These are more for everyday use than the mastermind session. Think of a *roundtable session* as simply getting a few people together and brainstorming ideas or looking for a solution to a problem. It's much less formal than a true mastermind session and can be put together on a moment's notice. Brainstorming sessions are less structured and aren't necessarily scheduled.

For example, if one of your top people has a problem the two of you can't seem to find a solution for, call a brainstorming session with your top people. Have them meet up somewhere, throw the issue out on the table, and let everyone talk. You'll be amazed at the ideas and solutions that come naturally to some that you may never have thought of.

When it comes to finding what your best sellers need, get them involved. By involving them in the process you can solve some issues as soon as they're uncovered.

The power of the mastermind

In *Think and Grow Rich,* a personal development and self-help book by Napoleon Hill published in 1937, Hill defines "Master Mind" as, "Coordination of knowledge and effort, in a spirit of harmony, between two or more people, for the attainment of a definite purpose."

I've been blessed to be involved in several mastermind sessions with some brilliant minds and had the opportunity once to be in one with Mark Victor Hansen, his wife Crystal, and about 16 other people. It was truly a once-in-a-lifetime chance to sit around in an intimate setting and talk to a man who has sold half-a-billion books and is generally regarded as one of the greatest marketers and entrepreneurs of our time. I was awestruck.

Mark shared several of his personal philosophies and habits with the group and challenged us to make a list of 200 people we'd like to spend time with. Think about that. Can you make a list of 200 people you want to spend time with?

With that in mind, he encouraged big, bold goals — after all, how does one sell 500 million books? He related one story about creating the Chicken Soup for the Soul brand with Jack Canfield. Instead of focusing on selling a million books, they focused on selling ten million. All of a sudden, a million didn't seem like such an insurmountable goal. It's all in your perspective.

Are you setting your goals high enough? What could you do to really raise the bar? Don't think about the "what if." Don't worry about failing — here's a newsflash: It's going to happen. Get ready for it. It's part of the gig.

Mark and Jack were turned down by over 100 publishers before getting *Chicken Soup for the Soul* published.

Don't be afraid to push the envelope and buck the trend. At one time, the *New York Times'* best seller list refused to acknowledge *Chicken Soup for the Soul,* telling Mark they "didn't include multiple author books."

He said, "You're sure?"

She said, "I'm positive. We *do not* include multiple author books."

He replied, "Well, you include the Bible and there are over 60 books with 40 authors."

Chicken Soup for the Soul made the best seller list the next week.

Among the many things I came away with was a sense of power — that I could accomplish great things. Greater than perhaps I even can imagine. Never underestimate the power of the mastermind. You'll learn, your people will learn, and the great thing is: You'll all learn more than you would have on your own.

Your top salespeople are the best of the best and the brightest of the bright. Use their talents and skills accordingly and never let them get complacent. Show them favor and pay attention to their needs and you'll be well on your way to building a winning team.

Creating a Winning Environment

Part of the formula for building a successful sales team is the everyday work environment. A negative, toxic environment produces negative, toxic results. Sadly, that type of environment still exists — I see it all the time.

If you're going to have a winning team, they can't hang out in losing surroundings. If you're going to take care of those superstars, you've got to give them the proper workplace for them to thrive.

Make it a point to let everyone know it's okay to have fun at her job. I hate it when I see managers setting such a serious tone that if you look like you're enjoying yourself, you're in trouble. Nobody wants to work in a place like that. Encourage fun. In fact, you should lead the fun movement — life's too short to take things so seriously.

When you create an environment so stiff and uptight that people can't relax and enjoy themselves — that's when mistakes happen, that's when things go horribly wrong. Let your team members let their hair down a little. I don't mean to imply you have to have a playroom, but you shouldn't make going to work seem like going to a funeral. And, we've all seen those situations!

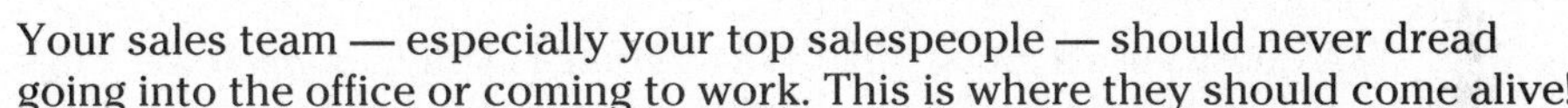

Your sales team — especially your top salespeople — should never dread going into the office or coming to work. This is where they should come alive!

Salespeople thrive when they open up and fly. Don't cage them and inhibit their flight and growth — encourage them to let go and see what happens!

Have your top salespeople help create their environment. In the book, *Nuts* by Kevin and Jackie Freiberg, the authors discuss how Herb Kelleher built Southwest Airlines by hiring (The Doubleday Religious Publishing Group) people who had a sense of humor. They tell one story about the tugs used to pull luggage carts around the tarmac at the airport. Kelleher and his Southwest managers decided to let the baggage handlers customize the paint job on the tugs — everything from painting them to look like their favorite driver's race car to adorning them in the colors of football teams. What happened as a result was that the baggage handlers took a sense of ownership and pride in their tugs and maintenance costs dropped dramatically. Simply because they were involved in creating their environment and making it fun.

Figure out how you can use a similar strategy. Does the break room need painting? If so, consider letting your team pick out the paint.

The best salespeople you will ever find are creative by nature. Don't stifle their creativity in any manner. Allow it to flourish.

Your superstars have achieved their level of success by not hanging around the Negative Nellies. They automatically move away from those people and their surroundings. So, don't wait for them to have to move — be out front and build a workplace, office, or environment where they can continue to be their best.

Finally, a winning environment is one where people know they're winning. They don't keep it a secret. Have you ever been to an auto dealership or a retail outlet where they ring a bell when a sale is made or announce it over the speaker? These people are having fun and they're selling! And, the customers get in on the act, too.

Lighten up. Buy a cowbell, a cymbal, a gong, or something and get out there and have some fun and sell something!

Your top salespeople are going to be top salespeople with your company or for someone else's. As Vince Lombardi once said, "The man on the top of the mountain didn't fall there."

These people ascend to the top wherever they are. You should make it your mission to keep them inspired and feeling as if they're a part of something special. And, just like treating a good customer well, if you don't, someone else will.

A quote I use a lot is: "If you're as good as you're going to be, life's as good as it's going to get." You should aspire to inspire. As a manager, you're most valuable to your top salespeople when you can push them to do things they didn't even know they could do. Never let them get complacent or comfortable. Keep challenging them to grow to achieve and to accomplish more — they owe it to themselves, to their family, and to the company.

Remembering that Everyone Needs Attention

Ask any parent and she'll tell you that everyone needs attention. Some need more than others, but everyone needs some. Salespeople tend to need a lot. It's part of what makes the good ones great — that desire to be noticed and succeed.

Every action by one of your salespeople creates one of three responses on your part whether you know it or not:

- **Positive response:** Praising, bragging, or otherwise acknowledging your satisfaction with their actions.
- **Negative response:** Criticizing or condemning what they did.
- **Indifference:** You show no emotion, either positive or negative. Their actions either go unnoticed or they fail to elicit any response.

A salesperson's preference is in that exact order, too. If you can't respond positively, she's rather you respond negatively than to totally ignore her.

Salespeople are extroverts for a reason. They need the attention — good or bad — to know how they're doing. The true superstars are constantly keeping score in their head even if you're not charting their progress yourself. They know how they are doing and they want you to know it, too. Oh, some may claim they don't need the pats on the back and accolades, but they do. Salespeople's psyches are fragile and can be broken by merely overlooking something they did.

Think of all of your salespeople right now — go ahead, it's okay, nobody's looking. Mentally, go through a list of each of them and focus on what you think they're doing. Now, this is what you think — not necessarily what they are actually doing. Here's the question: Would they like for you to notice their actions or not? Your top performers will always want to be noticed and those who are at the bottom of your sales charts are generally the ones who like to shrink into the woodwork and blend in. The good ones never blend in; they stand out.

Sometimes, your job is as simple as noticing what your salespeople have done. Just to know that you're paying attention to their efforts is rewarding in a small way and works to keep them motivated.

Never let your salespeople think that what they're doing doesn't matter or goes unnoticed. Whether it's good or bad, positive or negative, they need the attention. It's like a spouse or significant other who gives you the silent treatment. Geez! C'mon, yell at me already!

Give feedback — all the time

Providing accurate, honest feedback is a cornerstone of being a good sales manager. Nobody wants someone to just blow sunshine at her just as nobody wants to be constantly criticized. Your ability to not only observe the salesperson's behaviors, actions, and habits but to effectively communicate your thoughts and feedback is critical to your success in management.

You cannot do everyone's job for her. If you could, you wouldn't need her. If she could do the job without feedback and direction, she wouldn't need you.

The line of communication should run both ways; your salespeople should be able to come to you with questions or concerns, and you should be able to provide them with answers and guidance. It's how the system should work.

Unfortunately, sometimes it doesn't. If management doesn't want to listen and only wants to talk, that's a dangerous precedent to set.

While I'm talking mainly about the upper echelon of your sales team in this chapter, everyone needs your feedback and direction. The top performers just need it a bit more often. They want to know how they're doing, and they want to hear from you and know you're aware of their performance and results or lack thereof.

In Chapter 8, I discuss managing like a GPS system. Providing good feedback is a similar experience because your salespeople can't take corrective action until you take action. If their coordinates are a bit off, they'll continue to drift until you either make the necessary changes or give them the feedback that allows them to make the necessary changes to get back on track.

Before you give feedback, you must first observe your salespeople's actions, habits, and behaviors. You can't very well give feedback on something you know nothing about, can you? Whether you ride along on a sales call, watch them wait on a customer, or otherwise observe them in action, you have to take a backseat and let them drive — even if it means letting them fail.

Yes, sometimes you have to let a team member fail in order to help her learn. If she's in the middle of a presentation or working with a customer and does something wrong or makes a mistake, you can't jump in and rescue her. She can't expect Superman or Wonder Woman to come to her aid every time something goes haywire. She needs these learning experiences — and that's what they are. Getting good at sales is like learning how to ride a bicycle or roller skate — you get some bumps and bruises but you'll never learn without a few of them.

If at any time you observe a salesperson doing or saying something that's blatantly false or misleading, you must step in and correct her. Otherwise, save it for later.

After you have a chance to watch your salesperson do her thing, analyze what she did right, what she did wrong, what she should do more of, less of, and so forth.

Any time I worked with a salesperson, I carried a small pocket notebook. I'd keep it handy so I could make notes at any time and not try to commit everything to memory.

When the sales call, demonstration, or presentation is over, sit down with your representative and go over your thoughts. Again, be honest and forthcoming with what you tell her.

If your salespeople aren't doing something properly, you have to tell them. They aren't just going to snap out of it one day. That's what you're there for.

Repeat the entire process if you have to: Observe, provide feedback, observe, provide feedback. It's a simple two-step process, but one a lot of managers fail to go through.

Your job is not to be a friend and just tell a salesperson what she did right. Unless you cover the aspects that need to be improved, she'll never improve — and your superstars are always wanting to improve.

Keep them challenged

Just as they need feedback, elite salespeople need to be challenged. One of the traits you find in almost all top performers is a tendency to get bored very easily.

Successful salespeople get their challenge either from you or somewhere else. Don't make the mistake of losing top talent because they got bored.

Teachers cannot teach a classroom of students based on the ability of the weakest student in the room; neither can you as a sales manager manage your sales team based on the ability of the weakest salesperson. Your top performers thrive on challenges.

Although I like the term "raise the bar" about as much as I do "think outside the box" (which is not at all), you must constantly be pushing your top performers to do more. What's good enough today won't be good enough tomorrow. The world is changing and you and your company have to not only change with it, you need to instigate the change.

Your industry should see your company as the one pushing the envelope, not being dragged along kicking and screaming.

By implementing this philosophy with your salespeople, you'll instill in them the desire for continuous growth.

When you push your top performers, you end up pulling up the underperformers with them. However, by pushing the weakest salespeople, you don't do anything for the overachievers. You end up pulling the slower ones when you push the fast ones.

Give your top salespeople the ability and responsibility to make some decisions on their own. Perhaps you give them a little more pricing flexibility than you do the rest of your group. This allows them to control some of their own gross profit and provides them with negotiating skills they'll need to continue their growth in their current position and in their career.

If you give some salespeople extra leverage in certain areas, make sure you manage their performance. For example, if you provide them with the ability to negotiate prices, check that their gross profits increase — not decrease. When you provide your people with new challenges and tasks, make sure the results are what you want.

Another way to keep your top salespeople challenged is to give them some responsibilities when it comes to training new salespeople. If your top sellers know they're helping set the tone for someone else, most of them are going to automatically step up their game. It's a natural instinct.

Allowing them be a part of your training team keeps them on their toes because they know they're not only being watched by you, but they're setting an example, as well.

To continue to keep the great striving to achieve more, increase the number of calls you ask them to make, increase your expectations of them. But, do so in a positive manner that rewards their performance and doesn't demotivate them.

There's a difference between being happy and being satisfied in my mind. You can be happy with your performance or your team's performance, but never be satisfied. Never let them be content with what they've done in the past or what they accomplished yesterday.

I don't mean to create an environment of "what have you done for me lately." You'll know where the line is — you can feel it. Push your people enough to get them to push themselves, but not enough to where they feel the need to push back.

Don't let them get comfortable

Every now and then you have to do something to shake up the status quo — and keep your people from getting into a comfort zone. Nobody ever attained any level of success inside her comfort zone — she pushed herself or had someone push her to do things she thought she couldn't.

There are many ways to create a little excitement, but changing commission programs or dividing up territories isn't one of them. You need to find positive ways to keep your team from falling into that rut of the day-in-day-out grind.

Have you ever been in your car at a stoplight and had another car pull up next to you only to have it slowly roll forward or backward? You catch a glimpse of it out of the corner of your eye and for a split second you think you're the one moving? You know the feeling. You jam your foot hard onto the brake to stop yourself, even though it's not you in motion.

That's actually happening in your business every day. Your competition is inching forward maybe little by little, maybe by leaps and bounds, but they're moving forward. Now it's up to you to decide if you're going to slam on the brakes or keep pace with them and even lead the charge.

Keep your top salespeople thinking about the competition. Never let them take their eye off the desire to serve their customers and grow. It's that feeling of falling ever-so-slightly behind that keeps the great salespeople grinding it out day after day.

You've probably heard someone say, "Go as far as you can see and then you'll see farther." That's the attitude to instill in every one of your top performers. Go farther, do more, lead the way.

Once one of your people sets a new mark for sales or commissions or whatever, you'll be surprised how quickly others follow suit. You just have to get that one to step out there on faith first. (See the nearby sidebar, "Just because it's never been done . . . .")

Just because it's never been done . . .

You've probably heard the story of Roger Bannister breaking the record and running the four-minute mile. And maybe you heard that in the year after his accomplishment over 20 other runners broke it, too. Unfortunately, that's been embellished a bit, but it's still a story worth sharing.

For years, people were told that humans couldn't possibly run a mile in under four minutes. It was believed the speed needed to accomplish this was humanly impossible, that humans aren't built to run that fast.

Not everyone was satisfied with that answer.

On May 6, 1954, Roger Bannister broke the hallowed four-minute mile by covering the distance in 3 minutes, 59.4 seconds, disproving the theory it wasn't attainable. Within a year of Bannister's feat, another runner, Australian John Landy, broke the four-minute mark, too.

Within the next few years, others joined the four-minute mile club, and in 1964, it was accomplished by high school runner Jim Ryun. It has since been accomplished by five other high school athletes.

But, what if Bannister had never broken the mark? What if he'd accepted the fact that he wasn't supposed to run that fast? He didn't put limits on himself and once others saw what was achievable, they were free to do it themselves.

Don't let your best salespeople get complacent. Push them harder than you do everyone else and let them know the reason is because you believe they can achieve more; you believe they have more in them, and you believe they can sore to new heights. When you start believing in them this much, they'll begin to believe in themselves.

Never cut commissions or territories (if you can help it)

Maybe the biggest killer of motivation in a sales team is when management decides to cut commissions or decrease the size of their territory. There are few things you can do that will take the wind out of their sails faster. Avoid it at all costs.

Your top sales people spend years developing their territory or account base and (if they've been properly trained) see it as their own business. Their territory is their baby, and they don't want anyone coming along and messing it up or tinkering with it.

Commission plans are just as important. In Chapter 12, I stress the importance of double- and triple-checking commission plans before you roll them out because the last thing you want to do is to have to reel it all back in and start over.

I don't think there is ever a case in which a salesperson working on commission is overcompensated. Think about that: If she's on a good commission plan, you should want her to make tons of money because that means the company is making tons more.

More than once, I've seen salespeople leave a company and move to a competitor because of changes to compensation plans. And, if you want to find out who really controls their territory or account list, you'll find out when they leave.

A good commission plan is almost sacred. It's what has driven those few people to the top in your department and perhaps the top of their profession. Don't demotivate them by taking away what they've earned. It's not good business and it will cost you more than you know.

The reality is that the entire sales department will be affected if you change the compensation, commission, or territory of one person. What that does is send a message that if your salespeople get too big, you'll bring them back down and expect them to build it all back over again. They won't, and neither will anyone else in your department.

If your salespeople feel as if all their hard work will be met with a cut in commissions, you're in for a long hard battle to get your people motivated to grow beyond their current status. Why should they?

If there ever is a situation where you absolutely must change the commission program or cut a territory, do it all aboveboard with everyone's full attention. If there's even the slightest hint that you're trying to hide something or do it on the sly, you're toast. Done. Kaput. Make the announcement publicly and be prepared to defend your reasoning in a way that's easy for your team to comprehend — whether they agree with it or not. If it affects one of your top people, you owe her the courtesy of telling her face-to-face before the announcement as well. This is simply good business.

Chapter 15

Making Cuts: When It's Time to Let Someone Go

In This Chapter

- Deciding when to fire someone
- Knowing when the time is right
- Keeping it professional

You knew I'd have to talk about it sooner or later, and there's no getting around it. Part of the job of a professional sales manager is making the decision to and terminating an employee.

If you're new to sales management, let me go ahead and tell you firing someone doesn't get any easier with time. It's always tough because you're dealing with a human being and his ability to provide for his family. If it gets to the point where it doesn't bother you, perhaps you should do something else because you've become extremely jaded.

Like anything, there are good and bad ways to let someone go. It's never a fun process — for either party — but there are definitely ways you can make it worse.

In this chapter, I touch on the when, why, and how of the firing process. You can sugarcoat it with any word you want — termination, reduction in force, laying off, letting go, or whatever — you're still firing someone. I talk about what goes into the decision and how and when best to carry it out. This is one of those chapters you should probably bookmark or otherwise tag for future reference because if you don't need it now, you will eventually.

I can tell you now that if you take the rest of your job seriously, firing someone is going to be hard. If you've grown to truly care about your people as people, it's the hardest thing you do as a manager. In fact, I've had times when I've been physically ill leading up to firing someone. There's just nothing pleasant about it.

Even though the focus is on the person or persons you have to let go, your responsibility is to those you're keeping. If there's one way to find a sliver of positive, it's in the fact that you're protecting the jobs of the people you're keeping — that's where your allegiance lies.

Now that I've got you all excited to tackle this subject, let's get started.

Making the Decision to Fire Someone

The act of deciding to terminate someone's employment is certainly not one you take lightly. Generally the decision is brought about based on one of the following factors:

- **Action (gross misconduct):** The employee did something that violates his employment terms or company policy so egregiously that termination is the only answer. This can be anything from physical confrontation to sexual harassment and anything in between.
- **Behavior (misconduct):** The employee exhibits a pattern of behavior that doesn't conform to your standards. For example, he's habitually late or fails to turn in required paperwork.
- **Performance:** The employee isn't producing the sales numbers required to remain employed.
- **Market:** The employee is victim to your company's need to reduce workforce and either has the least time with the company or is the lowest producer. (Neither of these would've earned a termination had it not been for market conditions.)

I can think of very few situations in which salespeople should be a part of a reduction in workforce. If you have a team that's producing, they're needed more than ever if you have a downturn in your market or economy. Don't cut your profits in an attempt to cut overhead. More on this later in the chapter.

Prior to calling someone into your office, be sure you can answer the following questions:

- **Do you have all the facts?** Have you gathered all the information you need in order to make this an informed decision? Have you talked to everyone involved if it's an action-based dismissal? Have you got all the records and time sheets and so on if you're dismissing for behavior?
- **Are you prepared for the fallout?** Almost every salesperson has loyal customers. Be prepared to have someone out in the market immediately to talk to these customers before they're given a different story. Obviously, you can't get into specifics, but you need to be in contact with the salesperson's customers first. Don't forget about internal fallout as well if you fire a long-term employee.

- **Have you exhausted all other possibilities?** If you have a system of verbal and written warnings, make sure you've gone through that by the book. Never put yourself in a situation of terminating someone when his offense calls for a second written warning.
- **Is it the best time for you?** As crass as it sounds, you want to fire someone at a time that affects your customers and your company the least. Your loyalty lies with your remaining sales team and the company you all work for. There may be times when someone gets an extra week or two he doesn't deserve because it's not a good time for you to fire him.

Be professional and be prepared. Make sure you aren't putting yourself or your company in an unenviable legal position. And, always consult with human resources if you have questions.

Very few people should be surprised when they're terminated. A poor performer knows it's coming, especially if the reason is performance based and you've done your job properly with accurate, honest performance reviews. He knows his production isn't up to the standards you set for him. No matter what someone says or how he acts, seldom does being fired truly come out of left field.

The obvious fireable offenses

Of course, terminating any employee is tough. But, sometimes they make the decision rather easy for you — in fact, by their actions they make the decision themselves.

Your company's human resources department (HR) has a list of actions that constitute immediate termination in the company handbook. You need to be familiar with those actions and perhaps discuss adding some specific to the sales department with your HR director.

If you add actions to the immediate-termination list, provide the new list to all your salespeople and any new salesperson as part of the New Hire Packet. Outline the behavior you expect and the actions you won't tolerate in detail.

Obvious firing offenses include, but are not limited to

- **Physical assault:** Really no explanation needed here. However, you must stay out of the "he hit me first" arguments. Physical violence is physical violence. Only in the event it was used to stop the commission of a crime, bodily injury, or death is violence worth a second look before termination. But, consult human resources or your legal department for specifics.
- **Verbal abuse:** This one is not as cut-and-dried as physical abuse. Read the laws in your state on what constitutes verbal abuse or again, take this to your HR and legal advisors.

- **Alcohol or drugs on the job:** Another situation with little gray area. Under no circumstances should an employee be under the influence of drugs or alcohol on the job. In the event of an accident of any kind, you should immediately send everyone involved for a routine drug screen — every time.
- **Sexual harassment:** This has become much more visible in the past years. Sexual harassment by an employee can put your company in legal peril. If anyone even mentions it, you must investigate fully and take immediate action. Failure to do so could be deemed as approving of the actions. Once again, when in doubt turn to HR and legal.

While the offenses in the preceding list are standard across most organizations and departments, look at some sales-specific action, too:

- **Misrepresentation:** This one is all yours. You probably don't need human resources, legal, or anyone else to help here. If at any time, a salesperson intentionally misrepresents anything to a customer, it should be grounds for termination, no matter whether he misrepresents price, terms, or whatever. Deliberately lying to a customer should be dealt with swiftly and harshly.
- **Submitting false information:** Whether it's an expense report or a call report, false information is false information and there is no room for it in a professional sales organization. In fact, falsifying an expense report is most likely a criminal offense.
- **Misuse of company assets:** This may include cellphone, company vehicles, or company credit cards. Any of these would lead someone right out the door.
- **Non-disclosure of vendor incentives:** If you deal with manufacturers, vendors, or other suppliers who provide incentives for the sale of their product, those inducements should go through you. Unfortunately, sometimes salespeople work a deal with a vendor to circumvent the system and get paid under the table for selling the vendor's products. This is a blatant disregard for what's best for the company and what's best for the customer.
- **Disclosure of proprietary company information:** Salespeople are always in contact with pricing, terms, and other data, including product costs that are considered trade secrets. At no time should any of this information be discussed or shared with anyone outside the company without prior consent.

Those are just a few to get you started thinking. Your particular company or industry may have some specific only to you. The point is to get them clarified and have them in writing before you need them.

Getting fired for one of these offenses doesn't shock or surprise the employee. Everyone know that there are rules you don't break, and if you do, the consequences are spelled out well in advance and are the same for everyone.

Make sure you always state that your list doesn't include every fireable offense. Someone may do something that warrants firing but isn't on the list — you need to leave room to keep your company and your sales team safe from bad actors and bad actions.

In the unlikely event you're dealing with unionized employees, hand any termination issues over to HR and the legal department — that's what they get paid for.

Performance-based termination

When you have to terminate someone based on performance, it's not always as cut-and-dried as action-based or behavior-based offenses. Many times performance-based termination is the culmination of a process — you set out your minimum performance standards and determined someone isn't going to be a long term part of your team.

It's not easy, but keep in mind that you're only responding to the employee's actions or inactions. However, in order to cover yourself, follow a series of steps and handle it the same way every time:

1. **Establish and publish minimum performance standards.**

   It's important to not only establish your minimum performance standards but to publish them. Discuss them and ensure your entire team understands what is expected of them.

2. **Communicate breaches of standards.**

   When someone is falling below what you determined is acceptable levels of performance, communicate that (possibly verbally at first). Let your salesperson know that you're aware of his performance and that it doesn't meet the company's criteria. Make it exceedingly clear what future ramifications are regarding his lack of production.

3. **Counsel an underperforming salesperson.**

   If the salesperson's numbers don't improve after an initial warning, sit down for a more detailed discussion of how you can help him. Ask what he feels is keeping him from achieving your goals. Does he need more training? Does he need access to something that hasn't been available to him? Make sure he leaves the discussion with a set plan of action to improve his sales.

Don't assume you know what the problem is without sitting down with someone who isn't meeting standards and asking questions.

4. **Give a written warning.**

   The step before termination should be a written warning. Let the underperforming employee know for certain that his performance is substandard and subject to termination. Don't sugarcoat it. Make sure he knows the next step is the final one. This written warning should be signed by both parties and made a part of the employee's personnel file.

5. **Make the decision to fire a salesperson based on the data.**

   One of the reassuring things about performance-based termination is you can really take all emotion and judgment out of it. Either the salesperson is or is not living up to expectations. There really is no decision to be made. The salesperson makes this one himself. You simply have to follow through with what you've said you're going to do.

If you don't have a timeline for the process from slipping standards to termination, establish one and stick to it. Every time! Perhaps when a new salesperson is hired you put him on a 90-day probationary period and make clear he's expected to meet certain criteria.

The minimum performance standards are just that: minimum! You're not talking about someone who's just short of being a champion salesperson; you're concerned about people who are barely making the cut. You have minimum performance criteria, and they aren't meeting it. Others in your organization are not only meeting it, they're far surpassing it — that's why it's a minimum. Don't start to think you're letting go of one of your best salespeople. You're not.

After the 90-day probationary period if a new employee isn't up to the minimum, you can issue a verbal warning and give him two weeks to get his numbers up. At the end of that two weeks, you sit down and counsel him to see whether he's made any strides at all. You're now four months in with this person.

After another two-to-four weeks, issue the written warning and give him 30 days to either meet your standards or be terminated. This puts you pretty close to a six-month mark with someone. You're making a significant investment in him, and at this point you know if he's going to get it or not.

If you put a step-by-step process in place, you must follow it every time. You can't keep someone who is substandard because you like him or he's a friend of a friend. If you do, you're opening yourself up to some issues you probably would rather not face. You're going to have enough problems without bringing some on yourself. Don't put it off. Stick to the program.

Reduction in workforce

I hesitate to include this because I hope you never need it. I'm one of those people who believe salespeople should almost never be part of a workforce reduction, so I hope this section is a total waste of space.

If your sales team is made up of good salespeople they not only pay for themselves, but they contribute to the profits of the company. If they aren't, then you should have terminated them for performance and maybe you wouldn't be reducing your workforce now.

The only case I can think of when a sales force may need to be reduced is when two companies merge or one acquires the other and sales territories overlap causing a duplication of duties. That is really the only situation I can think to take a chance of losing a good salesperson.

In the event you find yourself in this situation it's important to convey to the salesperson that his termination doesn't have anything to do with his performance. Explain the situation and be as open as possible. Take time to answer questions and understand his position. He's done his job — sometimes exceedingly well — only to be without a job now. It's a very frustrating position to be in.

If your company allows, offer to write a letter of recommendation spelling out the reason for the reduction in force and note that the salesperson would be eligible for rehire (although he may be hesitant to give *you* another chance). The point is that you handle this termination differently from one where the employee brought it upon himself based on his actions, behaviors, performance, or lack of performance.

Reduction in force, down sizing, right sizing, layoffs — call it what you want, I can't stress enough how you should make every effort possible for it not to impact a salesperson who's productive.

When you've made the decision to let someone go (for whatever reason), write out what you want to say just as you would a sales script. I can't tell you the times I rehearsed what I said — to make sure I said what I wanted to and didn't say anything I didn't. Just like a sales script, this only a tool. Never sit down and read a termination letter to anyone. Give him the courtesy of speaking to him face-to-face, person-to-person and try to not make it some cold, sterile action.

The main purpose of the face-to-face meeting is to make it clear the other person knows he's getting fired. I once had a coworker sit down to terminate someone and in her desire to not hurt his feelings and soft-pedal everything, the two talked for over an hour and the employee still didn't know what was really happening. They talked about the employee's lack of performance, how this should've happened, that should've happened, and so forth. Everything was said except "I'm terminating your employment." In fact, at one time the employee asked, "Does this mean you're firing me?" Keep in mind, this was more than an hour into the conversation! By scripting or outlining what you want to convey, you'll do a much better job in getting your point across — and in the next section, I get into some of the specifics of how to do so.

Choosing Your Moment Carefully

Once you make the decision to fire someone, you have to notify the person to meet you at your office. While it should go without saying, never handle this type situation in front of other employees or customers. This is a strictly "behind closed doors" event.

As a matter of professionalism, call the person you're firing personally and ask him to meet you. If he asks what it's regarding, simply say you want to visit with him. If pressed, don't get into any specifics over the phone.

I've had people ask me point blank, "Am I getting fired?" This further solidifies the point that few are ever really taken by surprise. But, even in this instance, my response is something like, "I don't want to get into this on the phone, just meet me at my office in the morning."

You control the phone conversation and don't let the soon-to-be-fired employee pull you off into topics you should discuss face-to-face.

If you can't find a private place in your office, reserve a conference room or other area the employee is familiar with and can feel comfortable in. This day is harder for him than you and you should do everything in your power to make it as comfortable as possible.

Never pass off firing duty to someone else in your department. Don't delegate the responsibility to someone else just to get out of having to do it yourself. It's part of your job and part of being a leader. If you hand off terminations to a division manager or other mid-level manager, not only are you losing credibility with the person losing his job, but the person having to handle your business is likely to have a new opinion of you, as well.

Believe it or not, there is a best time to terminate someone. Now, this is assuming someone hasn't done something to bring about immediate termination, in which case you have to do what you have to do immediately if not sooner.

If you have to terminate someone because of an offense you have listed as punishable by immediate termination, that means immediate. Don't wait until the next day or a better time for you. Take a physical assault for an example (although it's a rather drastic one), but if an employee physically assaults someone and you wait to fire him, then another employee gets assaulted in the interim, you can be in some serious legal trouble.

As a manager, your job is to ensure a safe workplace. If you have the slightest inkling there could be a problem — whether by actions, words, or other intentions — you have a responsibility to act on behalf of the rest of your employees. Get HR and security involved if you must and have the fired person escorted off the property with his belongings.

In cases where the termination is your choice and you have some leeway in when and how it happens, I submit to you that some times are better than others.

I've seen people wait until Friday afternoon in order to hand out the pink slip or to call someone in to fire him. I totally disagree with this move. You're about to take someone's livelihood away. Why wait until Friday when his only option is to go home and mope around all weekend?

Any time I had to terminate someone and had a choice as to how and when to do it, I always chose Monday morning. Granted, it made for a less-than-enjoyable weekend for me knowing what I had to do Monday morning, but on the other hand, your salesperson can immediately go out and start looking for another job.

Firing an employee on Monday morning also offers you the opportunity to get it out of the way so you can control the information flow to your other employees and customers. Some customers and sales team members may be unavailable on a weekend if you wait until Friday.

By the same token, I always chose to handle these situations in the morning rather than at close of business. As their manager, I felt it my obligation to take care of them and look out for them even on the day I was about to terminate their employment. It just never felt right to me to have someone out representing my company — selling my products and services or waiting on my customers all day — on the day I had chosen to fire him. There's just something that feels wrong there.

If you're like me and struggle with firing someone on a personal level, I advise you to get it out of the way early and go on about your day. I've never gotten to where letting someone go doesn't bother me — it's just the way I'm wired. And, although I understand that the person I'm firing is losing a lot more than I am, I want to be able to put this unpleasant issue aside and focus on my job — which is leading my department to the best of my ability.

If you have to let someone go and you plan it for Friday, how well do you think you're going to perform your job the rest of the week knowing it's coming? How is your communication going to be with them in the preceding days? There are some things you just can't fake. They will smell it a mile away. Trust me.

So, if you have a choice, choose to fire someone early Monday morning. Do it, get it over with and both of you can go about your week.

Keeping It Professional

When the time comes, be sure you handle the termination with as much professionalism and control as possible. The following sections outline how you can have this very difficult conversation in a way that protects you and maintains the dignity of all involved.

Remember that you're dealing with a human being. No matter what you decide to use as your script or how you choose to handle the actual termination never, ever take away anyone's dignity. You're taking away someone's job, not his self worth. As unpleasant as the task may be, treat him with the same respect you'd like to be treated with. He has a family to go home to and his day isn't going to end like yours. Be aware that being fired puts people in a fragile emotional state. Everything you say can either pick them up or tear them down. Always allow them to walk out with their head held as high as possible considering the circumstances.

Use this as an opportunity to show compassion. It will make you a much better manager in the long run.

Have a witness

The decision has been made and you've decided on the time. Now you need to secure a witness to sit in on the meeting with you. Some may think this is for personal protection (I guess it could be, so choose a big witness), but it's actually to cover your tail and make sure all your t's are crossed and i's are dotted.

Your witness shouldn't be someone from your own department if at all possible. It's best if the witness is another member of management. Stress to your witness ahead of time that he's there simply to observe and shouldn't inject himself into the conversation even if the employee tries to engage him in it. His job is to simply witness the termination in the event his account is needed in the future.

Your witness should never participate in the conversation at all. He's there to observe and observe only. You're going to have a hard enough time controlling your own tongue without having to worry about someone else's.

As well as you've planned for today, the employee hasn't. His emotions are going to be raw. You need a witness to make sure things aren't remembered differently by the two parties later — and they will be.

Additionally, having a witness provides backup for you and the employee that you secured all the company property upon his exit. You probably have a list of all company-owned assets you need to retrieve, but if not, here are few:

- **Laptop or computer:** Get this immediately. Never give the employee access to it after you terminate him. I've had entire hard drives erased with customer lists and other information gone.
- **Cellphone:** Another item to collect immediately. Don't allow a fired employee to delete any numbers, texts, or emails. If he wants personal numbers removed, you can do that for him.
- **Sales materials/pricing:** Make sure you collect all sales materials, pricing plans, proposal, customer lists, and so on. Anything that can be used by the salesperson if he were to go to work at a competitor should be left with you.
- **Company credit cards:** Make sure you have fuel cards, credit cards, and any other cards before the employee leaves the premises.
- **Keys:** Whether it's keys to a company-issued vehicle or keys to the building, always collect them in front of the witness. Even the employee will want to ensure he isn't held responsible for these after his departure.
- **Passwords and access codes:** In today's world, everything seems to be password or access-code protected. Make sure you're able to get into the laptop, cellphone, and any other protected device before letting a fired employee leave the building. If terminated employees sign a statement saying they have returned all company property, include a paragraph stating that they gave you access to all company-related websites and so forth that are password protected.

After you cover the details of the termination, get all company property back, have the termination document signed by all — including the witness — and allow the former employee to add any statement he'd like to make to be part of the permanent record.

Your HR department should have a list of all company property assigned to the employee so you can simply go through the checklist. If it doesn't, take some time now to create one. You'll be glad you did when the time comes.

In addition to a witness, have someone standing by to drive the employee home in the event he has a company vehicle or takes public transportation to work. Don't terminate someone and then have him sit at a bus stop. Again, as a matter of professionalism, take it upon yourself to provide your former employee with a way home.

The person driving a fired employee should be someone you trust, because he's likely to get an earful from the now former employee, so he needs to be a 100 percent team player and not someone whose opinion and attitude are easily swayed.

Keep it civil

Any time you terminate an employee you can expect him to be upset. He's just lost his livelihood and is likely to be emotional. Keep your emotions and professionalism in check and be prepared.

Don't take anything a just-terminated employee says personally. Lashing out is a defense mechanism. Remember, he's been backed into a corner and is just reacting on instinct. His mind is running with everything from where he's going to work next, to how to pay the mortgage, to what he's going to tell his spouse. This is a very emotional time.

You're not qualified to fire me!

I once had to terminate an employee who had sold literally nothing in his first four months of employment. I don't mean his sales were low, I mean they were nonexistent. Nevertheless, the firing I thought the nonperforming employee expected came as a total shock to him.

When I called the employee in to meet me on Monday morning, he thought we were just having a friendly discussion. It was as if he had no real understanding of the fact that this was a business, even though about 30 days before the owner of the company and I had gone through our expectations and the need to pick up the pace with the whole sales team.

Anyway, on this morning I had my witness in the conference room with me and called the employee in. He saw the witness and knew what was going on. I asked him more than once to sit down so we could have a discussion and he refused.

His only response was, "You aren't qualified to run this department. How can you fire me?" His defense mechanism was to deflect onto me. "You're a horrible manager. How can you fire me?"

This was the refrain throughout the meeting as I took keys, laptop, and so forth. Rather than have someone take him home, I called a cab and paid the cab driver the estimated fare.

When it was over, the person I had witness said to me, "How in the world did you remain calm and not say something?" My response: "Well, I'm at work right now, and he's not."

If at any time a terminated employee gets verbally abusive or you feel a threat of physical violence, immediately end the conversation and call for security to escort him off the premises. (Hopefully, you have a witness in the room to help contain the situation, but know how to summon help quickly.)

Never forget the fact that you are the manager. You must put your emotions aside and simply take care of business. Keep your cool and don't let your former employee pull you into a shouting match or a he-said/she-said back and forth. You're a professional.

Also, be prepared for people to try to talk you out of firing them. They'll have excuses and reasons you've never heard of. They'll try to play on your emotions, and if you're even the slightest bit softhearted, you're going to be tempted to give them another chance. Don't. If you do, the situation only gets worse. The next time you have to have that exact same conversation with the exact same person, it will be even harder.

Have all your documentation ready, rehearse what you want to say, and know what you don't want to say. Be as calm as possible. If you get upset or angry, you're only going to add fuel to the fire.

Firing people is one of, if not the, hardest parts of being a manager. It's not easy, and it never gets easy. But, you must do what has to be done.

Choose your words carefully

The decision on the location, the words you use, your tone of voice, and everything in between must always be nothing but professional. You're taking a person who was a member of your team and closing the door on him. It's not a comfortable situation for anyone, but you can make it a bit more palatable by how you handle it.

This is no time for small talk. Don't try to ease your way into the conversation. Doing so only makes a bad situation worse. Once you sit down, get right to the point of the conversation.

I've used this sample script a few times in my career:

> (Employee), I've called you here this morning and asked (witness) to sit in because I've decided to terminate your employment. I know this is not what you want to hear, and I understand that, but the decision has been made, and I've decided to go in a different direction.
>
> I need to get your phone, keys, and laptop (and any other critical property) and will have someone help you gather your personal belongings. You'll be paid through today and human resources has all the information on continuation of your benefits. I wish it would've worked out differently.

That's it. I covered the high points and left little to the imagination. I made sure I got my point across in the most professional manner possible. Notice I didn't get personal, didn't rehash old issues, or get into specifics (I talk about that in the next section). I was brief, clear, and to the point.

The key points to cover in your termination speech are

- **Be specific about the purpose of the meeting.** I intentionally use the words "terminate your employment" so there's no misunderstanding. We both now know for sure what's happening.
- **The decision is made.** I always take responsibility for the decision — "I've decided to terminate your employment" — and let the person know the decision is final.
- **Don't be specific about reasons.** I simply say, "I've decided to go in a different direction." (I talk about why to be nonspecific in the next section.)
- **The need to recover company property.** Address this sooner rather than later. Have a list to make sure you get everything and don't forget about passwords and access codes.
- **Help gather personal belongings:** You can be sure a just-fired person isn't thinking clearly. You've just hit him with some of the worst possible news. Assure him you have someone to help get his things together.
- **Info on ongoing or terminating benefits.** I always prefer to have human resources go over the benefits. First, I didn't want to misspeak, and secondly it gives HR a reason to talk to the employee before he leaves. This is another safety net so everyone knows how things are handled.

After I delivered my short speech, I always gave the employee a chance to speak. Reactions ranged from tears to anger. Luckily I never had anyone get physical or threaten physical violence, but you should always be on guard for it.

Give the person a chance to talk and hear him out even though it's not going to change anything. You owe him the common courtesy to listen to what he has to say.

Try to find something positive to say to end the conversation. Don't promise to help the person find a new job or anything like that, but find something positive to leave with him. You can talk for a half-an-hour but your opening sentence and final words are the things that will ring in his ears for days, weeks, months, and maybe years to come.

If you have a severance package, this is the time to go over that information and let the (former) employee know how his last paycheck will be handled. Once you take him to HR for the benefit discussion, you should have another employee with him at all times.

Allow him to collect his personal effects and then have him taken home.

As you can see, some advance planning goes into this. In any situation where you're making the choice to terminate someone, take the time to step through how it's all going to be handled. Don't make a hard situation harder by having a fired employee sit around and wait for the human resources director while everyone walks by his office.

As you're planning, be careful about who and what is included in the plan. I had a manager many years ago who was terminating someone from out of town. The salesperson in question was going to be coming in for a three-day meeting but the manager had set the termination up for the day he arrived. Trying to cover all his bases and plan it out, the manager also cancelled the last two days of the person's hotel room knowing they wouldn't be needed. While this seems like really good planning, it backfired when the employee checked in to the hotel and the desk clerk said, "I see here that (manager) has cancelled tomorrow night and Sunday night."

As you can imagine the salesperson immediately knew what was going on and slept little that night and was not in the best of moods the next morning.

Planning is great, but be careful what you plan and whom you include in those plans. Be very careful not to do anything that could get back to the employee ahead of time — not because you don't want him to know, but simply because it's a very unprofessional way to find out he's about to lose his job.

You should also be prepared to give the departing employee an idea of what is going to happen next.

Someone who's just been fired isn't thinking clearly. The more you can have the process laid out for him, the smoother it will go. Being professional here includes taking control of some of the things the employee would normally do but is in no position to do right now.

Finally, either you or HR should be prepared to discuss all details of final paychecks, severance packages, and so on. Provide all this information in writing because a fired employee's head is spinning and he's never going to remember everything you go over with him. Seldom does anyone hear anything after being told you're letting him go.

Stay away from specifics

I've seen a lot of different views on how to handle an employee termination over the 25-plus years I've been in management. But, one thing almost everyone agrees upon: Stay away from specifics.

In my script in the preceding section, I use the words "I decided to go in a different direction." The reason I use that phrase is that there can be no argument about it. The person being fired can't dispute the fact that I made that decision.

Firing someone is not the time for discussion about whether you're going to let him go or not. That decision has been made, and it's not going to change. If you get into specifics about this or that, you're inviting a dialogue and the person you're firing goes into defense mode and likely tries to dispute your reasons or opinions. By staying away from any specific reason, you eliminate the entire argument phase of the conversation.

By using the phrase "going in a different direction," you don't make a statement that can be used against you or the company if the person chooses to fight the termination later. Whatever happens after you end his employment is a different direction, so you're speaking nothing but the truth.

Anyone losing his job will try to pull you into specifics. He'll want to know the why of it all. Stay away from answering that question. Anything you say he'll try to refute, and engaging him is only going to lead you down a rabbit hole you don't want to be in. Such a discussion would change the entire tone of the meeting. Even though you may want to give a reason, you shouldn't. Remember, whatever reason you give can be argued, but nobody can argue with your decision to go in a different direction.

Helping you avoid being drawn into a discussion about specifics is another reason to have your witness in the room with you. The witness hears and observes the entire process and may be needed later to back up the fact that you didn't fire the person for X or Y. Rather, the person was let go simply because you chose to go in a different direction.

If you haven't noticed, I highly recommend the phrase "I've decided to go in a different direction."

If the person asks whether you're letting him go because of something he did, simply respond with "I've just decided to go in a different direction."

I've had people almost play a guessing game and start listing things they did wrong — some of which I knew nothing about — to see if that was the reason I was terminating them. Again, don't allow yourself to be pulled into that trap.

Temper everything you say and do knowing it could possibly come back and be used in a court hearing in the future. Don't let your guard down, and don't get pulled into any conversation you don't control. You're likely to feel sorry for the individual and be emotional yourself, but keep your senses about you when it comes to what you do and say. It's all on the record.

Terminating an employee — no matter what the circumstances — is one of the hardest, least-liked parts of being a manager. There is no special speech or secret to handling it. I wish I could tell you something that would make it easier, but I can't. There is nothing.

If there's one thing I tried to focus on, it was the fact that my allegiance and responsibility was to the salespeople and members of my team who were staying — I owed it to them to uphold the standards I (and my company) had set for actions, behaviors, and performance. Letting someone slide just because you don't want to tackle the hard job of firing him isn't good for anyone and is especially unfair to those salespeople who do their job and perform at the highest level possible.

Chapter 16

Managing for the Future: Developing Careers of Future Leaders

In This Chapter

- Identifying future managers
- Looking at three types of employee
- Selecting and grooming and your replacement

One of the best pieces of advice I ever got was to hire someone who could replace me. Now, a lot of people are afraid to do that. They may think that person will make them look bad or outshine them. But, in my mind, it's the contrary: The willingness to hire the best possible talent shows a commitment to the future and not just today. Plus, if I hadn't hired people smarter than me, I would've been very lonely.

No business is really a business if it's not built for tomorrow. The world is changing at an alarming pace and in order to not only keep up, but to actually lead the charge, you need leaders at every level of your organization.

Some of your team members just want to maintain the status quo and keep their jobs. But others have career ambitions and think down the road. They understand the big picture and are focused on more than just getting through until Friday. Granted, those qualities must be inherent in a person — you can't really teach or guide someone toward that type of thinking or goal setting. But you certainly need to identify those select, ambitious few early on.

In this chapter, I take a look at how you take those select few to the next level, how you build from within and create an organization that will outlive you and those around you.

Managing Future Leaders

Leaders create more leaders. Managers develop more managers. Your job is to find those in your ranks who meet the criteria you set forth and guide, teach, coach, and mentor them to a career path that eventually pushes you out of a job.

As a manager, you have the hiring phase, the training phase, the managing phase, and the developing stage. You hire new people — in this case, salespeople — into your company, you train them to the best of your ability, you manage and stabilize their contribution to your business, and you develop their skill sets for the future.

As shown in Figure 16-1, there are stages in the career of a professional salesperson and you, as the sales manager, need to know at all times where each team member is.

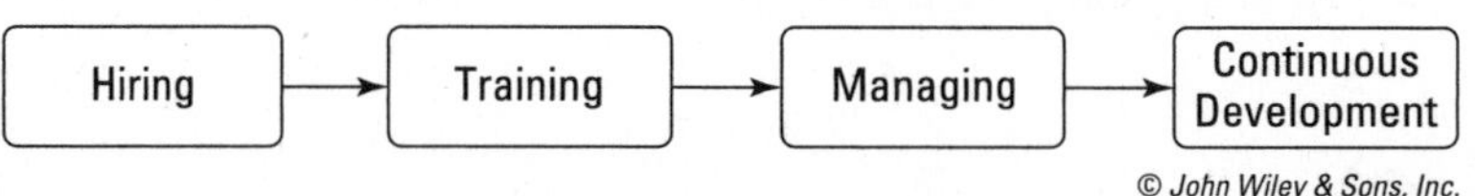

Figure 16-1: The life of a professional salesperson.

The tricky part for you is that you probably have at least one person in every one of those phases at any give time. Being a good, productive manager and leader means recognizing what stage each of your people is in and helping them get to the next.

I use the example of teachers and students a lot in this book, so think of it this way: you get them in kindergarten, take them through grade school where several will accelerate to middle school. From there a few will move on to high school. Your real challenge is to take the handful who want to go on to college and develop them into people who will run your company into the next generation.

It's not easy. Why? Because in elementary school everyone tells you they want to go to college. But, the reality is very few are willing to do the work required to get there. When you find them, whatever you do don't lose them. They're like gold or diamonds.

Steel magnate Andrew Carnegie once had more than 30 millionaires working for him. Now, this was back when a million bucks was a million bucks. Someone asked Mr. Carnegie how he had been so fortunate to hire so many millionaires. He said, "They weren't millionaires when I hired them."

Andrew Carnegie molded and shaped men to become more than they thought they could be. He not only built industry, he built people.

Are you prepared to take on that challenge? Are you prepared to help develop the leaders of tomorrow in your department and your organization? If so, one day you can say, "They weren't leaders when I hired them."

Identifying the Three Types of People in Every Organization

One of the wisest men I know taught me many years ago that there are three types of people in any organization:

- **Those who want more responsibility but can't handle it:** They want to be the boss or a manager, but they don't have the skills required to do the job.
- **Those who could handle more responsibility but don't want it:** These people have hit their comfort zone. They're happy right where they are. They don't want to be bothered after 5:00 p.m. and have no desire to grow or take on any leadership role. This type drives you crazy because of wasted potential.
- **Those who want more responsibility and can handle it:** This select few are the ones you must groom as your leaders of tomorrow. But, be warned: Of the three groups, this is by far the smallest.

In a completely unscientific estimate, I've found about 50 percent of people fall into the category of wanting it and can't handle it, 40 percent could handle it but don't want it, and only 10 percent are your true leaders of tomorrow, as shown in Figure 16-2.

In the next sections, I take an in-depth look at all three of these, share ways to identify them, and offer advice on what to do with them.

There's a place for each level of responsibility in an organization. Each of them plays a role, but you must both agree on the role she is going to play. You can't have someone who can't handle responsibility thinking she's in line for the benefits of the super group. (Being sales manager isn't all fun and games, is it?)

There's no way to create leaders of tomorrow without longevity. As a sales manager, you have to recognize those who can contribute long term and hold on to them. If someone is going to lead the next generation, you want her to do it for you — not your competitor down the street.

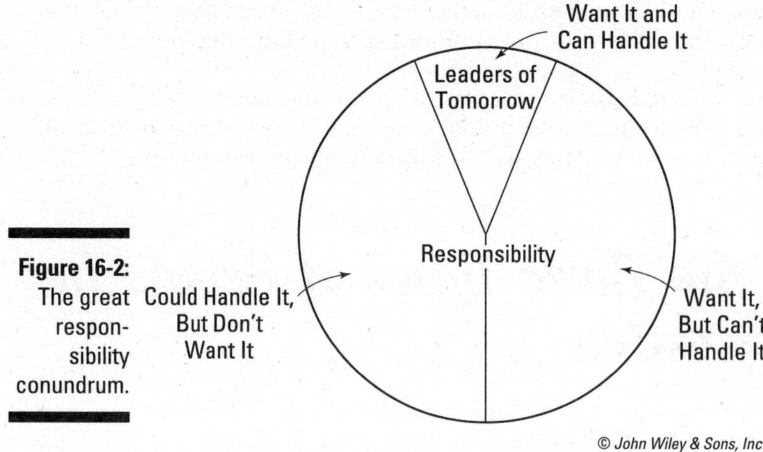

Figure 16-2: The great responsibility conundrum.

Are you creating a place where your people can see the big picture? Are you allowing your salespeople to think and dream bigger than their current position? If not, you're stifling the creativity and growth of the very people you covet.

If someone is content in her current position, that's fine. But, don't stop the dreamers and those who dare to set big, bold goals.

My mentor who hired me when I was 21 told me one of the things he saw in me was desire. During my interview with him, he asked where I saw myself in five years. I told him I wasn't sure about five years, but eventually I wanted his job. Gutsy? Not really. Isn't that what you want — someone who can see beyond this week's commission check?

Who's in your hall of fame?

A very successful auto dealer in Bossier City, Louisiana, recounted a story to me of how he recognized longevity. George Fritze built Red River Chevrolet into a thriving business despite many obstacles. He's landlocked — actually almost under an interstate and isn't part of the new wave of auto malls. Yet, his business continues to grow in part because of how he treats his people.

"We believe in recognizing our people," Fritze said. "We want them to feel like 'I am somebody' — to feel appreciated. They're certainly less likely to leave and go somewhere else. Many years ago we created a Hall of Fame and have pictures of long-term employees on our showroom wall. We recognize anyone who has been with our company longer than 20 years. We've got six people who have been with us more than 50 years and two with more than 60 years. We want people to feel like they are part of something bigger."

I would guess Mr. Fritze has little trouble finding people who want to be a part of his team.

As I look at the three types of people within an organization, think about your own staff: where does each of them fit in your mind? Do you think they see themselves in the same position?

If an employee aspires to something greater but you don't see that for her, she will go somewhere else to try to reach those heights. You have to decide if you're okay with that. Is this a person you have pegged for a future leadership role? If so, your vision for her better align with hers.

Those who want more responsibility, but can't handle it

The very first group of people I address is those who want more responsibility but can't handle it. You know the ones — they would love to be the boss but have a hard time managing themselves.

There's nothing wrong with the people in this group, they just don't have the leadership skills (yet) to take on challenges. Does that mean they can't be in that position some day? Absolutely not. It just means they aren't there today.

As a young sales manager, I was in charge of managing a team of about 20 salespeople, most of whom were much older than me. Many could've (and maybe did) see me as some young, punk kid trying to run the show. I made it a point to go out of my way to act older or somehow change who I was in order to fit what I thought they expected me to be. Big mistake. After a while it became apparent to me that I was making a bigger deal of my age than they were. They were looking for a sales manager, not a father figure. It didn't matter how old I was as long as I was able to see what they saw and understand where they thought they fit in the grand scheme of things.

I learned that it was more about how they saw themselves fit into the puzzle than how I fit into the puzzle. Once I recognized where they were along their career track (refer to Figure 16-1), I was better able to manage them and provide appropriate feedback and guidance.

I had several salespeople who fell into the category of wanting more responsibility but were unable to handle it. When we both understood what it would take for them to move to the next step, some were willing to do the work and others weren't.

You will find people who either want to be hired in as a vice president with an assistant and a corner office or think they can fast track themselves into that position overnight. If you take the time to show them that yes, they can get there and what it takes, you may be surprised at how many change their goals. Not everyone is willing to work to get to the next level.

My late father used to tell me, "If it was easy, everybody would do it." There's a lot of truth in that. If you give people a title and a raise, they are all in, but if it takes effort, sacrifice and work some decide they're content right where they are.

The biggest mistake you can make with your people who fall into this group is to let them think they have a management position or promotion coming to them just because of seniority. Remember, it's important for both of you to understand where they are and don't think you are always the one who is confused. Many times they're the ones confused about where they are along their career path.

When you identify salespeople who want more responsibility but can't handle it, you must decide if they will ever be able to handle it. Is this where they are now or where they're going to be forever? If the potential is there, work with them to develop and hone leadership and management skills. If they aren't management material, make them the best salesperson they can be. Success equals happiness. It's not so much about what their title says on their business card as the contribution they can make to the overall success of your organization. It takes great people at every position — not just management. Don't waste good people just because they can't advance past where they are.

Some of the greatest salespeople I've ever known would've made horrible sales managers, and they knew it! Not everyone is cut out to run a department or manage others. Never see that as the sign of a bad salesperson — you'll cost yourself some great people that way.

Those who can handle responsibility but don't want it

The group of salespeople that will drive you craziest and have you ready to pull your hair out are those who could handle more responsibility but don't want it. These people have hit their comfort zones; they aren't interested in growing or progressing. They like to show up to work, do their job extremely well and then go home and not worry about anything until it's time to show up again.

You know these people have the potential to be so much more, and it's frustrating to see that potential wasted. Some people just don't aspire to be more than they are. Of course, there's nothing wrong with that, there's a seat for them on the bus, it's just not the driver's seat as much as you'd like for them to take the wheel. For whatever reason, these people can't see themselves as leaders. They have all the characteristics and qualities you'd normally look for in a leader, but they just cannot see themselves in that position.

If you're a good manager, few things bother you more than wasted potential. Seeing someone you know could excel choose to play small instead of growing is extremely frustrating. You'll likely find it hard to grasp their reasoning, but it's not for you to understand — just accept it and move on.

Don't let your frustrations affect your relationship with the people in this group. Some people are just made to come in, punch the clock, do their job and leave. If they truly don't have the desire to advance, there's not a lot you can do about it.

Some great salespeople fall into this category. A lack of desire to be a manager doesn't preclude someone from being a great salesperson. Focus on the strengths these types have and help them get the most out of those instead of worrying about what they aren't going to do or be.

Don't force the square peg into a round hole

Steven was a one of my top salespeople. He knew his product, could sell to anyone, and had been with the company for many years. So, when it came time to promote someone to division manager, he was the obvious choice.

There was only one problem: he didn't want to be a division manager. He was happy right where he was and was making a good living at it. His customers loved him, he was never away from home, and in retrospect, and he had a pretty sweet deal going.

But, I wanted him to be my division manager. Well, that's not entirely true — I needed him to take the position because I had nobody else who was ready. After Steven there was a tremendous drop off in talent and experience.

He was the obvious choice and the person everyone anticipated would get the job after I got promoted to vice president of sales. I hadn't really spent a lot of time grooming Steven to be my replacement; it was just kind of assumed he would be the perfect fit. And we all know what happens when you assume.

When he told me he really didn't want the job, I was floored. I couldn't believe it. Just because I was the type personality who wanted to progress, having someone as talented as he was not want to was foreign to me — it just didn't make sense.

How can you not want a promotion? These are the things I lived for — it was why I was working. I wanted to keep climbing the corporate ladder. Well, Steven didn't. Had no interest in it. None. Zip. Nada.

It made absolutely no sense to me — I really couldn't fathom why someone wouldn't want it. But, that was because that's the way I was wired — it wasn't necessarily the way Steven was.

We talked on more than one occasion about how great it would be for him to take the job. (Great for me.) We talked about how it was the natural next step for him. Each time we talked, I tried harder and harder to sell him on the idea that it really was what he wanted he just didn't know it.

(continued)

(continued)

Looking back on it, it was all from a selfish standpoint. I needed Steven to take the job. He was my only option. I didn't have a plan B ready and I had already taken my position. If he turned it down I was going to be in a pickle finding someone from within or doing something I didn't want to do — bring someone in from the outside. I was going to have a learning curve in my new position and really didn't want to take on the added pressure of training someone completely new on the ways of our industry and company.

After several meetings (a few of which found me almost begging), Steven agreed to be my division manager. It was something we both regretted almost immediately.

I had taken a great salesperson and made him a poor manager. He was now in a role he was totally unprepared for and uncomfortable in. His customers didn't care for the salespeople we assigned to them — they wanted Steven.

His family didn't like the new hours, travel, and other responsibilities that came along with the job. It was, in a word disastrous — disastrous for me, for him, and for the company. It was just a bad situation all the way around.

And, it wasn't really anyone's fault but my own. I was trying to force a square peg into a round hole and it didn't work. In my haste to make myself happy and do what was easy for me, I made almost everyone else miserable. After only a few months, Steven and I agreed to start training someone to take his place — it would be much better for me to have to train one manager than to have all these other people in an uproar.

It was a lesson I'll never forget. You cannot make a great salesperson a great manager if she doesn't want to be one. You'll end up losing a great salesperson. Luckily for me, Steven stuck it out and assisted in the transition for the new person and stepped right back into his old role.

Which brings up another point: if you have someone take a new position — especially if she's doing it for the good of the company — never put her in a position where she cannot go back to her old job. If she's willing to step out on faith for you, don't burn the bridge behind her. If you do, you'll never have anyone want to take a promotion again.

It's not up to you to try to move someone from one of these groups to another — even as badly as you want to sometimes. Your job is to determine what group your employees are in because the people you need to really focus on and develop are the few who fall into the third group: those who want more responsibility and can handle it.

You got to where you are today because you wanted more responsibility and could handle it. As hard as it may be for you to process some people don't want your job. They're extremely happy in their own little world, and the last thing either of you need is for you to rock that boat.

The select few who want responsibility and can handle it

It's natural to find yourself gravitating toward this group — those who actually want additional responsibility and can handle the job of taking it on. You'll know who they are even though they make up only an estimated ten percent of your sales force.

When you identify these people or tag someone for future management, do everything within your power to keep them in your organization. Keep them challenged, keep them hungry and keep them moving forward. They don't like to be stagnant.

Although you may set up your own criteria and traits you look for, some I've found run through virtually 100 percent of people willing and able to carry your organization into the future:

- **Positive attitude:** These people tend to exemplify what it means to be positive. They're almost always upbeat and see the glass as half full rather than half empty — and their attitude tends to be infectious. Others like to be around them and seek them out in a crowd
- **Motivated:** These people don't have to be hit with jumper cables every morning. They're ready to go, motivated, and looking to grow. They tend to have a magnetic personality that draws others toward them. Leaders are like that — they create an aura others want to follow.
- **Goal oriented:** You rarely meet a successful leader who isn't goal-oriented. Your future leaders have very specific goals about where they want to go, what they want to do, and how they plan to accomplish it. Most of them can tell you where they want to be a year from now, five years from now, and more. These members of your sales team take it upon themselves to establish weekly, monthly, and quarterly sales targets — and usually hit them.
- **Problem solvers:** This one is big to me. We all know people who are problem finders. They love to and almost live for the chance to point out flaws instead of using that same energy to find a solution. In contrast, your managers of the next generation are problem solvers. They see a problem and take it upon themselves to either correct it or bring you the solution. They're always thinking of how to do things bigger, better, and more efficiently. If a customer has an issue, they don't say, "that's not my job." They solve the problem first and then look for the cause afterward.
- **Action oriented:** Leaders take action. Sure, they're thinkers, but they are also doers. Once a plan is in place they are generally the first out making it happen or at least testing the waters.

- **Creative:** Your leaders of tomorrow are creative — creative in their approach to their job and with ideas on how to help their customers. They aren't satisfied with a "that's the way we've always done it" attitude. They tend to question a lot of things, and at times you may find yourself disliking this trait. Get over it. You want creative people leading your organization — they're the pioneers.
- **Hungry for knowledge:** These people are sponges — soaking up everything they can. They have a true desire to learn, whether it's through asking questions, reading, attending workshops, or whatever. This is by far the most desirable characteristic because it can't be faked — a person either wants to learn or she doesn't. I've always heard, "readers are leaders." You'll find a lot of readers in this group — and not reading junk, either. They're reading the latest sales books, blogs, or otherwise seeking knowledge.
- **Positive people skills:** True leaders have to have the desire to help others. They take less credit and more blame and are as happy for other people's success as their own. They don't lead people as much as they have people follow them.

If a member of your sales team demonstrates more than two or three of the traits in this list, let her know you see bright things in her future. These people thrive on feedback, and you want them to know that if they aspire to grow, you want that growth to occur under your roof.

I think there's a reason why this is the smallest of the three groups: commitment. A lot of people have the desire, they just don't have the discipline it takes to follow through and learn what they need to know, do what they need to do, and sacrifice today for the good of tomorrow.

We live in an era of immediate gratification, and building for the future is not as prevalent as it was in previous generations. Today we have microwaves, fast food, and instant access to everything under the sun. Fewer and fewer people really want to work to build something — they want it all now.

These people are few and far between. If you have one, don't let her go. If you have a really good one, *never* let her go! It may be a long time before you have another opportunity to develop someone like that.

Responsibility is a funny thing. Some run to it while others run from it. No matter which way they run, if they're great salespeople there should be a spot for them on your team as long as the responsibility they're shunning isn't the basis for their job. It's one thing to not want more responsibility, but it's an entirely different thing to not accept the responsibility that comes with the job.

Though they are willing to work for what they want, the salespeople (or really anyone) who fall into this category tend to be impatient. They know where they're going and want to get there as fast as they can. They don't want a lot of red tape holding them up.

Communicate with them regularly and provide proper feedback on where they are and what the next steps are in their journey.

Look for ways to include these people in industry programs allowing them to learn and grow. I've found this group of young leaders to be very much into personal development. You should spend as much or more on their personal development as they do. Their growth into management should be just as important to you as it is to them.

Building Yourself Out of a Job: Grooming Your Replacement

It may sound strange to hear that you should build yourself out of a job, but that's exactly what you should be doing as a manager. You should always be looking for who's going to take your place tomorrow.

When you find that person or those people, you must start preparing them to take over in your absence.

A management team I was a part of used to ask, "If I were to get hit by a truck tomorrow, who would take my job?" We always wanted to know that if something happened to us, the company would survive.

If you think of it in those terms — if something happened to you today, who would fill your role? Are they ready? Would the company suffer? I'm not trying to sound morbid, but you have to think in those terms.

No business should ever be so dependent on one person that it would collapse if she left or something happened to her. Apple survived the resignation and untimely death of Steve Jobs; Walmart has continued to grow after leader and founder Sam Walton passed way in 1992. But, many organizations don't fare as well simply because they have a poorly thought out plan or worse — no plan at all.

In 2013, *Forbes* magazine published the results of a study by Professor Sascha O. Becker at the University of Warwick in the U.K. and Professor Hans K. Hvide at the University of Bergen in Norway. The study surveyed more than

300 privately owned companies up to ten years old whose majority owner and founder had died. They compared those organizations to similar companies where the owner or manager was still living. Amazingly, the companies who lost their leader suffered up to a 60 percent sales decline in four years and employment was down 17 percent. Those numbers are scary! The professors hypothesized the owners were the glue that held the business together.

Even though you may not be an owner or founder of your company, your department is a microcosm of your entire organization.

I've heard of companies where the key executives or department heads wouldn't fly on the same flight (and I'm not talking about just knowing the secret formula or recipe). Why would you ever have your company in a position where an accident beyond your control could totally wipe it out? In my opinion, this is poor management. At any given time you should be prepared or at least preparing for the next person to step up and take your job. Don't see it as a threat but as a way to set your department, company, or organization up to survive the future.

Not having a clear plan for the future of your department or your company is akin to firing one of your salespeople and worrying more about them than about those who still work for you. If you think only about the person you're letting go, you're ignoring those left behind. By the same token, you have to build yourself out of a job in order to take care of the people at the company long after you've left it. That's just being a good manager.

Is this difficult? You bet! Heck, it's hard to even really think about if you consider it from the standpoint of someone taking over after your death. But, what would happen if you got promoted tomorrow? What would happen if someone above you passed away and you had to take her position, who would be the person to step up and fill your shoes? These are all questions you should be in a position to answer at a moment's notice.

What's your plan? Are you building yourself out of a job by developing talent under you? If not, start immediately, if not sooner.

Developing the leaders of tomorrow

After you realize that you need someone to take over for you one day, it's time to get to the job of developing that talent and making sure your department and your company are set for long-term growth and prosperity.

Developing leaders at every level

Many years ago, I helped create a program called Leaders At Every Level at a company where I was executive vice president. We challenged each department head to identify at least one person in her department who fit the criteria to be a future leader and invite that person (or persons) to participate in the program. Keep in mind, initially we knew only that these people could handle more responsibility — we weren't sure if they wanted it or not.

After the candidates were selected, they were interviewed by a panel of managers and given the opportunity to join the program. Some did, and others chose not to.

The program consisted of monthly meetings in which these future leaders were exposed to other departments — the inner workings of the company — and invited to participate in other management functions. Additionally, they had monthly meetings on their own where they were tasked with solving problems given to them by the management team.

For instance, if we had a production issue or delivery issue or whatever, we threw that over to this group and let them take a stab at solving it or handling that particular issue. Sometimes we took their findings, and other times we didn't. It was a great exercise for everyone involved.

The true win was that it gave them real-world experience in dealing with things they would have to work through in the future as a manager or department head. It also gave them a respect for what their current leader was dealing with on a day-to-day basis.

We sent members of this group to trade shows and other seminars and management training. Everything was paid for them. But, they were required to report back to the entire management team what they learned or what they discovered at each of these events. We weren't just going to pay for a vacation trip. It was meant to be a learning experience.

Our Leaders At Every Level program was a huge hit. We developed several future leaders who are still with that company today almost 20 years later. Would they have been if we hadn't had that program? Maybe. But, I firmly believe the training and experience they got proved to be invaluable in future decision making and management.

I talk about many things you must do to be a good sales manager, but when it comes to your leaders of tomorrow, you have to concentrate your time on those who are going to actually be the leaders — those who display the desire for more responsibility and demonstrate the ability to handle it.

Don't forget to make sure this group is challenged in their current job. Never let them get complacent or stale. Ensure they are on a growth path you both have identified will take them to where both of you want them to eventually be.

After you select or identify your future leaders, you must hold them to a higher standard than the rest of your salespeople or employees. Any lapse in judgment or breach of company policy should cause you to seriously examine your decision.

In our Leaders At Every Level program (see the nearby sidebar, "Developing leaders at every level"), if one of our future leaders missed two meetings within a year without cause she was dismissed from the program. If you're going to make a commitment *to* a select few, you must demand a commitment *from* them!

Your future leaders are the leaders of tomorrow — not today. They're going to make mistakes. That's the entire reason you create training programs or groups — so they can learn from them. When they make a mistake, don't overlook it — work through it as a group and let them know how and why they could have taken a better path. These are knowledge-seekers . . . let them learn.

Whether you develop a full-blown program or simply start letting these people attend seminars and workshops to develop their skills, it's important to keep them engaged. Have some sort of program for them to attend or participate in regularly.

Create a job description for what you do. Yes, you. In the event someone has to take over for you, there should be written documentation for everything you do — daily duties, procedures, and so forth. Don't expect everyone to know what you do every day.

When you start to develop your leaders of tomorrow, that mentality tends to be a mindset that permeates the organizational chart. You'll have people above you and below you thinking in the same way. And when that happens, your company will soon be prepared for almost anything.

Letting your people push you up the ladder

In working to build yourself out of a job, one of the greatest lessons you learn is the fallacy of climbing the corporate ladder. I submit to you that if you climb the ladder, you're very likely to fall and that sudden stop at the bottom tends to hurt. We've all seen people who advanced their own careers with no regard for who or what was in their way. That's a really shaky philosophy and one that leads to more of those falls than you can imagine. I personally wish the phrase had never been coined, but it's become part of the business lexicon. Everyone wants to climb that ladder.

I want you to shift your mindset and think of your ascent up the corporate ladder a bit differently. Instead of climbing it, what if you developed leaders below you at such a pace that they literally pushed you up the ladder? What if you do so well at building yourself out of a job and developing the leaders of tomorrow you're forced to take on more responsibly and therefore gravitate toward a more senior position yourself? This career path is not only much more stable, but it's also one with more integrity and morals.

As you start to develop future leaders, you must also be thinking about where you're going next. What position will you take?

Take the example of a fictitious sales territory to see how getting pushed up the ladder can play out. You hire Janis to be a salesperson in this territory because it's very obvious early on that Janis is a go-getter. She doesn't just talk a good game, she's making things happen. Within a few years, Janis has built the territory to a point where you need to hire someone else to help cover it. This person is now put alongside Janis with the understanding that Janis needs to train him to be another Janis. You're developing a leader for tomorrow, and Janis is building herself out of a job.

You sit down with Janis and make sure she's ready for what is ultimately coming — does she want to advance in the company? Is she ready to take on the responsibility that is almost inevitably coming down the pike? She is.

This new salesperson, call him José, is caught up in Janis's attitude and work ethic and soon becomes another leader for you. José is killing it and Janis is there with him every step of the way — teaching (and learning) how to grow a territory. Meanwhile, you're formulating a plan for the next 24 months, knowing it won't be long before you're going to have to hire someone else for this now red-hot territory that Janis and José are dominating.

In walks Marta. Marta has all the attributes of a superstar. You can see that she has what it takes to be something special. Where are you going to put her? Do you place her in a territory where everyone is dragging around and complaining or do you put this A student in the best classroom? At this point, you promote Janis to territory manager, and she *and* José bring Marta into the fold and make her a part of their team.

Note what happened here: Janis is now developing a leader for tomorrow (Marta) and building herself out of a job with José. It's a beautiful system to see it happen — and it's happening every day in small amounts. But, it's up to you to see those, take advantage of them, and have them grow your company.

What do you think would've happened if a manager (not you, of course) had ignored Janis's performance and just left her out there killing it? Building a great territory but not being recognized or rewarded for it? I'll tell you what would happen: That manager (again, not you) would be competing against Janis, who is now working for your competitor.

A great manager has this happening in multiple territories or departments all at the same time. If you're in a retail clothing store, it should be happening in menswear, formals, shoes, and every other department under your tutelage. You cannot sit back and wait for a superstar salesperson to get her territory built before moving on to work with another up-and-comer. You have to juggle these all at once. And communication is essential. Know what's happening with all these people — let them tell you what they need to grow.

As each department or territory grows, the salespeople growing them are inching you up the corporate ladder. Eventually one of these people will be ready to take over as sales manager, and you will move up to a level above.

If you're training the people below you to do your job, but the person above you isn't giving you the feedback and information you need to grow into her job, you need to have a conversation sooner rather than later. Just as Janis doesn't want to build a territory and be taken for granted, neither do you.

Once you have the talent to develop and build sales teams, you will never look for work — work will look for you!

Selecting Your Replacement

So, it's come down to this, huh? The end of the road, the last hurrah. Before the credits roll in this book let's talk about actually selecting your replacement.

You've proven to be more than just a good sales manager — you're a great one. Your team is consistently outperforming their goals, and your department is tops in your entire company. You've made a name for yourself as a talent evaluator and as someone who builds winning teams.

Now, it's time for you to advance your career — all the hard work, long hours, and struggles are about to pay off. But, there's one more thing. You can't take the promotion, the huge raise, and the company vehicle until you find someone to take your place — someone competent enough to step right in and pick up where you left off.

The company needs another you. And since you can't clone yourself (as of the writing of this book), you need to do the next best thing and hire your replacement.

You've looked forward to this time for years — this is what you wanted. Now let me give you a little advice: When it comes to selecting and hiring your replacement, take your time. Don't hire in haste and then have to micromanage the position forever. Just as I talk about in Chapter 5: Hire hard and manage easy or hire easy and manage hard. I'll take the former.

If there's one thing I can impress upon sales managers who are hiring or promoting someone to take their place it's this: Start with your own weaknesses and find someone who is strong there. If you're weak in the detail areas of your job, choose the candidate who's strongest in that area. All things being equal go with the person who is going to fill gaps in your own skill set. Very simply, these people will make you a better manager as you both progress through the company. Not to mention the fact you don't need two managers — one reporting to the other — who both share the same weakness. It can cause a huge disconnect in the business.

So, identify your weakness or weaknesses first and fill those gaps. You'll be glad you did.

As you continue your career path, you never stop learning — just like you impress upon your salespeople. Perhaps the best way to demonstrate that is through your own actions and willingness to admit where you need help.

When looking for or selecting your replacement, find someone whose personality matches with yours. Although you don't want someone who's going to agree with everything you say (assuming you're being promoted to her supervisor), if this is her first foray into management she's going to need a lot of guidance in the beginning. You want someone you can communicate with, someone who understands you, and whom you understand. In layman's terms — you need to jive.

Just because you're getting promoted, and someone is taking your old position, don't leave her holding the bag. Make yourself as available as possible to ensure her success and that of the team. You owe it to her and to the salespeople you helped groom. Always leave the department better than you found it. If there's one thing I can say about my career, I always tried to leave situations better than I found them.

Finally, when hiring someone to replace you, get someone you like and who likes you. You never know when you'll be working for her one day. The rungs of that corporate ladder aren't always connected, and you just may hire your future boss.

Part VI
The Part of Tens

To read about ten habits of great sales managers, go to `www.dummies.com/extras/salesmanagement`.

In this part . . .

- Understand how to display leadership and be the best you can be.
- Be mindful of behaviors or actions that can damage your credibility beyond repair.
- Recognize the signs that indicate a member of your team is struggling.
- Check out apps that can help make your sales management life that much easier.

Chapter 17

Ten Traits of a Successful Sales Manager

In This Chapter

- Exhibiting leadership
- Committing yourself to success
- Being the best you can be

Anyone can grab a box of business cards or a nameplate for his desk and call himself a sales manager. But, to truly rise to the level of a successful sales manager, you must display certain traits daily. Some of these you can develop, but the vast majority are born into you; they're part of your DNA and the fabric of your being.

Succeeding in your role as sales manager takes more than being a good salesperson. Managing and motivating a sales team requires you to wear many hats including teacher, counselor, confidant, and critic. This chapter looks at the traits effective sales managers need to have.

Having the Heart of a Teacher

As a professional sales manager you spend more time teaching, coaching, and training than anything else. So, it only makes sense that you must be good at it. However, you also have to love it . . . and I mean *love* it.

You have to truly enjoy taking a new salesperson, planting the seeds of knowledge, watching him make mistakes, showing him how to take corrective action, and ultimately seeing him succeed. The feeling you get from that will be greater than if you did it yourself.

The most successful sales managers live to watch others succeed. The most successful sales managers look at mistakes not as mistakes but as teachable moments. When you start to manage this way, your salespeople will no longer be crippled by the fear of making an error or messing something up.

Having the Curiosity of a Student

One of the great paradoxes of being a professional sales manager is that almost every time you begin to teach or train someone, you end up learning something yourself. However, you have to have your mind tuned to receive that lesson. Unless you're set on the right frequency, the message disappears into space. Set your mind to the frequency to learn, to absorb, and to come away from every training session better.

You must always search for and be aware of opportunities to learn and continue to grow as a manager. Some of the greatest lessons I've learned came when I was teaching someone else.

Set an example by discovering a love for learning and trying new and different techniques. Never let yourself fall into the "that's the way we've always done it" trap. It's a creativity killer.

Read, listen to audio books, attend seminars or webinars, and do whatever it takes to continue to learn and grow as a professional. If you set an example of someone who understands there's always something more to learn, you're setting an amazing example for your department.

Exhibiting Fairness

Being fair to your team is critical. We all know and understand that in the broad sense, life isn't fair. But in your dealing with your sales staff, you must always be fair. You cannot play favorites, and although you manage every personality type differently, your treatment of each must be transparently equitable.

When in doubt simply ask yourself, "What is the fair way to handle this situation?" Whether you're mediating a dispute, dealing with pricing for a customer, or assigning sales territories, never let your fairness be called into question. Even if it isn't a win for you personally, you earn respect from your salespeople and your clients simply by responding fairly.

Understanding Empathy

First you must know the difference between empathy and sympathy. *Empathy* means "I know how you feel because I feel the same way or have felt the same way in the past." On the other hand, sympathy says, "I understand how you feel but I don't necessarily have those feelings myself."

The reason you must understand empathy is because as a leader you must have a true understanding of what your team is going through at all times. Good, bad, or indifferent, you must know what the experience is like with ever fiber of your being.

When one of your salespeople comes to you with an issue or an objection he's hearing from customers, you have to know what he's feeling, not just understand it.

Now, just because your top performer is in a slump doesn't mean you have to let it bring you down, but you must be able to speak from an empathetic position because you know what those feelings are like because you've been there. Conversely, when one of your weaker salespeople scores a huge win, you should feel that as well. You are on a high as much as he is.

Know the difference between empathy and sympathy, and your team will greatly benefit.

Being a Good Listener

One of the skills you teach salespeople time and time again is to be a good listener. And you need to practice what you preach. You can't very well ask your team to listen and truly hear their prospects and customers if you don't show them the same courtesy and concern.

Just as you have them listen with more than their ears, so should you. Hear what your people are saying, not just what they tell you verbally. (Head to Chapter 4 for more on communicating with your team.) You learn a lot more by listening than by talking, and the more time you spend in management and away from the field, the more important the feedback coming from the field. Your sales team is your eyes and ears for the market, and they need to know you care about what they know.

Remaining Humble

The first thing I tell salespeople I train or coach is that I'm not better or smarter than they are, I simply have the ability to look at their situation with a different perspective. You, as a professional sales manager, will be most successful by taking the same tack daily with your people.

Learn to feed your ego on your team's success and you'll have more success than you ever dreamed possible. It truly isn't about you. You're there to make your salespeople look good, not vice versa.

Living with Integrity

When all is said and done, your integrity is really all you have. The greatest managers I've ever worked for were people I knew had their hearts in the right place. They did the right thing because it was the right thing to do without regard for the monetary benefit.

Your actions and words should display the highest moral, ethical, and honest behavior. If a salesperson sees you cut corners, cheat, or otherwise do something to compromise your principles, he'll think that type of behavior is not only acceptable but encouraged.

Never compromise your integrity. No sale, customer, or deal is worth it.

Being Accessible

Don't confuse being accessible with having an open door policy or some other simple attempt to show concern. To truly make yourself accessible is not only the mark of a professional manager, but a successful one, too. Never be too busy to do what is most important. Being accessible many times simply means prioritizing correctly. What is most important at this moment?

Being accessible also can mean lending an ear, an opinion, or just being there for someone. When you're with someone, be present yourself. Make the person you're with feel as if he's the most important person in the world. When you give someone your time, you're making an investment he can seldom repay.

Possessing a Positive Attitude

Having a great attitude when things are going well is easy. It's when the chips are down and the tide has turned against you it's most important. Your salespeople and even other departments draw their attitude and opinion from you and imitate how you respond to crisis situations.

Focus on the positive. Look for solutions, not problems. By displaying a positive attitude, you make several things happen:

- You don't let the small things drag you down.
- You find a lot of the things you used to worry about are the small things.
- People want to be around you. You give off an aura — a vibe, if you will — that just attracts other people to you.

Showing great leadership and management doesn't mean you necessarily know all the answers; it means you display a good, positive attitude even when you don't.

Embracing Change

The world is ever changing, and you must embrace the change. The truly successful sales managers and leaders see change as an opportunity — an opportunity to learn, grow, and improve their business. With the advent of social media, the Internet, and other technologies, business is changing at a rapid pace. You must see that as a positive.

Change can include changes in upper management, ownership, company direction, philosophical direction, and more. Although some of those may challenge you, never let them stop you. As the great motivational speaker Jim Rohn said, "Your life does not get better by chance, it gets better by change!"

Too many people see change as negative because of the uncertainty. Embrace it, grab it, and run with it! See it for what it is: innovation and opportunity!

Chapter 18

Ten Things that Destroy Your Credibility

In This Chapter

- Protecting what you've worked for
- Earning respect daily

What takes years to build can be destroyed in a matter of moments with a poor decision, a bad choice of words, or a knee-jerk reaction. In order for your sales team to have confidence in you as a sales manager and a leader, you have to earn their respect each and every day. Never take it for granted, and never put it in jeopardy.

Many careers have been derailed by things that were forgiven but never forgotten. This chapter looks at ten sure-fire ways to destroy your reputation and diminish your team's trust in you.

Being Dishonest

In balancing your role as a member of management and the leader of the sales team there are times where you're aware of situations, upcoming changes, or other information you're not ready or able to share with your salespeople. Tell your team up front that there will be certain information you cannot share but that you'll always have their and the company's best interest in mind. I don't consider withholding that type of information dishonest. However, telling your team that something is going to happen when you know it's not is another story.

Understand that your personal character is on display at all times. Never do anything that can remotely be considered dishonest in the eyes of your people, your company, or your customer.

Even little white lies display a propensity to be less than trustworthy. Never create a scenario in which a salesperson might ask herself, “If my manager would do that to a customer (or the company), what would she do to me?”

On the other hand, being completely honest will reap reward after reward. Let your team know they can depend on you not to tell them what they want to hear but the truth whether it’s good, bad, or otherwise.

Acting Like a Know-It-All

Have you ever known someone who was an expert at everything? No matter the subject from underwater basket weaving to wild game hunting, she’s an expert and has done it bigger and better than anyone else. These people aren’t a lot of fun to be around, are they?

Instead of spending your time putting your knowledge on display, try to find out more about each member of your sales team. What are her likes, dislikes, hobbies, and so forth? Let her brag. Just as you’d get a customer talking when you were a salesperson, as a manager you need to let your representatives talk.

And, if you were the 1981 State Underwater Basket Weaving Champion, bite your tongue and keep it to yourself. Nobody really cares.

Showing Favoritism

Although you must manage everyone differently, treat everyone the same. Even though every person has different quotas, goals, and aspirations, your interaction with every member of your team should be almost identical.

Will it be exact? No, it never is. But, be very careful not to have favorites who always get preferential treatment. You may gain a few but you’ll lose the masses.

Failing to Follow Through

Your sales team counts on you to assist them in selling. While that is a very simple statement, it’s critical you follow through on what you tell them you’ll do.

If you're tasked with helping one of your reps put together a presentation, do your part and then some. Follow through on all your promises, and live up to expectations in everything from scheduling regular performance reviews to placing a phone call to a customer or potential customer.

As an aside, as the sales manager, always take it upon yourself to ensure that other departments follow through on their promises, as well. If production is supposed to have a sample available for a customer review, hold them accountable. Your salespeople learn from your example.

Placing Blame

Guess what? Something's going to go wrong. An order is going to get fouled up, a customer is going to be mad, and perhaps a sale is going to be lost. That's all a part of business. Never accept substandard performance out of your department or others, although you have to know you're going to get it sometimes.

Your customer doesn't care what happened or who's at fault. Neither does your salesperson. The last thing people want to hear is their manager playing the blame game. It's not the weather, the mayor, the transportation department, accounting, or anyone else's fault. Your time is much better spent solving the problem than figuring out whom to blame. Save that until after the problem is solved.

Taking Too Much Credit

Hand-in-hand with placing blame is being that person who always seems to find the limelight. Any time something goes right, she finds a way to have a hand in it and get credit. Don't be that person. Your team will respect you much more if you give that credit away and make others look good. People know. You don't have to toot your own horn.

You'll be a very successful manager if you make it a point to take more blame and less credit than you deserve.

Procrastinating

Nothing is more frustrating for a salesperson than a manager who procrastinates. I've been there; I know. The salesperson ends up making up stories to tell her customer why something isn't complete after it's been buried on your desk and forgotten. Don't make anyone ask you four times for help on an issue or situation — don't make her ask more than twice at the most.

If you need to write everything down, do so. Personally, I take written notes a lot! I love technology and use a calendar app and a note app on my phone (which I talk about in Chapter 20), but I have a legal pad and a notebook where I write down almost everything — especially projects or programs I'm working on for others.

If a salesperson needs you to approve a presentation or program for a customer, don't cost her credibility, and perhaps a sale, because you put it off.

Changing Commissions Unjustly

Ah, the slippery slope of compensation. It seems everyone wants the sales department to sell more until she's selling so much that she's making too much money. "We can't pay somebody that much!" I've heard it more than once. If you stay in management long enough you will too, and you'll have to defend your salesperson's paycheck. As long as someone is being paid on the gross profits she generates, why would you cut her commission?

At times, upper management may see nothing but the commission and need to be reminded what an asset a certain salesperson is to the company and that she's not just a payroll number.

Nothing demotivates your people and potentially costs you a superstar quicker than pulling commissions. But, that's not going to stop other members of management from wanting to do so. You need to hold your ground. Unless there's a very good reason (for example, people aren't being paid on gross profit), leave the commission program alone.

Sharing Privileged Information

In your role as a manger, you have access to a lot of personal and private information from company-related information to personal details regarding your department and team members. Treat that information as if you are guarding Top Secret government information. It's not cute to show off just because you know something. It's poor form, bad management, and in some cases leaves you and your company exposed to legal issues.

If you're ever in doubt, don't discuss it. Keep it to yourself. If someone wants to share information with you that you don't believe she should, don't let her. By refusing to be involved in that behavior, you display a solid character.

This isn't high school. If you have time to gossip, you're probably procrastinating on something else.

Showing a Lack of Concern

If something is a legitimate issue for one of your salespeople, it needs to be an issue with you. And it's as important as she makes it. If something is a big deal to one of your team, at least give her the courtesy of listening to her complaint. If you show a true, honest concern for the wellbeing and success of your team members, you'll be successful yourself.

Chapter 19

Ten Signs of a Struggling Salesperson

In This Chapter

- Recognizing the warning signs of burnout
- Restoring a struggling team member's confidence

The job of a professional salesperson can be extremely stressful, especially for those who work on straight commission. As a sales manager, you deal with a variety of situations involving salespeople who struggle, fail to make quota, and simply fall into a slump. Only a very few salespeople go through an entire career without experiencing a slump at least once. It's part of the job; it happens. But, the mental aspect of it can be very taxing for even the strongest salesperson.

Anyone who has been in sales for more than a few months has had the thought — however fleeting — that he'll never sell anything again. And then the panic sets in. How a salesperson responds to self-doubt varies, but you'll do well to watch for the warning signs of someone struggling with confidence issues so that you can help him pull out of his nosedive.

As a professional sales manager, you have to be a bit of counselor at times. Your people look to you for guidance in more than just the standard sales process sense. Don't forget that they're people first with real needs, real wants, and real issues. Pay attention and you'll build a strong team that sees you as a strong leader.

Failing to Make Required Calls

If you expect your salespeople to generate a certain amount of calls or leads weekly or monthly, one of the first signs to watch for is someone who falls below those numbers. It's a classic warning sign that the person has crawled into a shell and isn't out seeing prospects.

You'd think the best way to get out of a slump or a downturn would be to get out and make calls on prospective customers. But a slumping salesperson's brain doesn't work that way. In fact, it works the exact opposite. He gets to the point of fearing rejection so much that he avoids the confrontation by failing to make the required number of sales calls.

Determine whether the problem is based on ability or unwillingness. If it's a matter of ability, you need to work with the salesperson to improve his skills. If it's unwillingness, it's time for a face-to-face meeting to determine whether he wants to remain on your team. If he does, he must meet the requirements you set forth.

Frequent Tardiness

If one of the members of your sales team is always on time and all of a sudden begins to drag in late, miss appointments, or fail to meet other deadlines, raise your antenna. Keep an eye on him because he's likely to be in or about to be in a position of needing some management help to rebuild his confidence. At least give him a motivational jumpstart.

Know what your individual salespeople respond to. Knowing whether to offer tough love or a shoulder to cry on gives you the ability to help your salespeople when they fall — and they will.

Before you jump up with a verbal warning and then a written warning, find out why the person is having a problem being on time. Is it a personal issue? Problems with transportation? Or perhaps just a lack of concern. The first two you can work with — the third one, not so much.

Placing Blame

Not only is blaming a classic sign of problems, it's a crutch you cannot allow your people to use. Period. I've seen salespeople come up with every reason in the book why someone didn't buy, but the bottom line is this: If the prospect gave his time and attention, then the prospect did his part.

A professional salesperson can look himself in the mirror, admit fault, and begin to work on the areas he needs to improve. Less self-aware salespeople who are struggling may blame the government, the weather, the time of year, the economy, the company's advertising program, and any other crazy inanimate object or item that can't defend itself. Don't let your people begin playing the blame game — it will never end.

Disappearing during Work Hours

Sometimes people come in late, and sometimes they sneak off early too. A professional salesperson must have enough self-discipline to manage his own time because he works in the field away from direct supervision. As a manager, you must have confidence your people are doing their jobs even when you can't lay eyes on them.

Are you getting voice mail when your salesperson should be answering his phone? Is someone missing appointments and always having an excuse as to why?

If one of your salespeople is hard to find during regular business hours, it's a sign he's going through a bit of a downturn and needs a manager to step in and help.

Salespeople aren't generally required to clock in and clock out, but they are expected to work during their work hours. I've had instances when I secretly followed a salesperson to see what he was doing when he left the office. If you find the company vehicle in the salesperson's driveway during work hours, you may need to cut ties.

Lack of Participation

Someone who starts skipping sales meetings, company functions, and other team-oriented activities exhibits a classic symptom of a struggling salesperson. When someone falls into the almost depressive state of mind of a struggling salesperson, the last thing he wants is to be around work. On the other hand, someone who is firing on all cylinders loves to be around fellow salespeople and to participate in activities that can make him better. Take note of who does and doesn't volunteer to participate in some of the extracurricular activities created to build a team atmosphere.

Be aware that this lack of interest can come on in an instant. Someone may be the first person at the company picnic and then all of a sudden fall off the map because he's going through a tough time. This is usually how it happens and what you need to look for.

If one of your team misses a required function, take action and discipline him just as you would for any other offense. Salespeople represent your company, and you want a team of people who want to represent it.

Falling Customer Satisfaction

Of all the signs, having dissatisfied customers is one you can't ignore. If customer service scores begin to slide, you have to take action. You can't hope your salesperson improves or snaps out of his slump. As the sales manager you must respond and respond quickly.

A salesperson who's struggling may be avoiding his customers, thinking, "If I call on that customer he may have a problem or tell me he's quitting me. If I don't call on him, I can't get bad news." Your salesperson is trying to protect himself by avoiding confrontation. It's up to you to manage him through this, build his confidence, and get him back in the swing of things.

Deteriorating Physical Appearance

Although physical appearance isn't at the top of the list, it's usually the first thing you notice when a salesperson starts losing interest in the job. Whether it's his body, his clothes, or even his vehicle, if someone who generally takes pride in his appearance suddenly shows up disheveled, unshaven, or with hair and makeup a mess, you've got not only a salesperson in a slump, but one who's asking for help — he's not hiding his distress.

If someone lets himself go, he's asking you to step in and find out how you can help. Do so and don't ignore it. "Martin, you know one thing I've always appreciated about your professionalism is how you kept up with your car and materials. But, it seems as if lately, you've kind of let them go. What's going on? How can I help?" You don't have to get too personal, but if you have the right relationship ahead of time, he'll appreciate the concern.

But, no matter the relationship, be careful. People in this state can act erratically and be impulsive.

Increasingly Negative Attitude

Perhaps the one sign that drives you the craziest is when one of your top performers falls into the puddle of a negative attitude. Don't let him sink too deep before you step in. Again, this one is easy to notice: everything is wrong, he snaps suddenly, he's mad at the world, every customer is a blankety-blank — you know the drill. He finds everything to complain about, and nothing is ever going to get better. My personal opinion is that this negativity springs from part of the creative brain that actually makes successful salespeople successful — until it turns on them. Then it can be harmful — very harmful.

The problem really explodes when the struggling salesperson starts to affect other members of your team. The rest aren't going to start dressing sloppily, missing meetings, or failing to take care of their customers just because someone else does, but negative attitudes spread like wildfire. Stop it before it infects the rest of your group and becomes an epidemic.

Let the salesperson know you've noticed a change in his attitude and find out what's causing it. As his manager, you have to let him know he has the potential to infect your entire department, and you aren't going to let him do that.

Noticeable Lack of Motivation

You've probably already seen this: someone who is usually happy-go-lucky falls into a nasty mood and doesn't want to do anything positive. He's simply not motivated to grow his business, go the extra mile, or do the things that once made him successful. Recognize it as a cry for help — this person is slumping and needs your help even if he's not comfortable coming out and asking for it.

As the manager, take the lead and talk to him. Let him know you need him to be a leader and find out what's got him down. Many times, just knowing you still have confidence in someone can rebuild his confidence in himself. But, you've got to have your eyes open to see it.

Taking an Abnormal Amount of Time Off

I'm not talking about taking regularly scheduled vacation or time to recharge the batteries. I'm referring to people who call in sick, miss extra days, have something going on that pulls them away from work frequently. This can be a defense mechanism to avoid rejection. Like so many of the other signs in this chapter, taking a lot of time off is evidence of call reluctance and the fear of rejection.

You have to display empathy and put on your counselor hat to help correct this behavior. Again, you need to determine whether this is caused by an inability to do something or an unwillingness to do it. The answer obviously dictates how you respond.

Chapter 20

Top Ten Apps for a Busy Manager

In This Chapter

- Using apps to take notes, scanning docs, and sending messages
- Availing yourself of customer service management apps
- Scanning docs, listening to podcasts, and reading books with apps
- Using a GPS app to find your way to clients and appointments

I remember when a phone was something I used just to just make a call. Now I have an entire big box retail store in my pocket. Just about everything you could possibly want is available on an app for your iPhone or Android.

Every sales manager should embrace this technology. There are as many lists as there are apps: I put together my list of apps I use daily to help me do my job better.

And, that's the key. Too many times we let technology drive us instead of letting it help us. Anything that causes you to do more work or costs you time isn't helping, no matter how cute it is or how many of your friends want you to check in on it or like their status.

I deliberately chose to leave out social media apps. Yes, they can have business applications but most of them are time-wasters. Instead, I focus on products I think can make you more productive, more efficient, and a better salesperson.

Evernote

This app is, in a word, great. From taking notes to saving Internet clippings to filing pictures and saving critical data, I use this one daily. You may start using Evernote (`http://evernote.com`) just as a note-taking app, but you'll soon find so many ways it can save you time and effort. You just need to invest a few hours to learn it.

Find an article on the Internet you want to save for later? Simply clip it from the Evernote web-based app and read it on your phone or iPad later. Want to save an email into a file for later review? Evernote is the answer. It syncs across all platforms — make a note on your phone and it's available on your laptop or iPad.

Maybe the best part is the free version is more than most people need. Download it at `http://evernote.com`. I was a user long before I upgraded to the paid version. Evernote has the capability to be your favorite app — it certainly is mine!

Any.do

Another app I use daily. This is my to-do-list app. Now, let me say I tried a lot of apps — a *lot* of apps — before settling on Any.do (`www.any.do`). Another app that syncs across platforms, this is the simplest, cleanest to-do list I've found. There's a premium version available but the free version does everything I want and more!

I'm not one for big, bulky to-do lists; I just like to see what I've got on my list today. Any.do is more than adequate.

Audible

Another app I use daily is Audible. ***Note:*** This app requires a subscription from `www.audible.com`. Once a member, you have a world of audiobooks available in the palm of your hand. With a set of earbuds, you can listen to some of the latest business books, classics, or even just some mind-numbing entertainment while you drive, fly, work out, or simply fill time between meetings. You purchase a set amount of credits and each book you download is a credit — and it's yours to keep forever. Download it on your phone and listen on your iPad later — it keeps up with where you left off.

Audible regularly offers bonuses, such as getting three books for two credits, or buying one book and getting one free. If you love to read but just don't have time, Audible is a great option.

Many of us who are old enough to have had a backseat full of motivational cassette tapes can now use Audible in their place.

Downcast

Your iPhone comes with a default podcast player. However, Downcast (http://downcastapp.com) is just a free, cleaner, simpler interface to listen to your favorite podcast. I was introduced to Downcast by a friend and now couldn't tell you which folder I hid the old standard app in on my phone.

I subscribe to way too many podcasts, but no matter what your interests or tastes, Downcast makes it easy to subscribe and have podcasts automatically download when a new episode is released.

One of the things I like best of all is the ability to go back and listen to old episodes of new podcasts I discover. Try Downcast; I think you'll end up migrating all your podcasts from others players to this great app! It's a very clean, easy-to-use player.

E-Readers

Getting an e-reader is a no-brainer in my opinion. Everyone talks about how technology makes her job harder and not easier, but the advent of the Kindle and other e-readers is one of the greatest innovations of my lifetime! You may even be reading this book on an e-reader! If you're not listening to books on Audible, you can be reading them on an e-reader. And, as iPhones get bigger, they become a lot easier to use with reader apps.

Again, as with most, this syncs across devices. If you sign out on your iPhone and back in on your iPad, you get the option of going to the last place you were on the other device.

You can download the e-reader apps for free in the App Store or Google Play on your Android and then shop to your heart's content — filling your library with everything from the latest mind-numbing, fun read to the classics.

Pocket

A little-known app I love is Pocket (http://getpocket.com). It's not only free, but it's another app I use every single day. Pocket is aptly named because you use it to basically save things to your pocket. And, you guessed it . . . it's free!

Web articles you want to read later? Save them to Pocket. Find something online you want to cut a piece of and save? Send it to Pocket. Best of all, you can read it later and then email it to people, post it to social media (tweet out a link), or otherwise share the article with others. Keep articles forever in Pocket or read them, share, or delete them. Where Evernote is an all-in-one, Pocket is, just as its name suggests: a pocket for you to keep articles you want save. I use it as a kind of middleman between the article and Evernote. Evernote is the filing cabinet and Pocket is the inbox on my desk, so to speak. If I want to save the article for later, I send it from Pocket to Evernote. If not, I just delete after reading.

Customer Relationship Manager Apps

I'm not going to even get into how many CRM (customer relationship manager) apps there are out there, but whatever program you use, download the app and have it at your disposal at all times. Between sales calls you can input new contacts, see what your sales process looks like, and do any number of other scheduling tasks you normally do from your laptop.

Scanner Pro

Scanner Pro (`http://readdle.com/products/scannerpro5`) has been around awhile, but I just started using it recently, and now I don't know how I lived without it. Need to scan a document? You need Scanner Pro and you can do it from the front seat of your vehicle!

Simply line up the document and take a picture. Scanner Pro then works its magic, removes shadows, wrinkles, and other abnormalities and makes a clean document that looks like you ran it right through a scanner. I've used Scanner Pro on papers that had been wadded up and it made them look brand new. You can then save the scan as a PDF and email it or file it.

You have to pay for the app, but it's well worth the price. (I love this app!)

Calendars 5

Just like the to-do-list apps, there are hundreds, if not thousands of calendars out there, and I've tried a lot of them. Yes, the default calendar on your phone is probably serviceable, but I like Calendars 5 (`http://readdle.com/products/calendars5`) because of its simple design, clean interface, and ability to color-code my appointments and tasks. You don't have to keep a separate calendar for all different aspects of your life; you can manage them all in one place. This one has become my favorite! And, once again it's free (do you see a pattern developing?).

Color-code your sales reps and keep up with vacations, meetings, and other important dates applicable to each person. Then you can sort and search as you like.

WAZE

I may have saved the best for last. Though it is frowned upon by some police agencies because it lists red-light cameras and police ahead, WAZE (yep, it's free) (`www.waze.com`) is the single greatest GPS (global positioning system) app I've ever seen.

Why? It's run by other motorists reporting traffic, accidents, debris, closed roads, ice, fog — you name it and WAZE knows about it and steers you clear of it. After you input your destination, WAZE calculates the best route at that time based on real-time reports from others users.

I've had it take me on streets I didn't know existed in order to avoid a backup. Please note, you should *never* input information as you drive, simply use it as a guide, and it will save you hours over a very short period of time.

Index

• Numerics •

• A •

• B •

• C •

• D •

• E •

• P •

• S •

• T •

• V •

• W •

Notes

Notes

About the Author

Butch Bellah is an expert sales trainer, an accomplished speaker, and an author. He works with salespeople and organizations to help them gain more appointments, win more business, and retain more customers.

With an extremely successful career spanning more than three decades, Butch has made tens of thousands of sales calls, gained thousands of new clients, and sold hundreds of millions of dollars of product. He's also worked with hundreds of salespeople to help them do the same through his training and coaching.

Butch began a career in the distribution industry when he was 21. He was a division sales manager at 25, vice president of sales at 30, and bought the company with a business partner just five years later. During that time he was instrumental in growing the company from a small, local wholesaler to a one of the largest food distributors in the nation with annual sales of more than $200 million. During his rapid ascent to sales and financial success, Butch also spent ten years as a professional, stand-up comedian honing not only his public speaking skills but enjoying what he calls "the best sales training I ever received."

He formed B2 Training & Development to bring his knowledge and experience to others and provide them with tools to not only survive but thrive in today's competitive landscape.

Butch is a past president of Sales and Marketing Executives and has been named one of the Top 100 Sales Experts and Top 50 Business Coaches to follow on Twitter. His first book, *The 10 Essential Habits of Sales Superstars: Plugging Into The Power of Ten* was published in 2014.

He and Angie, his wife of 30years, live just outside Dallas, Texas, with their dogs. They have three children: Jonathan, Whitney, and Sidney and are anxiously awaiting their first grandchild. Butch can be found online at `butchbellah.com`.

Dedication

This book is dedicated to my late parents, Don and Maudie (Toot) Bellah, who instilled in me at an early age the idea I could do and be anything I wanted. Also, for my late brother, Scott. I miss the three of you every day and wish you could be here to see the fruits of my labors.

Author's Acknowledgments

First and foremost I want to thank God for the talents and abilities I've been gifted with. I also want to thank my family for their sacrifices while I chased the dreams I've had. To my wife Angie and our children: thank you for letting Dad keep playing. To my mentor and friend Noble Feldman: I'll never be able to repay you for all you've done for me. To my first sales manager, Mike Radney: thanks for seeing something in that 19-year-old kid and introducing me to the teachings of Zig Ziglar and other master motivators.

The team at John Wiley & Sons: There's no words to express my appreciation for the confidence you place in me with this project. It has been an absolute blast and true learning experience. Thanks to my Acquisitions Editor Stacy Kennedy who helped me flesh out the initial ideas and direction of this book. My Project Editor, Michelle Hacker, the person who answered every email, every crazy question and was by my side through the entire journey: thank you! My Technical Editor James Clark, thank you for all your help and support. For the rest of the Wiley team including my Development Editor Tracy Brown Hamilton and Copy Editor Kathleen Dobie, your dedication and tireless work have helped make this book happen. It's an honor to work with you all.

Publisher's Acknowledgments

Acquisitions Editor: Stacy Kennedy

Project Manager: Michelle Hacker

Development Editor: Tracy Brown Hamilton

Copy Editor: Kathleen Dobie

Technical Editor: James Clark

Production Editor: Siddique Shaik

Cover Image: © sorendls/iStockphoto

FREE copy of Butch's book!

The 10 Essential Habits of Sales Superstars: Plugging into the Power of Ten

"A terrific handbook of practical, bare-bones sales training. It's brief but thorough and easy to understand and apply. As Dad would say, 'We don't always need to be told, but we often need to be reminded.' Kudos to Butch Bellah!"
Tom Ziglar, President/CEO, Ziglar, Inc.

"Butch Bellah packs a lot of rock-solid advice into this little book. Apply just one habit and your sales will increase; apply more and you'll get 10x the results."
Jill Konrath, author of *Agile Selling* and *Snap Selling*

"*The 10 Essential Habits of Sales Superstars* is just that: Essential. This should be a part of every salesperson's library and arsenal. Read it. Learn it. Use it. When it comes to sales books, this one should make the Top Ten List."
Robert Terson, best-selling author of *Selling Fearlessly: A Master Salesman's Secrets For the One-Call-Close Salesperson*

Go to **ButchBellah.com/free10habits** to get your copy!

Hire Butch to Speak or Train!

ANY employee who interacts with a customer is in sales, no matter what his or her business card says! Are ALL of your employees prepared at EVERY level of your company? ONE customer's bad experience can go viral immediately via social media!

Businesses of all sizes and organizations of all kinds have benefited from Butch's sales advice. Turn ALL of your employees into sales professionals by arming them with knowledge that will boost the bottom line AND customer loyalty.

Call (337) 384-9204 or email butch@butchbellah.com to schedule a speaking engagement or training session. Check out ButchBellah.com/speaking to see a video of Butch in action!

"Butch is a highly intelligent trainer whose many years of sales experience has helped my company bring on a large account. Knowing the culture of the market helped Butch teach us to refine our presentations to address our customer's key concerns."
Peggy Peterson, President, MesaTech Corporation

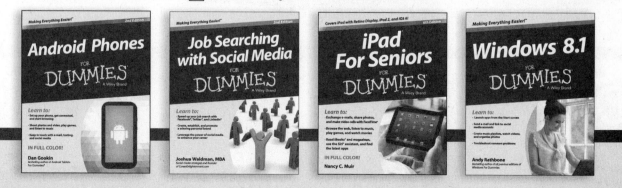

For Dummies is the global leader in the reference category and one of the most trusted and highly regarded brands in the world. No longer just focused on books, customers now have access to the For Dummies content they need in the format they want. Let us help you develop a solution that will fit your brand and help you connect with your customers.

Advertising & Sponsorships

Connect with an engaged audience on a powerful multimedia site, and position your message alongside expert how-to content.

Targeted ads • Video • Email marketing • Microsites • Sweepstakes sponsorship

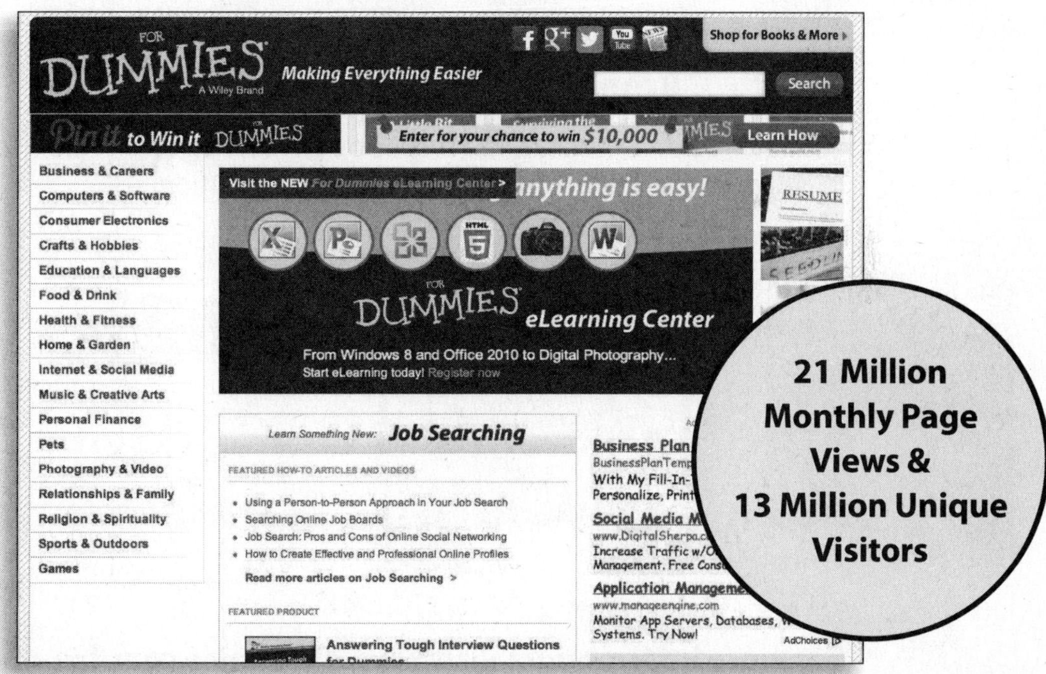

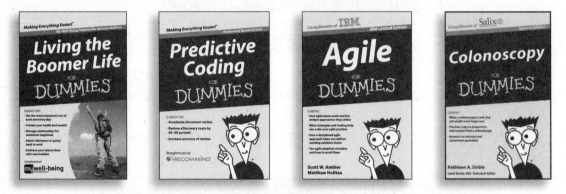

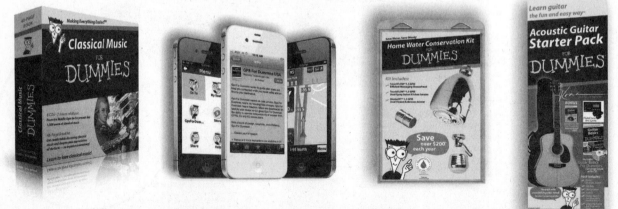